ORIGEN
and the
DOCTRINE OF GRACE

The Fernley-Hartley Lecture 1960
A Synopsis of which was delivered at
Trinity Methodist Church, Duke Street, Southport
on 5th July 1960

ORIGEN
AND THE
DOCTRINE OF GRACE

by

BENJAMIN DREWERY
M.A.

Minister of Wesley Memorial Methodist Church
Oxford

LONDON: THE EPWORTH PRESS

FIRST PUBLISHED IN 1960

© THE EPWORTH PRESS 1960

Book Steward
FRANK H. CUMBERS

SET IN MONOTYPE BASKERVILLE AND PRINTED IN
GREAT BRITAIN BY THE CAMELOT PRESS LTD
LONDON AND SOUTHAMPTON

TO THE UNDYING MEMORY OF
MY FATHER
WHO BY HIS LOVING GUIDANCE AND EXAMPLE
STIMULATED AND FOSTERED MY STUDIES
GUARDED AND CONFIRMED MY CALLING
CHERISHED AND ENRICHED MY LIFE

PREFACE

THE SUBJECT of 'Grace in the Greek Fathers' was suggested to
me for post-graduate study by Dr R. Newton Flew, formerly
Principal of Wesley House, Cambridge; but soon after those
memorable college years in which, under his firm and kindly
guidance, I began to explore this field, it became clear that I
could not hope to deal at all adequately with the Greek Fathers
as a whole until I had mastered the one by whom (whether in the
way of attraction or repulsion) they were all, both as theologians
and exegetes, decisively influenced. The current revival of interest
in Origen, which has been responsible during these years of my
studies for an unbroken flow of fascinating works on him, en-
couraged me to hope that some day my own contribution might
take its place in what has become an 'ecumenical conversation'
on the merits (or demerits) of the famous (or notorious) Christian
Platonist of Alexandria.

The invitation to deliver the Fernley-Hartley Lecture at the
Methodist Conference of 1960—for which honour I wish to thank
the Trustees most sincerely—gives me an opportunity to present
some of the first-fruits of my studies; and this book has the twin
positive aims of introducing my author to a public from whom
most of his work is still effectively hidden in dusty tomes of Greek
and Latin, and of looking at him from the standpoint of the
doctrine of Grace, which has not (to my knowledge) been attempted in any detail before. I hope that later I may have the
opportunity to relate my findings both to the patristic tradition
as a whole, and to the modern studies—English, French and
German—which are throwing such floods of light on Origen and
his fellows; but the scope and purpose of the present book have
meant the exclusion of both these related fields.

The translations of Origen's text, of which much of the book
consists, are all my own—although I have of course found valuable
guidance in many modern versions, among which that of the
First Principles by G. W. Butterworth and that of the *Celsus* by
Dr Henry Chadwick are in a class of their own; and I am deeply
indebted to them. But my studies since college days have been
pursued privately, in the midst of the somewhat engrossing

vii

labours of a pastoral ministry; and my greatest debt has been to the inspiration and encouragement afforded me by my congregations in Middlesbrough, Croydon and Oxford. With them it has been my joy to share, in both thinking and living, the treasures of the Christian revelation.

Dr Nicolas Zernov, whose work for Christian unity in Oxford (and beyond) is such an example to us, asked me once why English Free Churchmen are so little interested in the Orthodox Church. 'We have', he said, 'our invaluable links with the Anglicans; but we long to know and be known by the Free Churches as well.' This little book, by a Methodist, on the grandfather of Eastern Orthodoxy, may furnish evidence that we are by no means as disinterested as Dr Zernov supposes. I have made no attempt to conceal my real (if critical) admiration for my author, and my work rests on constant study of the whole range of his writings. I only hope that my own limitations have not unduly obscured his greatness.

An earlier Fernley-Hartley Lecturer, the Rev. Gordon S. Wakefield, was able to conclude his preface with a felicitous tribute to the help and forbearance of his wife in words quoted from one of his own Puritans. I am less lucky in my author, whose reaction to women is to allegorize them with all possible speed; but I am not less fortunate in my wife, whose understanding and sacrifice have made my work possible. Nor must I fail to thank most cordially my secretary, Mrs Violet D. Hacker, who has typed the whole of a rather difficult script with exemplary patience and efficiency, or my colleague, the Rev. Donald G. Knighton, M.A., whose meticulous and stimulating help has been at my disposal throughout the writing and revision of this book.

BENJAMIN DREWERY

OXFORD
March 1960

CONTENTS

NOTE ON TEXTS

THE TEXTS used in the preparation of this work are those of the Prussian Academy—*Die Griechischen Christlichen Schriftsteller der Ersten Drei Jahrhunderte*—for all the writings of Origen they cover. For the rest I have had recourse to Migne's *Patres Graeci*, except for J. Armitage Robinson's *Philocalia*. For the *Commentary on John* I have used both A. E. Brooke's edition and the later text of Preuschen in the Prussian Academy series. The more recently discovered Greek fragments of lost commentaries are quoted from:

JTS Vol. III (fragments of the *Commentary on Ephesians*)
JTS, Vols IX, X (fragments of the *Commentary on 1 Corinthians*)
JTS, Vols XIII, XIV (fragments of the *Commentary on Romans*)
R. Cadiou, *Commentaires Inédits des Psaumes*

References to *Greek fragments* of a work which has survived *in extenso* only in a Latin version are given explicitly (e.g. *Comm. Rom.* [Gk], §10); otherwise (e.g. *Comm. Rom.* 1.2) the Latin version is meant.

BIBLIOGRAPHY

As this work is a study of primary sources, references to secondary authorities and modern works have been kept to a minimum. Excellent bibliographies are to be found in the works of Chadwick and Hanson (below); to these should be added such of the modern writings listed in my Introductory Chapter as have subsequently appeared. (see p. 12).

Among the references in my text or footnotes are the following:

Origen: Contra Celsum. Translated with an introduction and notes by Henry Chadwick (C.U.P. 1953).

Origen on First Principles. Translated with an introduction by G. W. Butterworth (London 1936).

Origen's Treatise on Prayer. Translation and notes, etc., by E. G. Jay (S.P.C.K. 1954).

Origen's Prayer and Exhortation to Martyrdom. Translation and notes by J. J. O'Meara (Ancient Christian Writers, No. 19) (London 1954).

Origen's Doctrine of Tradition, by R. P. C. Hanson (S.P.C.K. 1954).

Allegory and Event, by R. P. C. Hanson (S.C.M. 1959).

The Doctrine of Grace, ed. by W. T. Whitley (S.C.M. 1932).

The Doctrine of Grace in the Apostolic Fathers, by T. F. Torrance (Oliver & Boyd 1948).

Other references will (I hope) explain themselves.

ABBREVIATIONS

REFERENCES TO THE WORKS OF ORIGEN: (see the list of his writings on pp. 4ff)

Princ.	= *De Principiis*
Cels.	= *Contra Celsum*
Comm. Mt., etc.	= Commentary on Matthew, etc.
Hom. Lev., etc.	= Homily on Leviticus, etc.
Frag.	= Fragment (of a passage from a Commentary or Homily, etc.)
Comm. Mt. XVI.8 on 20²⁵⁻⁸	= Origen's Commentary on Matthew, Book 16, paragraph 8, which comments on St Matthew, Chapter 20, verses 25-8
Hom. Jer. VIII.2 on 10¹²	= Origen's Eighth Homily on Jeremiah, paragraph 2, which expounds Jeremiah, Chapter 10, verse 12
Comm. Ser. Mt., 100	= *Commentariorum in Matthaeum Series*, excerpt No. 100 (see p. 5 below)
Sel. Ps. 29²ᴬ	= Origen's note on Psalm 29, verse 2A [NB: I enumerate the Psalms according to the English versions, not the LXX].

Italic figures indicate page numbers in this book.

INTRODUCTION

I. THE LIFE AND WRITINGS OF ORIGEN

ORIGEN WAS incomparably the greatest scholar and theologian of the Eastern Church in the early centuries. His fame has been great and lasting; but (as Macaulay said of Boswell) it marvellously resembles infamy. He was never canonized, although his voluminous writings were the great fountain-head of Eastern thought for generations. The reaction against him culminated in the anathematizing of his teaching by Justinian and the fifth ecumenical Council of Constantinople in A.D. 553; and with this verdict Luther, for example, who knew little of Origen and disliked intensely what he knew, would have cordially agreed. It is only in modern times that there has been anything approaching a return to Origen, and scholars are not wanting—Protestant and Roman alike—who would not only vindicate his importance but defend his orthodoxy. Whether this is justified or not remains open to question; but it is certainly true that in asking whether Origen is orthodox we need not be bound by the ancient verdicts. For one thing, we approach him with different questions in our own minds. For another, we are not disposed to pay too much reverence to the early canonizations, remembering that Jerome and Cyril were among their number.

Origen (c. 186–c. A.D. 255) was born in Egypt, probably at Alexandria, and given the best Christian upbringing and education then available. From his earliest years he was conversant with the Bible; and his almost fanatical loyalty to the faith was shown when at the age of seventeen his father Leonidas became a victim of the persecution of Septimius Severus: not only did he most strongly urge his father to accept martyrdom ('Take care not to change thy mind on our account'), but fired with the ideal of martyrdom as a vocation, was only prevented from achieving it for himself by his mother, who at the critical moment hid all his clothes 'and so laid upon him the necessity of remaining at home' (as Eusebius puts it). One is reminded of the felon who walked to the gallows under an umbrella, lest he should catch cold; and this is the first hint of that instinctive celibacy—that shrinking from sex—which leaves strong marks not only on his life but his theology. He was an ascetic through and through.

The Alexandria of Origen's day was the great meeting-place of philosophy and religion. There was a secular university, with unique libraries and a large staff of professors; there was also a strong Christian Church, which ran its own 'Catechetical School' (for the teaching of catechumens before baptism). To this Origen was appointed as master by his bishop, Demetrius, while still only seventeen. He immediately gave up all other activities and sold all his secular books. He threw himself with the utmost ardour into the study and teaching of Scripture, 'persevering', as Eusebius tells us, 'in the most philosophic manner of life, at one time disciplining himself by fasting, at another measuring out the time for sleep, which he was careful to take, never on a couch, but on the floor. . . . he considered that those sayings of the Saviour . . . ought to be kept [literally] which exhort us not [to provide] two coats nor to use shoes. . . . He is said . . . to have walked for many years without using a shoe of any description'.[1] The presence of women at his lectures and the consequent possibility of scandal suggested to him a literal acting on the words of Matthew 19^{12b} ('there are eunuchs which made themselves eunuchs for the kingdom of heaven's sake'), and his self-mutilation was later brought against him by such as Demetrius, who had begun to dislike him on other grounds.

His success as a teacher, however, was unparalleled. As time went on he handed over the teaching of the catechumens to Heraclas, a pupil, and confined himself to advanced instruction. The school, indeed, became the first Christian University, where Christian ideas were treated in a liberal and even speculative manner, with constant reference not only to heresies but to pagan philosophies, in an atmosphere redolent of the Platonic tradition. Nothing is more characteristic of Origen than his Platonic determination to follow the argument wherever it leads—ὅπου ὁ λόγος ἄγει—combined with his attempt, successful or not, to replace the Platonic λόγος by the biblical Λόγος, the Incarnate Word of God. As a scholar he sought to master all branches of learning, with theology as their crown, and his lectures attracted not only Christians but heretics and pagans. His conversion of the

---

[1] *H.E.*, VI.3, transl. Oulton (Loeb edn.).

wealthy Valentinian heretic Ambrosius was of great practical importance to him, for this new friend supplied him with shorthand writers and copyists and thus enabled him to begin his vast series of literary works. Nor was he a mere recluse: he visited Rome with Ambrosius; he visited Palestine (and in particular Caesarea); he was consulted by the Governor of Arabia, and even (at Antioch) by the Emperor's mother, Julia Mammaea; he attended the lectures of Ammonius Saccas, the neo-Platonist and teacher of the far-famed Plotinus, to equip himself for meeting difficulties brought by his non-Christian students.

Suddenly the scene darkens. Not for the last time, a theological college principal was becoming too powerful for the ecclesiastical hierarchy. Origen was only a layman—and he was becoming the unofficial arbiter of the whole Eastern Church! Relations between him and his bishop became strained, and reached breaking-point when Origen allowed himself during a stay at Caesarea to be ordained priest by his friends the Bishops of Jerusalem and Caesarea. Demetrius, who had not been consulted, secured from his synods Origen's condemnation and later his degradation from the priesthood. Demetrius's attempt to obtain the backing of his brother-bishops by a series of letters was successful at Rome but had no effect in Caesarea, where Origen settled (in A.D. 232), and continued his literary and educational work. Among his pupils were now the famous Firmilian, already Bishop of the Cappadocian Caesarea, Gregory Thaumaturgus (the 'wonder-worker', later Bishop of Neo-Caesarea in Pontus), and his faithful patrons Alexander of Jerusalem and Theoctistus of his own Caesarea. He regularly expounded the Scriptures publicly, in Church, and near the end of his life these 'homilies' were taken down for publication. All the time he was writing, travelling, learning, settling difficulties and converting heretics in the Churches. He made a long visit to Athens, for study and writing. Twice his work was interrupted by the periodic persecutions suffered by the Christians in that age—the persecution of Maximin (235-7), when Origen retired to Cappadocia as the guest of a Christian lady named Juliana, and that of Decius (250-1), when Alexander of Jerusalem died in prison, and Origen himself was tortured. His health was weakened, and he died about A.D. 255, leaving a reputation quite unique as preacher, scholar, devotional writer, commentator, theologian—and a corpus of writings challenging comparison in everything except distinction of style with the greatest names in the history of Christianity.

What, then, went wrong? The admiration accorded his writings became more and more reserved, and it became Origen's unhappy fate to touch off controversy after controversy, until the final condemnation by Justinian and the fifth Council. I cannot retrace here the intensely tangled story of the next three hundred years. There is no more revealing commentary on human self-seeking and ecclesiastical intrigue than the parts played in the Origenistic dispute by Jerome and Rufinus. What lay behind it all? Personal and political factors, no doubt; but theologically one may point above all to two things—his methods of biblical interpretation, and his misfortune to be a doctrinal pioneer. We need only to remember the trial of Robertson Smith to realize the extent of positive hatred to which the former can drive the most sincere of Christians; and the pioneer of dogmatic definition becomes outdated and 'unsafe' by the very progress that he has initiated. His gaps and flaws, his blind-alleys become increasingly evident; and he suffers from later and lesser followers who expand—often improperly, and with insufficient regard to his work as a whole—hints and speculations that are subsequently seen to lead to heresy. Origen has been called the father of Arianism, and if one looks merely at phrases like ἕτερος κατ' οὐσίαν ('different in being', of the Father and the Son), the accusation seems plausible. But his doctrine as a whole—not only the distinctive teaching on the eternal generation of the Son, but the full range of treatment he gives to Christology and the Work of Christ—is in a different world from Arius. There is no theologian, not even Karl Barth, who loses more by the summaries and criticisms of 'secondary authorities' than Origen. That is why I have attempted, in this book, to let him speak for himself.

The writings of Origen may be classified as follows:

(1) The *Hexapla* (only extant in fragments)—a six-column text of the Old Testament, setting out in parallel columns the Hebrew text; the Hebrew text in Greek characters; the Greek version of Aquila of Pontus (a convert from Christianity to Judaism, who compiled this version, with literal fidelity to the original, as a counterblast to the Christian use of the LXX—*c*. A.D. 128); the

Greek version of Symmachus, an Ebionite, compiled toward the end of the second century, and attempting to improve the literal version of Aquila into something more idiomatic, for the benefit of non-Jewish readers; a revised recension of the LXX itself, with Origen's own attempt to harmonize it with the Hebrew; and the Greek version of Theodotion, *c.* 150, a Jewish convert, of Ephesus, which was a free revision of the LXX.

The object of this gigantic enterprise was critical; but whereas the modern scholar would compare manuscripts, Origen compared versions, in order to establish as closely as possible the wording or meaning of the Hebrew, which he recognized as the ultimate authority.

(2) *Commentaries* and *Homilies* on most books of the Bible.

In addition to the full commentaries, Origen left many sets of notes on separate words, phrases, or verses of Scripture. Some of these survive in the Greek (e.g. the *'Selecta in Psalmos'*), some in rather more elegant Latin translations made later by other hands. (The so-called *Commentariorum in Matthaeum Series*, consisting of 145 excerpts from Origen's Commentary on Matthew [covering 22^{34}-27^{66}] is an anonymous Latin translation of a part of this work which is otherwise not extant.)

The *'Homilies'* were sermons actually preached by Origen and taken down in shorthand by copyists. Eusebius tells us that Origen did not permit this to be done until he was over sixty and had now gained 'immense facility' in preaching 'from long preparation'.[2] It is commonly said that these works (e.g.) 'belong to the history of Christian spirituality and mysticism rather than to biblical science';[3] but they are of the greatest interest to the student of theology. In them Origen lets his allegorism have full scope, and one often feels that like other preachers he gives us more of his heart in his sermons than in his more formal works. It may be true, as Kidd says, that 'the mixed congregation of Caesarea was not altogether an encouraging audience for a great scholar; and he is oppressed by a sense of the need for Reserve';[4] but one would suppose that this worried him less and less as the years went by, and the need for Reserve in any case applied only to choice of subject. Great preachers cannot help betraying their real thoughts, often unconsciously and by implication. It is certainly true that the Homilies do not form a

---

[2] *H.E.*, VI.36.1.   [3] Quasten, *Patrology*, II.47.   [4] *History of the Church*, I.405.

separated group of 'devotional' writings which Origen consciously kept clear of theology and even 'biblical science'.

(3) *De Principiis*, Περὶ Ἀρχῶν, 'On First Principles', a dogmatic treatise in four books. This is the first attempt ever made to construct a system of Christian theology. Origen takes his place beside St Thomas, Melanchthon, Calvin, and our modern dogmatists like Barth and Schmaus. The four books deal respectively with God, the world, human freedom, and the revelation of all this in Scripture. Origen's indomitable pursuit of every difficulty into the realms of speculative philosophy should not blind us to his conscious loyalty to Scripture: he begins with the Κήρυγμα, and his failure to think out every problem in Christological dimensions is partly a measure of the intractability of the problems, and partly the penalty of the pioneer.

(4) *Contra Celsum*, an apology for the faith written in answer to a detailed and far-reaching attack by Celsus—an eclectic Platonist—nearly seventy years earlier. Celsus' work, *The True Doctrine*, attacks Christianity from two points of view: first, the Jewish, in which Celsus puts into the mouth of an imaginary Jew his objections to Jesus Christ; secondly, his own. Celsus is no godless rationalist. He believes that the 'true doctrine', known by the wise and godly from the beginning, has been perverted by the Jews and is in danger of destruction from the still more corrupt descendants of the Jews—the Christians. Like George Bernard Shaw, he shudders at the absurdity of worshipping a recently executed Jew; but unlike Shaw he knows his subject, and his real concern is a return to the true faith of our fathers. Origen's enormously copious reply, in eight books, was written in response to the appeal of his patron Ambrosius.

A definitive translation with notes, by Dr Henry Chadwick, was published in 1953 (Camb. Univ. Press). This is indispensable; but the general reader should remember that throughout Origen is arguing *ad hominem*, and that although he shares many of the philosophical presuppositions of his adversary, much of what is most characteristic of Origen is missing—e.g. his allegorizing of Scripture. The book was not written for 'true Christians' but for outsiders, or at any rate for those 'weak in the faith' (Preface, § 6). Hence although it contains masses of positive teaching, its chief value in an inquiry like the present one is partly in its discussions of themes (like Providence) where there is some common ground between pagan philosopher and Christian theologian, and partly in its incidental confirmation of doctrines expounded more positively elsewhere.

(5) (a) *On Prayer*. A short treatise addressed to Ambrosius and an unknown lady, Tatiana, dealing with prayer in general and the Lord's Prayer in particular. (A valuable translation with notes and essays, by Canon E. G. Jay, was published in 1954 [S.P.C.K.].)

(b) *Exhortation to Martyrdom*, written at Caesarea in A.D. 235 during the persecution of Maximin, and addressed to Ambrosius and Prototectus (a presbyter of the local church). Origen urges his friends to stand fast in tribulation; martyrdom is a duty of every true Christian, because all who love God wish to be made one with Him. A brave confession of the faith is a sure guarantee of salvation. Apostasy and idolatry are the greatest sins—they lead to union with the idols, which will be severely punished after death. Only those who take upon themselves the cross with Christ will be saved, and the greater the sacrifice, the greater the reward. By martyrdom a man can offer himself as a true priest in sacrifice to God, for 'just as Jesus redeemed us by His precious blood, so by the precious blood of the martyrs others may also be redeemed'. Origen had certainly earned the right to urge such things on his friends, whatever we think of the implicit theology of this conclusion.

(c) *De Resurrectione* (of which only fragments remain).

(6) Other writings, mainly extant in fragments only, and one or two letters, need not be specified here. But mention should be made of:

Philocalia, a collection of twenty-seven 'choice passages' from the writings of Origen, made toward the end of the next century by Gregory of Nazianzus and Basil. This anthology is of high intrinsic merit, and frequently gives us the original Greek of passages which survive in the Origenistic corpus only in Latin translation—never wholly reliable (see below).

Origen has no real distinction of style, and no great dexterity of phrase. He is inordinately diffuse. In reading him one is constantly reminded of Bright's description of Gladstone: 'When

I speak, I strike across from headland to headland. Mr Gladstone follows the coastline; and when he comes to a navigable river he is unable to resist the temptation of tracing it to its source.' I have done my best in the following pages to temper his eloquence by tactful selection and omission. But one main cause of his prolixity may be accounted to him as a merit—he never loses any opportunity of quoting Scripture. Not only did he know his Bible apparently by heart, but he can discharge in one volley a whole mass of relevant quotations from all parts of the Bible on practically any given point. His learning is often, to our mind, wrong-headed and woodenly mechanical; and his apparent lack of any sense of humour, or of any real awareness that the biblical writers were human beings, with human feelings and failings, leads him into occasionally fathomless absurdities of exegesis. But no biblical theologian has ever surpassed his high seriousness of purpose, his untiring search for the truth, or his sustained conviction that the key to every page of Scripture is the Word of God in Christ.

Origen sets out his doctrine of the interpretation of Scripture in a famous passage:

> *Princ.* IV.2.4: 'The right way, as it appears to us, of approaching the Scriptures and extracting their meaning—the way that we have tracked down from the writings themselves—is as follows: . . . the reader should portray the meaning of the sacred writings on his own soul in a threefold fashion, so that the simple man may be edified by what we may term the *flesh* of the Scripture, i.e. the sense most ready to hand; while the man who has made more progress may be edified by what we may term its *soul*; while the man who is fully mature (like those mentioned by the apostle—'Yet among the mature we do impart wisdom, although it is not a wisdom of this age or of the rulers of this age, who are doomed to pass away. But we impart a secret and hidden wisdom of God, which God decreed before the ages for our glorification' [1 Cor 2⁶ᶠ]) may be edified by the 'Spiritual Law' [Rom 7¹⁴] which 'has a shadow of the good things to come' [Heb 10¹]. For just as a man consists of body, soul and spirit, so in the same way does Scripture, which has been divinely ordained by God to be given for men's salvation.'

These three senses—the flesh (or literal sense), the soul (or moral sense), and the spirit (or mystical sense)—do not, however, all apply to every passage; and Origen shows in practice a tendency to fuse the latter two, and derive the resultant moral/mystical meaning from the text by allegory.

Nothing has aroused more interest among British theologians since the war than this question of allegory and typology in the interpretation of the Bible. A whole series of writings, largely by Anglicans, has culminated in the magnificent *Allegory and Event* (SCM, 1959) by Dr R. P. C. Hanson of Nottingham—the crown of his Origen studies, and among the most forthright and fascinating works of theology ever published. I am not, however, concerned in this book with the question of allegory as such, but with the resultant Christian doctrines that Origen expounds—however he reaches them. It is nevertheless important that the readers I have in mind should appreciate the problem of the validity of allegorical interpretation.

Probably every Methodist preacher has tried his hand at 'Wrestling Jacob', and followed the lead of Charles Wesley in allegorizing it into the wrestling of the human soul with God in prayer. Valuable devotional lessons, no doubt, are to be drawn from the old story in Genesis; but the question is, how far is such an allegory a legitimate interpretation of the text? Was it in any sense in the mind of the author? If not, are we justified in applying a theory of biblical inspiration whereby any given text may be expounded not so much according to the conscious intention of the author as according to the presumed will of God for the reader—that is, in line with the divine impact on the reader of the revelation of God in *Scripture-as-a-whole?* Thus, whatever the author of Isaiah 53 meant by the Servant, may we maintain that God clearly means us to understand it as a delineation of the suffering Christ, and that this procedure is justified by the recurrence in *Scripture-as-a-whole* of patterns of action and types of person which lead to and culminate in the story of the Incarnate Christ? 'Tracking down', in Origen's fashion, the mode of interpretation 'from the Scriptures themselves', one could point not only to the example of St Paul ('they drank from the supernatural rock which followed them, and the rock was Christ' [1 Cor 10⁴]) but to the precepts of Jesus ('Beginning with Moses and all the prophets, He interpreted to them in all the Scriptures the things concerning Himself.' . . . 'everything written about me in the law of Moses and the prophets and the psalms must be fulfilled' [Lk 24²⁷, ⁴⁴]). 'You search the Scriptures, because you think that in them you have eternal life; but it is they who bear witness to me, and you refuse to come to me that you may have life' [Jn 5³⁹ᶠ].

So much seems reasonable and to the Christian even necessary. But when Origen, the prime allegorist of Christendom, gets to work the thing repeatedly becomes incredible. Look at his exegesis of Judges 6³⁶ᶠᶠ (Gideon and the sign of the fleece) (*Hom. Judg.*, VIII.4, see below, pp. *84*f), or of 1 Samuel 1 (Helchana and his wives and children) (*Hom. 1 Sam.*, 5, pp. *43*f). Clearly the authors of Judges and 1 Samuel never dreamed such things as Origen imputes to them. But neither did the author of the Pentateuch dream that the rock was Christ, or that the wrestling of Jacob had anything to do with prayer. And it is at least questionable whether the prophet of the suffering servant was thinking of the future Messiah. Yet we feel that these last three 'types' or 'allegories' are legitimate, whereas Origen's Gideon and Helchana are not. What is the difference?

I have never seen a satisfactory answer to this question. It is easy to talk of Origen's clumsy literalism, or of the place of common sense in the application of the allegorical method, or to say that acceptance of the principle of Christological interpretation of the Old Testament does not justify any and every typological venture. Such answers merely repeat the question. Fortunately, I am not called upon in the present study to give my own answer; but I would ask the reader to keep the question in mind as he reads the numerous examples of allegory in the following pages.

What I am concerned to stress, to Origen's very great credit, is his two-fold insistence on the *unity* of the Bible and the *Christological interpretation* thereof. He may blunder in the detail of application—and once he sets off after a false hare, none can run farther or faster into absurdity. But in these two points he is very largely a pioneer, as he also is in his doctrine that God's grace is operative not only in the writing of Scripture but in its understanding. The Bible is, from every point of view, the 'book of grace'.

Note on Origen and His Latin Translators

Of the enormous list of works by Origen given above, only a small part is extant in the original Greek. This is largely in consequence of his successive condemnations. Much of the rest, however, survives in later Latin translations, mainly by Jerome and Rufinus, of the late fourth and early fifth centuries. Unhappily, these translations—or at any rate the translations of Rufinus, which cover the most important writings—are notoriously unreliable. The story of Jerome and Rufinus and their translations is a particularly unedifying one, and reflects little credit on either. Rufinus in particular deliberately emended his author's text at points where Origen's orthodoxy was currently questioned, in order to safeguard his own reputation; and his omissions, additions, and alterations can be seen at a glance in Koetschau's edition of the *De Principiis*, in the places where the original Greek survives. But besides this dishonesty, Rufinus is guilty of another charge—he is hopelessly paraphrastic. Origen is copious enough already, but the work of Rufinus, purporting to be a translation, 'represents a working over rather than a translation . . . and is in places so unreliable that it continually needs checking to be of any use'.[5]

The points at which one must be particularly wary of Rufinus are those on which Origen's orthodoxy had come to be impugned —the 'subordination' of Son and Holy Spirit, the pre-existence of souls, the purely spiritual resurrection, and the ultimate salvation of all beings, including the Devil. The 'tradition of the Church' had grown to be at variance with him on these matters, and the authority and status of that tradition left less and less room for the venturesome speculations of the pioneer from liberal Alexandria. Rufinus dare not be on the wrong side of the fence, and on these matters he will insert, omit, or conceal in a cloud of paraphrase the Greek of the original.

Why, then, use the Latin at all? Because, comparatively, so little of the Greek survives, and because in the present inquiry these doctrines are not *directly* in question. It may be that grace is ultimately involved in them all; but at least the doctrine of grace was not *as such* in question in the later disputes. Subordinationism, for example, concerns the Person of Christ: my direct concern is the Work of this Christ, 'subordinate' or not, for and within man.

I have, however, genuinely sought throughout to use the Greek remains of Origen himself as my primary authority, and the Latin translations mainly for illustrative purposes.

[5] Koetschau, quoted by Hanson, *Origen's Doctrine of Tradition*, p. 41.

2. THE DOCTRINE OF GRACE

The extraordinary revival of interest in Origen in recent years has issued in a stream of learned and absorbing books, which look at him from many different points of view. The translations of the *Contra Celsum* by Chadwick and the *Prayer* by Jay throw revealing light on his philosophical background and his theory and practice of devotion. The studies of Hanson (*Origen's Doctrine of Tradition* and *Allegory and Event*) look into his biblical scholarship and interpretation. The pioneer work of Volker (*Das Vollkommenheitsideal des Origenes* [1931]) and Molland (*The Conception of the Gospel in the Alexandrian Theology* [1938]) has been followed by a remarkable series of studies, mainly in French, such as Bertrand's *Mystique de Jésus chez Origène* (1951), Crouzel's *Théologie de l'Image de Dieu chez Origène* (1956), Balthasar's *Parole et Mystère chez Origène* (1957), Marguerite Harl's *Origène et la Fonction Révélatrice du Verbe Incarné* (1958). Origen plays an important role in such a recent study as Turner's *Pattern of Christian Truth* (1954).

My own small study claims no comparison at all with these works of scholarship. Its main aim is to introduce my author to Methodists—not of course to the scholars of my Church, but to the ordinary members who have an interest in theological studies and a desire to find their way into unfamiliar fields. But it may be that the choice of the doctrine of Grace has a value of its own. After all, the burning question about Origen is still his orthodoxy. Was his condemnation justified? Is it possible that the points on which his critics settled were peripheral, and that in his fundamental presentation he was loyal to the Christian revelation? If so, what better touchstone of orthodoxy could there be than the doctrine of Grace?

The doctrine of Grace itself has, of course, become another focal-point of research and controversy in recent years. As the ecumenical movement opens our ecclesiastical windows, we not only discover something of the treasures bequeathed to other Christian communities, but we are forced to look more closely at our own. I should make bold to say that every major divergence in theology, worship and ethics between the main Christian Churches today revolves ultimately into different conceptions of Grace; and if we are ever to undercut our differences, it can only be by a common return to the full, fresh and determinative doctrine of the New Testament, and above all of St Paul. Here there is no danger of deadening 'archaism'. To seek to impose the exact pattern of Church government, of behaviour, and even of worship that can with varying degrees of clarity be deduced from the New Testament records of the primitive communities would indeed be to 'quench the Spirit' and reduce the living Church to a dead relic. But the New Testament doctrine of Grace is the sum and substance—the whole point—of the Christian Gospel, and the new truth into which the Spirit leads us as history unfolds can never add to or alter the seminal and decisive revelation in Christ which Paul designates χάρις—only give us fresh insight into its range and application. 'The religion which underlies the New Testament writings is a religion of grace, or it is nothing', says Moffatt (*Grace in the New Testament*, p. xv); 'Grace in the New Testament is the basic and the most characteristic element of the Christian Gospel' says Torrance (*Grace in the Apostolic Fathers*, p. 34); '*La grâce n'est pas dans le christianisme une notion secondaire surajoutée par une spéculation théologique . . . , mais elle est* l'essentiel et le tout du christianisme *au point qu' on peut dire que parler du christianisme, c'est parler de la grâce, . . . que traiter d'un point quelconque de la doctrine chrétienne, c'est traiter d'un des aspects de la grâce. . . . la grâce n'est rien d'autre que cette vι. de Jésus-Christ en nous. Ainsi le christianisme, c'est la grâce, et la grâce, c'est le christianisme*', says the Roman Catholic Jean Daujat (*La Grâce et nous Chrétiens* [1956]), pp. 9f.[6]

In 1948, when I was studying theology at Wesley House, Cambridge, a book appeared which cast a searching new light on the early history of doctrine. Dr Sanday used to speak of the experience when 'a number of threads seem suddenly to come

---

[6] For a vigorous counter-statement see the final essay in *The Doctrine of Grace*, ed. Whitley (SCM, 1932), by the former Bishop of Gloucester, A. C. Headlam (pp. 373ff), who suggests that it has been a 'great mistake to exalt the doctrine of grace into the importance which it has held, especially since the Reformation, in Christian theology. It means, in fact, the substitution of an abstract scheme oɪ salvation in the place of personal adherence to and faith in our Lord, which is, I would hold, the really fundamental principle of Christianity' (p. 374). This statement, and the whole of the essay, exhibit in startling relief the distance we have moved, and the fresh insights we have gained (for example, into the theology of the Reformation and counter-Reformation) in the last quarter of a century. So too, in a different way, does *Grace and Personality* by John Oman (3rd edn, 1925). If ever two men needed the 'Barthian corrective', they were Oman and Headlam. Headlam, indeed, was years behind the very book to which he wrote the postscript.

together and unite in a definite conclusion'.[7] We had all been conscious that there was something wrong with the theology of the Apostolic Fathers—a decisive falling-away from the level of the New Testament. It was left to T. F. Torrance to focus this decline and give it a name.[8] It was the doctrine of grace that went wrong; it became detached from the *person* of Jesus Christ; the great presupposition of the Christian life ceased to be the decisive act of God which cut across human life and set it on a wholly new basis, grounded upon the self-giving of God in Christ, and became God's call to a new life in obedience to revealed truth—man's acts toward God, his striving toward justification, moralism replacing grace. The twin factors of Judaism, with its insistence on law, and Hellenism, with its humanist naturalism, coincided under the wing of Christianity; and the Apostolic Fathers present a theology which was corroded from both sides, because it had lost hold of the basic significance of grace.[9] Legalism and moralism were the 'enemies within the gates', and are with us today.

What, then, of Origen? Here was a man of the next age, rooted and grounded in the learned Hellenism of Alexandria, with a range of knowledge and a penetration of mind that the somewhat pedestrian Apostolic Fathers could never even have appreciated. Did he still further corrode the New Testament doctrine of grace? Torrance claims that what was lost by Clement and Ignatius and their fellows, was not recovered—and even then not in full—until the Reformation. But in Origen was a theologian concerning whom it is at least possible that because the Church condemned him it failed sufficiently in other directions to assimilate him—that quite apart from his heresies and his allegorism, his deeper and wider knowledge of Scripture and philosophy might have corrected some of the defects of his predecessors. This it is our task to investigate, and our method will be to let him speak for himself.

I have no 'private and peculiar' doctrine of grace to set over against the great Alexandrian. I look to the New Testament, and above all to St Paul. But if a summary is needed I should unreservedly commend the essay of W. Manson in *The Doctrine*

[7] Peake, *Recollections and Appreciations*, p. 42.
[8] *The Doctrine of Grace in the Apostolic Fathers* (Oliver & Boyd, 1948).
[9] Torrance, ibid., Pref.; pp. 133ff.

of Grace (ed. Whitley), which has always seemed to me to set the stage for a whole generation of theological conversation. 'Grace for St Paul signifies the generous love or gift of God by which in Christ salvation is bestowed on man and a new world of blessings opened. It implies that what saves man is not something proceeding from himself or from his own nature, or from his own will or effort, but something "wholly other", which proceeds from God and which is "exhibited" (Rom 3²⁵ᶠ) on the Cross of Christ' (pp. 43f). This, says Dr Manson, is the 'fundamental Christian sense of grace to which all uses of the word in the New Testament go back, and by which in the last resort all these other uses must be justified' (p. 44). Dr Manson does full justice to the centrality of the Cross in this theology, 'as a historical revelation of the divine passion to forgive and save a lost world' (p. 45).[10] God's grace 'has for its object to disclose' (i.e. 'wisdom') 'and bring in' (i.e. 'righteousness') 'for Christians a higher world of spiritual good, in which we must see the translation into present actual experience of the eschatological promise of salvation' (ibid.). 'In particular this grace of God has found concrete embodiment in his [Paul's] apostleship to the Gentiles and in the admission of the latter into the people of God' (p. 47).[11]

The grace of God—the initiative of God in salvation—takes effect in human hearts in various ways, 'now as giving men a new status, now as conferring various special gifts, now as inspiring to fresh tasks and responsibilities' (p. 49). But the 'primary sense of God's graciousness as expressed in His great gift of salvation in Jesus Christ' is always retained (p. 50).

In the Church are 'various spiritual aptitudes and functions which have their source in God's will to give', and which Paul calls χαρίσματα—'grace-gifts' (cf. Rom 12⁶). But Paul guards against any conception of χάρις as an immanent power or influence or quality at work in the world, which might depersonalize it (and, we might add, degrade it into an ecclesiastical instrument). 'To detach grace from the person of Christ and to think of it as acting impersonally upon man is inevitably to land in determinism. That was Augustine's mistake.'[12] 'It was doubt-

---

[10] Cf. Torrance, op. cit., p. 137: 'The most astonishing feature was *the failure* [of the Apostolic Fathers] *to grasp the significance of the death of Christ*.'
[11] This point was brought home by Armitage Robinson's *Commentary on Ephesians*. We shall see what a prominent part it plays in Origen.
[12] Torrance, op. cit., p. 33, note 2.

less for that reason that whenever Paul spoke of grace-gift in a detached sense it was not χάρις he used, but χάρισμα, and what is more, he did not derive χαρίσματα from χάρις but from Πνεῦμα'.[13] That is to say, the grace of God—the generous gift of salvation and a new life through and in the sacrifice of Christ—is made available for believers, and issues in 'spiritual aptitudes and functions' in their lives, through that personal presence of God with man that we call the *Holy Spirit*. He grants, He controls, He withdraws—and no Christian, no Church can so appropriate God's grace as to live to himself or to itself, with secure control of its administration. The Christian, the Church are alike under judgement, and the living 'gifts and graces' which are made available for them stem from the sacrifice and victory of Christ, perpetually renewed, and are granted through the living presence of the Holy Spirit.

[13] Ibid., p. 33.

CHAPTER ONE

GRACE IN ORIGEN—THE WORD AND THE IDEA

THERE IS NO formal and comprehensive definition of Grace (χάρις, *Gratia*) in any of the voluminous writings of Origen. This suggests from the start that χάρις was never for him—as it was for Augustine—a *problem*, much less a battleground. '. . . in patristic and particularly in Eastern Greek literature, there are no special researches about this most essential element in Christianity. . . . what partial declarations there are on this subject are neither strictly dogmatic nor sufficiently definite.' This pronounces Gloubokowsky,[1] and whatever we think of his bland suggestion that the Greek Fathers did not theorize on Grace because they instinctively enjoyed it—'theory began in the West with the disorderly life of individuals'—we shall certainly not find in Origen discussions about grace infused and imputed, grace prevenient, concomitant and subsequent, grace forgiving and enabling, grace habitual, actual and sanctifying, grace efficient and sufficient, grace resistible and irresistible, grace general and special. But if we have any sense of the continuity of Christian thought, we shall be surprised if the later struggles have not been at least foreshadowed in Origen by latent tensions and potential stresses; just as, if we have any sense of the shifting responses of Christian thinkers to changing contemporary questions and challenges, we shall be prepared for a (perhaps unconscious) modification of standard Pauline usage by a man as sensitive and flexible as Origen. Nevertheless, we shall approach him with our minds as far as possible emptied of later doctrinal controversy and let him speak for himself.

Our first step will be to formulate as precisely as possible the definition of χάρις which the wide range of references in Origen would suggest.

---

[1] *The Doctrine of Grace*, ed. Whitley, p. 62.

§ 1. DEFINITION

(A) GRACE IS THROUGHOUT A MATTER OF DIVINE GIVING

Grace is God's free giving—generous, abundant, a reward of our endurance but not measured by it.

Hom. Ezek. VI.6: 'Grace comes to us from God and we are filled with His gift.'

Martyrdom 2: '(We shall face affliction with proper endurance) if we turn our mind from our troubles and look not on the present evils but on the things laid up by the grace of God[2] for the athletes in Christ who have kept the rules, because of their endurance of these present evils. For God makes His favours [εὐεργεσίας] to abound, and gives not merely what the struggles of the contestants have merited, but what befits His own non-grudging and generous nature, who in His wisdom makes great His graces to those who show with all their power . . . that they love Him with all their soul.'[3]

Grace is the unexpected, unearned forbearance of God.

Hom. Josh. XVI.3 (of the two advents of Christ): 'Happy are all who are conquered by Christ in His first coming. For it is a sheer boon [χάρις] to them that they are already subjugated while many others are still fighting. For at His second coming the prisoners are taken by force [ἀνάγκῃ].'

(This passage I have translated from the Greek of Procopius 1024 c.)

It is the very opposite of a reward.

Comm. Rom. (Gk), § 22 on 4[4t] (*JTS*, III.357): 'None of God's gifts to humanity is made in payment of a debt, but all are of grace.'

Ibid. § 34 on 6[23] (ibid. p. 368): '(Paul's) distinction is rightly made: "wages" is used with reference to sin, "grace-gift"

---

[2] χάριτι Θεοῦ not, as O'Meara, with ἀθλήσασι, but with ἀποκείμενα.
[3] Cf. for this *idea* of 'grace abounding', *Hom. Num.* XI.6: 'He is the bread which though always eaten always remains—nay, is always increased. . . . The more you take the Word of God, the more insistently you eat that food, the more exceedingly will it abound in you.'

(χάρισμα) with reference to God. For God's gifts are of grace, not like wages which are owed.'

Comm. Rom. IV.5, on 4¹⁶ᶠ: '(St Paul's view of) the distinction between reward and grace . . . is that reward is something owed, while grace is not owed but a work of sheer kindness. [And at Rom 4¹⁶ᶠ], wishing to show that God gives the reversion of the promises not in payment of a debt but as an act of grace, Paul says that it is given not as a reward that is due but as a gift to faith. Just as for example the fact that we exist cannot possibly be a reward of our works but is due to the grace of our Creator. . . .'

It is God's giving to us, which even when in return for is yet in deliberate excess of our giving to Him.

Hom. Lk. XXXIX: 'God asks for things from us, not that He has need of anything,⁴ but in order that He might graciously

---

⁴ Cf. *Hom. Num.* XXIII.2 on 28² [τὰ δῶρά μου δόματά μου], interpreted by Origen as 'your gifts to me are actually my gifts to you'. [Baehrens compares Philo's comment on the same passage (*Quod Deus Immut.*, 6): εὐχαριστητέον . . . διὰ τίνων δὲ ὅτι μὴ διὰ τῶν ὑπ' αὐτοῦ δοθέντων, 'we must offer a sacrifice of thanksgiving . . . and what can we give except what He has given us?'] 'Everything (says God) that mankind has it receives from me. Lest therefore anyone should believe that in offering gifts he is conferring some benefit on God, and should thus stand guilty of sacrilege through the very act that he intended as worship (for what sacrilege could equal that of thinking that one can minister to God in need?) God must . . . first teach men the lesson that his offerings are rather giving back than giving away.' Ibid. XII.3 (on the same passage): 'What . . . can a man offer God? Just this . . . "gifts to Me that I have already given" . . . what has God given man? Knowledge of himself. What does man offer to God? His faith and love. That is what God seeks from man (quoting Deut 10¹², q.v.).' Cf. *Sel. Ps.* 292ᴬ: 'None can "exalt the Lord" if the Lord has not uplifted him. . . . To exalt the Lord means to hold an elevated and lofty doctrine concerning Him. . . . To uplift one's own soul in all virtue and in the life of wisdom is to exalt the One who dwells in that soul.' Cf. *Hom. Josh.* XII.2: 'None boasted of His victory or ascribed it to His own courage, but because they knew that it is Jesus who gives the victory, "not a man moves his tongue" (Josh 10²¹). The apostle well understood this when he said "Not I but that grace of God that is in me" (1 Cor 15¹⁰). (Origen quotes Lk 17¹⁰ [unprofitable servants], and adds): here too in the same way, he seems to be debarring vainglory after success.' Ibid. XII.3: 'May my Lord Jesus grant me (after winning the battle of life) . . . to lay the victory not to my own credit but to that of His cross.' Baehrens quotes parallels in the Greek tradition: Philo, *Quod Deus Immut.*, 7: 'God needs nothing'; Xenophon *Memorabilia*, I.6.10: 'To need nothing is divine, to need as little as possible is to get as near as possible to the divine.' This latter quotation is particularly instructive. Both Christian believer and pagan philosopher could say 'God needs nothing', and both would be expressing the thought of divine transcendence. But whereas the pagan naturally goes on to commend an aloof independence as the target of our ethical strivings, the Christian concludes differently—'He *needs* nothing, but He *wants* us'. 'He hath loved, He hath loved us', says Charles Wesley, '(not because He *has* to, or because He *needs* something we can give but) because He *would* love.' Hence the coincidence of phrase between Origen and Xenophon ('what sacrilege could equal that of thinking that one can minister to God in need?' and

give us in return [ἀντιχαρίσηται] things of His own. . . . God graciously gives us in return good things—with an addition. For to him who made his one mina into ten (Lk 19¹¹ff) He gave in return the ten minas, adding to them another that belonged to the man who did not work.'

It is God's freely-given help to man, and its limits are not so much our needs as our receptive capacity and God's judgement of what will really benefit us.

Comm. Eph., § 17 on 4⁶ (JTS, III.413): 'God does not *have* to "measure out" His Spirit and His grace—"to His greatness there are no limits" (Ps 145³). The point of the "measure" is to spare the recipients, who can only cope with what is fitting for them to take.'

Comm. Jn. XXXII.7 (6), on 13¹⁰ [the feet-washing. Why wash the already clean? Origen finely quotes Matthew 25²⁹ ('to him that hath shall be given') and after a long discussion makes the point that this feet-washing does more than meet our needs]. Ibid. 9 (6): 'for the grace-gift [χάρισμα] of God surpasses our need, even as does being in the glory of sun, moon and stars, or in the holy resurrection of the dead.'

Comm. Rom. IX.3: '(Paul teaches that) there are three ways of receiving grace, . . . his point is that we have some part to play in the matter, but that the greatest fact consists in the bounty of God. First . . . there is the "measure of faith" by which a man receives grace; then, it is given "for a man's profit"; lastly, the Spirit apportions it "as He wills" (cf. Rom 12⁶ with 1 Cor 12⁷, ¹¹). Now it appears to be our responsibility that sufficient faith should be found in us to merit higher grace;⁵ but God's judgement determines for what profitable

'To need nothing is divine') proves nothing as to any 'corroding Hellenism' on the former's theology. It is true that the impact of Greek philosophy on Eastern theologians threw up new questions which had to be answered: in this case, what is the relation of the God whom we agree to be wholly transcendent to the created world and to humanity? Those like Cullmann who would 'throw out all Hellenism with a pitchfork' seem to envisage every possible contact and relationship between Hellenism and Christianity as a degradation and corrosion of the Gospel. But *this* relationship—that of question and answer—they never consider, and it is surely legitimate and salutary. Indeed, one may wonder how Christianity will ever make its way in the world if it so shuns other faiths and philosophies that it will not even answer the questions they pose. Herein, I think, lies the real and permanent value of Origen as a speculative but loyal Christian theologian. (Cf. of course St Paul—Ac 17²⁵).

⁵ Note (and continually watch for) this remarkable collocation of grace and merit. Cf. e.g. Comm. Song Songs, II, p. 147 (translated below, p. 35): '*per gratiam, si meruerit.*'

and useful ends it should be given, and of course the decision to give it at all rests entirely on Him. . . . I think I have sufficiently laid down above the difference between the faith that is required from us and faith given us by God through grace . . . : the faith which hopes, believes and trusts with no shadow of doubting is our own; but the mode of operation of faith itself, our knowledge of it, and the perfected understanding of the things we believe, is given by God.'[6]

Comm. Jn. I.20 (22): (The Incarnation and Death of Christ took place because of man's sin, and would not otherwise have happened) 'We must ask, too, whether He would have become a "shepherd" either, if man had not become "ranked with the unthinking cattle and likened to them" (Ps 49[12] LXX). For if God saves men and cattle, He saves the cattle by graciously granting [χαρίσαμενος] a shepherd to those who cannot cope with [χωροῦσι] the king.'

Sel. Ezek. 16[8]: 'God is above feeling and change. He is uncreated. But the acts of His providence are as various as are those whom His providence rules, for He is maker of all. Some of these acts, for example, provoke to anger, others to envy. In the same way do His spiritual servants receive dispensations of His grace, glory and splendour, given from the one omnipotent God who is Himself above change and feeling.'[7]

It is granted to those who by faith and virtue are prepared to receive it.

Comm. Jn. Frag. 44 on 3[27]: 'The grace-gifts of God are given to those who by faith and virtue have become prepared to receive them.'

Comm. Eph., § 17 on 4[6] (*JTS.* III. 413): 'Grace is given "according

---

[6] For this dichotomy of faith, see pp. 25ff.

[7] The question arises whether God's grace is not equally shown in the 'dispensations which provoke to anger or envy'. Cf. *Hom. Jer.* XII.8: 'Paul had grounds for pride in his sights and visions, his signs and wonders, the toils he undertook for Christ, the churches he founded. . . . But since pride over even these achievements cannot be without peril, the kindly Father gave him, by way of a gift of grace [ἐν χαρίσματος μοιρᾷ], a "messenger of Satan" (2 Cor 12[7f]) . . . a gift of providence to forestall his pride. And the Lord made answer to him—"My grace is sufficient for thee".'

In *Sel. Ezek.* 16[8] here, χάρις is *not* specifically used for the whole idea of an unmoved and transcendent God accommodating Himself in His providence to the desires and passions of changeful man—the one pure unoriginate light broken up, as it were, through the lens of creation into the innumerable shades and colours to which sinful and ignorant man can respond. χάρις is merely one of the kindlier 'accommodations'. But the larger *idea* of grace is the whole point of the passage, as it is of the preceding extract from *Comm. Jn.*

to the measure of the gift of Christ", if not "from works" (Rom 11[6]), at least on condition of *some* qualification on our part. For grace is given "from faith" (Rom 4[16]), its purpose being to co-operate towards the adornment of faith with works . . .' (and quotes 1 Cor. 15[10]).

Hom. Lk. III on 1[11]: 'Sensible objects make no contribution to their being seen; the sound eye is directed to them and sees them whether they will or no. Divine objects, however, are not seen without their own empowering it, even when they stand before us. God was seen by Abraham or by other holy ones through divine grace. The eye of the soul of Abraham was not the only cause, but God offered Himself to be seen by the righteous man, who was worthy of seeing Him.'

Comm. Jn. VI.33 (17): 'Of the four (evangelists) who tell us that John confessed he had come to baptize with water, only Matthew (3[11]) adds "to repentance", teaching thereby that the benefit from baptism depends on the intention of the person baptized. If he repents he receives it: if he comes for baptism without repenting the benefit becomes all the sterner a judgement. It is to be noted also that in the case of the stupendous miracles of healing performed by the Saviour—tokens as they were of the perpetual liberating power of the Word of God from all illness and disease—it was none the less through their challenge to faith that the miracles physically benefited the recipients; and it is the same in the case of the washing with water—a token of the purified soul, washed clean of every stain of evil: it is none the less to the man who offers himself to the divine power of the invocation of the adorable Trinity that such washing becomes in itself the origin and fountain of divine grace-gifts [χαρίσματα].'

Although God's grace may be prompted or limited by our virtue, faith, or receptive capacity, that very faith and virtue are represented by Origen (although not fully and consistently—see below, p. 25) as God's gift; and the response we make to God's grace is itself prompted and empowered by that grace.[8]

Grace, for example, is the divinely-given ability to praise God.

Sel. Ps. 71[8]: 'If the mind is not filled with the grace of God, it cannot sing the praises of His glory.'

---

[8] Cf. the passages quoted under p. *19*, note 4, above.

It is the power Christ gives us to do good works.

Comm. Ser. Mt. 45 on 24²⁰ᶠᶠ (the Sabbath): 'Everyone . . . who lives in Christ lives ever "on the Sabbath" and rests in peace from evil works, but does the works of righteousness without ceasing. But many who have the name of Christ but not His grace, live in sabbatic holiday from good works and do bad ones.'

It is the offer of divine power to fulfil our various Christian callings.

Comm. Eph., § 17 on 4¹¹ᵗ (*JTS*, III.414): 'If to be a "teacher" is a grace-gift "according to the measure of the gift of Christ", it is clear that a "shepherd" also, who tends his flock wisely, needs a grace-gift to do so. And how can one be an "evangelist", the "feet" of whose soul (if I may put it so) are not "beauteous"? For this, God must grant the "beauty". (And so with prophets, apostles).'

Comm. Rom. I.2 on 1²: ' "Called . . . applies to all who believe in Christ . . . but each, according to the providence and choice of God, is called apostle, prophet [etc.] . . . , and the saying . . . "Many are called, but few chosen" (Mt 22¹⁴) is fulfilled in accordance with the divine ways of grace. . . . It is, however, possible for a man to be called as an apostle [etc.] . . . but to fall from his calling, if he neglects the grace of that calling . . . [i.e.] "called but not chosen".'

It is Christ's enabling us to die with Him.

Comm. Jn. Frag. 79 on 11¹⁶: 'Then [Thomas], as a true disciple, resolving to follow wherever He should go, sought that the other disciples too should by the grace of Christ lay down their lives with Him.'

Ultimately indeed it is God's very gift of recognition that He is our God.[9]

Comm. Mt. XVII.36 on 22²³ᶠᶠ: 'He is the God of the living . . . who perceive the grace He gave them when He announced Himself as their God and said "This is my eternal memorial" (Ex 3¹⁵). And so Abraham, Isaac and Jacob live perceiving God and His grace.'

---

[9] Cf. *Hom. Lk.* III above, p. 22, where grace = God's offer of Himself to be seen by man.

It is God's giving of Himself to be the God of those who live by Christ.

> *Hom. Jer.* IX.3 on 11⁴: ' "You shall be my people and I will be your God." He is not the God of all men but only of those to whom He graciously gives Himself [οἷς χαρίζεται ἑαυτόν], as He did to the patriarch to whom He said "I am your God" (Gen 17¹), . . . [Origen quotes Mt 22³²: "not the God of the dead but of the living"]. Who is the "dead"? The sinner—the man who does not possess the One who said "I am the life" (Jn 11²⁵), the one whose works are dead (Heb 6¹). If then He is "not the God of the dead . . .", and we know who is the living—the one who guides his life by Christ and remains with Him—and if we desire God to be our God, let us bid farewell to the works of death. . . .'

It is God's bestowal of Himself on Jesus Christ and Christ's true disciples (including the saints of the Old Testament) not only as God but as Father.

> *Comm. Mt.* XVII.36 (continuing the extract p. *23*—): 'of the One greater than [the patriarchs]—our Saviour—He is not only God but Father. . . . This Jesus Christ . . . has graciously bestowed [ἐχαρίσατο] on those who are truly His disciples that the same One should be not only their God but their Father [and quotes Jn 20¹⁷: "I ascend unto my Father and your Father, and my God and your God"]. It is my opinion that He bestowed the same gift on Abraham [etc.] also. . . .'

> *Comm. Jn.* VI.3 (2) on 1¹⁶ᶠᶠ: 'He who "lies on the bosom of the Father" has not "made Him known" now for the first time, as if none previously existed who was fitted to receive what He expounded to the apostles. For He who existed before Abraham teaches us that Abraham rejoiced to see His day. . . . Further, the words "from His fulness we have all received" and "grace for grace" . . . show that the prophets too were able to accept the gift from the fulness of Christ, and received the second grace in place of the first. For they, too, led by the hand of the Holy Spirit, after their initiation by allegory, attained to the vision of the truth. That is why not all the prophets but only "many" (Mt 13¹⁷) longed to see what the apostles saw. For if there was a difference between the prophets, it lay in this, that the higher class who had been perfected did not long to see what the apostles saw, for they

had already seen it; but those who had not, like them, achieved this ascent to the heights of God's Word had come to yearn for the things made known to the apostles through Christ. . . .'[10]

Ibid. 4 [as evidence that before the Incarnation 'the saints had achieved a larger understanding than ordinary believers of the mysteries of the deity, since the Word of God was teaching them before He was made flesh', Origen refers to John 5[17] and Matthew 22[31ff]. His contention that 'those who had been perfected in previous generations had no less knowledge of the revelations given by Christ to the apostles, since the same One disclosed these things who taught the apostles the secrets of piety' is further illustrated by Romans 16[25f] (quoted as far as 'of the prophets' and proceeding 'and of the appearing of our Lord Jesus Christ']—[2 Tim 1[10]].[11]

Comm. Jn. XIX.5: '[None of the Old Testament writers address God as "Father"] perhaps because they did not know the Father; they pray to Him as God and Lord, awaiting the One who pours out the Spirit of adoption not less on them than on those who believe in God through Him after His appearing. Unless indeed Christ *did* appear to the eye of their minds, and they *did* gain, being perfected, the spirit of adoption, but did not venture to speak or write of God as Father openly and to all, lest they might anticipate the grace that through Jesus was poured out on all the world, as He called all men to adoption.'

'*Not fully and consistently*' (p. *22* above): *in other passages Origen gives a kind of dichotomy of faith and virtue—grace is God's gift of virtue, etc., to supplement or strengthen our own.*

Comm. Rom. IX.3 (pp. *20*f).

Comm. Inéd. des Psaumes p. 84 [L, 12a]: 'To every one that hath shall be given. When by the efforts of our own free will we are

---

[10] Note how Origen's pedantic literalness of interpretation here makes Matthew 13[17] mean exactly the opposite of its true significance.

[11] Note the interpretation of the enigmatic 'grace for grace' of John 1[16]. Origen does not, like Chrysostom, refer the first 'grace' to the Old Testament law (an interpretation excluded by verse 17) but to the revelation given to the highest minds of the Old Testament by the pre-incarnate Christ—an 'initiation by types' into the second 'grace', which is the 'vision of the truth', the 'heights of God's word'—a degree of understanding of the 'mysteries of the deity, taught by the same Christ who revealed the 'secrets of piety' to the apostles. The *content* of the first grace, then, is (like the second) primarily intellectual, but with a practical reference ('piety'). For another interpretation of 'grace for grace' see *Comm. Jn. Frag.* 11 (p. *26*)·

become pure in heart, then God too establishes a pure heart within us.'

Ibid. p. 107 [CXVIII, 32b]: 'God's grace is not given to those who lack zeal in the cause of good, nor can human nature achieve virtue without help from above.'

Comm. Jn. Frag. 11 on 1¹⁶: 'Part of our virtues we possess from our own resources, and we have gained it through our own choice; the other part is from God—that is, if we have such faith in the Saviour and His Father as our free will allows: and for this we may have recourse to Him as did Jesus' disciples with their "increase our faith"—where "increase" implies that they were asking Him for God-given faith in addition to what they had gained of their own choice. Paul expressly says that "in proportion to our faith" (Rom 12⁶) (i.e. the faith within us that is due to the exercise of our own free will) "the gifts of the Spirit are bestowed". "To another is given faith, by the same Spirit" (1 Cor 12⁹). If faith is given to a man in proportion to the faith he already has, it is clear that the God-given faith comes alongside that which we have achieved of our own resources. And so with the other virtues. Since then virtue is a grace, since it makes its possessor a "favoured one" [κεχαριτώμενον, the angel's word to Mary at Luke 1³⁸], it follows that the part which comes from God comes alongside that already achieved by our own purpose; and this is the meaning of "grace for grace" being given us by God.'¹²

Comm. Rom. I.12 [speaks of God's gift of faith and adds]: 'blessed are they . . . to whom the apostle decides to pass on this spiritual grace for the strengthening of their faith.'

Ibid. IV.5 [continuing the extract above, p. *19*]: 'But if that very thing which is said to be "from faith" (Rom 4¹⁶) should appear not to be a free gift (Latin—'*gratis*'), as if faith must first be offered by a man before grace is deserved from God [we must look as a corrective to other words of Paul—

---

¹² Here, I think, is a clear example of Origen straining a text to fit his preconceived ideas. Part of our virtues we have bred and cultivated from our own resources: God increases this by a divine contribution—χάρις ἀντὶ ἀρετῆς! But because John 1¹⁶ says ἀντὶ χάριτος, Origen hurriedly inserts a note about all ἀρετή being χάρις, in the sense of making its possessor κεχαριτώμενον [which could either mean 'gracious', i.e. 'winsome', or 'recipient of (divine) grace'] and offers this as an exegesis of John 1¹⁶! We must be aware of ascribing to Origen a 'total ethics of grace' on the strength of such sentences as 'since then virtue is a grace'.

Compare the different and much more biblical exegesis of John 1¹⁶ at *Comm. Jn.* VI.3 (pp. *24*f).

1 Cor 12⁸—where] he says that among other things the gift of faith is also granted by the Holy Spirit (cf. 1 Cor 12⁹, Phil 1²⁹). [Origen then quotes Luke 17⁵ ("increase our faith") to show that] the apostles, understanding that the faith which springs up within a man cannot be perfect unless the faith coming from God is added to it, say to the Saviour "Increase our faith". [and so Romans 4¹⁶]: even that very faith by which we are seen to believe in God is confirmed in us by a gift of grace.'¹³

Hom. Lk. XXXIX (continuing the extract above, pp. *19*f): 'For he who has achieved virtue from his toil and sweat receives an addition from God: for example, when a man has achieved faith by the exercise of his own free will, he will be granted a grace-gift of faith [χάρισμα πίστεως, 1 Cor 12⁹], and (in sum) a man who has improved some one of his natural resources by care and attention will be granted what is still lacking from God.'

Comm. Ser. Mt. 69 on 25²⁹ [After an almost verbatim reproduction of the above from *Hom. Lk.*]: 'For we must apply not only to wisdom but to every virtue the words of Solomon (Wis Sol 9⁶): "For though a man be never so perfect among the children of men, yet if thy wisdom be not with him, he shall be nothing regarded." Thus a man perfect in chastity or righteousness or virtue or piety who has not, however, received that chastity [etc.] that comes from the grace of God, will be "nothing regarded". Hence if we wish to be granted this more perfect virtue, and that it should abound in us, let us first use every means to acquire diligently that which is perfect on human standards; and having done so, let us show our awareness that this is "nothing regarded" without the grace of God, let us "humble ourselves under the mighty hand of God" (1 Pet 5⁶), and pray . . . that the perfection of all the good in us may be given from God, and that He may make us perfect and acceptable to God, as it were His sons.'

---

¹³ Surely in this passage the inconsistency *saute aux yeux.*

(B) GRACE IS ESPECIALLY OPERATIVE IN SCRIPTURE, BOTH IN THE INSPIRATION AND POWER OF THE WRITINGS AND THE INSIGHT GIVEN TO UNDERSTAND THEM. THIS IS PARTICULARLY TRUE OF PROPHECY

The whole of Scripture was written under the influence of heavenly grace, which was the very presence of God in His inspired book.

Hom. Ex. VII.8 on 16¹²: (if this passage is interpreted literally, as by the Jews) 'what is there in it to show of the divine gift, of the disposition of heavenly grace? Do you suggest that we can find God in the fact that flesh is eaten at evening without bread, and do you assert that the glory of God shines forth if, again, bread is eaten without flesh?'¹⁴

Princ. IV.1.6: 'The sojourn of Jesus (upon earth) showed clearly that the Law and the prophets, previously not beyond suspicion of *not* being divine, were in fact written under the influence of heavenly grace.'

Frag. Prov. (ex *Procopii Epitome*) on 1⁶: '(do not wonder at the parabolic and mysterious passages of Scripture) for such was the work of the grace which disposed the word of God.'

These words of heavenly grace were filled with power; as contrasted e.g. with Plato, they have not only the truth but the power to drive home that truth to the human soul.

Comm. Mt. X.17: 'Jude wrote an epistle which was short, but filled with the powerful words of heavenly grace.'

Celsus VI.2: 'The divine scripture says that the spoken word, even if it is most true and convincing in itself, is not sufficient to reach a human soul unless some power is also given by God to the speaker and grace flowers on¹⁵ what is said, and it is only by God's gift that this power is possessed by those who preach with effect.'¹⁶

---

¹⁴ An amusing instance of what I should describe as Origen's 'atomistic inspirationalism'.

¹⁵ χάρις ἐπανθήσῃ τοῖς λεγομένοις is a rare instance of χάρις in Origen retaining its classical connotation of 'beauty'. Cf. possibly *Sel. Ps.* 452ᴮ (pp. *36f*): 'words of grace.'

¹⁶ The context here is Origen's answer to the criticism of Celsus that the *truths* in Scripture have been better expressed—in a finer style—by others, especially Plato. This very modern complaint is not dismissed by Origen with mere abuse of the Greeks—'for mankind has derived help from him (Plato) also' (cf. *Cels.* VII.42 [p. *58*], where Origen quotes some famous words from Plato's Timaeus and describes them as 'noble and impressive') but by distinguishing 'truth' from 'power to convert and confirm'. He quotes in this respect 1 Cor 2⁴ᵗ.

This grace is operative in the whole of Scripture—Old Testament and New Testament.

Cels. VI.57: 'God admonishes those who hear Him throughout the whole of scripture and through those who teach by God's grace.'[17]

For the Old Testament cf. *Hom. Ex.* VII.8, *Princ.* IV.1.6 (p. *28*).

For the New Testament cf. *Comm. Mt.* X.17 (above) and— *Hom. Lk.* I on 1[1] ('many have attempted'): 'There is here an implied censure on those who undertook rashly and without a grace-gift [χάρισμα] to compose Gospels. (e.g. the "Gospel acc. to the Egyptians", "Gospel of the Twelve", etc.). But Matthew (etc.) did not "attempt", he "wrote"—under the leading of the Holy Spirit.'

Correspondingly, God gives grace to understand His word, especially the more difficult passages, as the grace at work in the Bible is naturally sometimes mysterious to man—e.g. the how and why of biblical parable and miracle.

Sel. Ps. 1[2]: '. . . nothing good can come apart from God, and this is above all true of the understanding of the inspired Scriptures.'

Princ. Pref. 8: '. . . the scriptures were composed through the Spirit of God and have not only the obvious meaning, but also another which is hidden from most readers. . . . There is but one opinion in the whole Church on this, namely that although the whole law is spiritual, the spiritual significance is not recognized by all, but only by those to whom is given the grace of the Holy Spirit in the word of wisdom and knowledge.'

Hom. 1 Sam. 2: (This book is so difficult that it cannot be expounded 'without the grace of God-given ability'.

Hom. Jer. VI.3: 'Let us exhort God to grant that, as the Word grows in us, we may receive a rich large-mindedness[18] in Christ Jesus and so be able to hear the sacred and holy words.'

Hom. Isa. II.1: 'And so, if at times we do not understand what is said, we shall not lessen our obedience or betake

---

[17] For the Christian 'teaching grace' cf. *Comm. Song Songs* III, p. 187 ('the grace of teaching, of instructing, of preaching the Word of God').

[18] ἀδρότητα καὶ μεγαλειότητα. The idea, if not the word, of χάρις is fully present.

ourselves to easier material, but wait for the grace of God
to suggest to us an answer to our question, whether by direct
enlightenment or through the agency of another.'

Cels. I.44 (on the credibility of the story of the Baptism of
Jesus): 'A man who has been adorned with the grace-gift
called the "word of wisdom" (1 Cor 12⁸) will also explain the
reason for the opening of the heavens and the form of the
dove, and the Holy Spirit's appearing to Jesus in just this
living form and no other.'

Comm. Mt. XV.37 (after a lengthy discussion of 20¹ᶠᶠ—
Labourers in the Vineyard—Origen concludes): 'Probably a
man wiser than I and judged by God worthy of a more penetrating and richer grace-gift of wisdom in exposition from the
Spirit of God, and of the gift of knowledge in the word by the
Spirit (1 Cor 8¹²) . . . (could give a better exposition here
than mine, but I have done my best.')¹⁹

Ibid. XVI.13 (after expounding 20²⁹ᶠᶠ): 'May God grant to
whom He chooses a richer word of wisdom and a word made
more penetrating by the light of knowledge, that my own exposition compared with one based on such grace-gifts may
resemble a candle in the light of the sun.'

Frag. Prov. on 1⁶ (p. *28*).

*For the understanding of the more recondite passages greater degrees of
grace are given: but the gift as a whole is rare.*

Comm. Mt. XVI.17 (Origen's modest conclusion to his exposition of 21¹⁻⁵): 'This is the best I can do. . . . Let the man who
is able to receive greater grace for the understanding of this
passage speak more and better words.'

Sel. Ps. 119⁸⁵: 'Many have sought to interpret the divine
scriptures . . . but not all with success. For rare is he who has
the grace for this from God.'

*This interpretative grace is contrasted with the power of our own minds—
although our minds need to be such that they can mingle with the mind
of Christ, and our hearts pure enough for the Holy Spirit to write upon.*

Comm. Mt. XIV.11: (None can fully interpret 18²³ᶠᶠ) 'unless
Jesus, who privately explained everything to His own disciples
(Mk 4³⁴), has made His dwelling in his mind and opens all

---

¹⁹ For the parables in particular cf. *Comm. Mt.* XIV.11, 12 (below).

the dark, hidden unseen, treasure-chambers in the parable. . . .
Now I have not yet received a mind sufficient and capable of
being mingled with the mind of Christ and thus able to attain
to such things.'

Ibid. 12: '. . . would that there could be found a heart
fitted and, through its purity, able to grasp the explanations
of the parables, that on it letters might be inscribed by the
"Spirit of the Living God" (2 Cor 3³). [Some say that it is
impious to commit such "explanations" to writing, even if you
can explain the parable] but I, admitting that I fall short of
the ability to sound the depths of their meaning, and achieving as I do only a somewhat limited understanding of the
implications, shall nevertheless maintain that, whereas there
is much that, after long and searching examination, I believe
I discover, whether by the grace of God or by the power of
my own mind, but I do not dare to entrust to writing—there
is much too that I must in some degree at least expound, for
my own training and for that of my readers.'

Ibid. 18: 'The words "a woman is bound to her husband . . .
I suppose I too have the Spirit of God" (1 Cor 7³⁹ᶠ) were
spoken by a Paul who was confident in his possession of divine
grace. N.B. in this passage, to the words "in my own opinion"
he wisely adds "I suppose that I too have the Spirit of God",
lest that "opinion" of his should be decried as empty of God's
Spirit.'

*Prophecy in particular depends on grace; this is true not only of the canonical
prophets but of all who have the 'grace-gift of prophecy'.*

Sel. Deut. 1⁹ᶠ: (Moses says that Joshua has succeeded him) 'in
the grace of prophecy and leadership'.

Frag. on *1 Sam.* 19²³ᶠ: 'The grace of God causes Saul to prophesy.'

Hom. Lk. IV: 'For the Spirit and power—or spiritual grace-
gift—came to Elijah as to every other prophet.'

Cels. VIII.46: [Elisha (2 Kgs 4⁸¹ᶠᶠ) prophesied 'by the grace
of God' about the birth of a child.]

Comm. Lam. Frag. 116 (Klostermann) on Lam 4²⁰ (on the
grace-gift of prophecy, granted by Father, Son and Holy
Spirit): 'Paul, speaking of the grace-gifts, among which is prophecy, says, "All these are inspired by one and the same Spirit,

who apportions to each individually as He wills" (1 Cor 12[11]), that is, with sovereign freedom, not because He has to.[20] . . . The target of all prophecy is the prophetic grace-gift, and that is Christ, i.e. comes from Christ. For Christ is the end of the law and the prophets (Rom 10[4]).'[21]

> *Comm. Mt.* X.22 (p. *46*).

This grace might consist in simple prevision, or the insight to interpret the Scriptures allegorically, or to distinguish between true and false prophets themselves; for prophecy proper always judges and condemns sin.

Sel. Ezek. 3[10]: 'If a man has found from God the grace of prevision of the future . . .'

Comm. Jn. I.*30* (33) [where Origen interprets Psalm 104[15] ('wine gladdeneth the heart of a man') allegorically—this being the only manner of interpretation] 'worthy of the prophetic grace'.

Hom. Lk. I: 'Among God's people of old many professed to be prophets, truly or falsely; and to the people was granted the grace-gift of "distinguishing between spirits" (1 Cor 12[10]) which enabled them to judge who was a true prophet and who false.'

Hom. Jer. I.*7* on 1[10] (Jeremiah, says Origen, never *actually* 'destroyed cities', so we must allegorize): 'All who receive words from God and have the grace of heavenly words receive them for the purpose of "destroying nations". . . . You must not think here of nations and kingdoms literally, but of human souls under the kingship of sin, . . . and hence you must allegorize nations and kingdoms into the evil things in the souls of men which are uprooted and overthrown by the words of God given to Jeremiah or whoever it may be.'

The grace can be lost by sin, but is never inactive, and when forfeited by one man is forthwith transferred to another.

(Gk.) *Hom.* § 9. on *1 Sam.* 28: 'He alone loses the grace of pro-

---

[20] τουτέστιν αὐθεντικῶς, οὐ δουλικῶς. In this phrase is implicit a whole theology of grace. The Holy Spirit is not a 'servant'—not a bank-clerk who 'has to' cash our cheques because we have deposited sufficient (in the way of merit) to meet them. His hand cannot be forced. He remains the sovereign dispenser of a grace that is free.

[21] This sentence illustrates the obscurity of many of the fragmentary survivals of lost commentaries. τὸ οὖν χάρισμα τὸ προφητικόν, πρὸς ὃ βλέπει πάσης τῆς προφητείας ἡ ἔκβασις, Χριστός ἐστιν, τουτέστιν ἀπὸ Χριστοῦ. 'τέλος γὰρ . . . κτλ.' The meaning, however, is clear: Christ is the inspiration of prophecy in the double sense of being its object and source.

phecy who after prophesying has done things unworthy of the Holy Spirit, causing the Holy Spirit to leave and fly from him. . . . The grace of prophecy is not idle; no grace-gift is idle in a holy man.'

(C) GRACE IS OPERATIVE THROUGHOUT THE WHOLE OF EVERY MAN'S SALVATION

Salvation is of Jesus Christ: and the Person and work of Christ were throughout empowered by divine grace.

E.g. the grace of John the Baptist's commission to prepare the way for Jesus—

Comm. Jn. VI.21 (12) (of John the Baptist): 'For in truth, while many prophets are his equal, none is his superior in the (measure of) grace given unto him.' Ibid. 32 (17) (John the Baptist speaks): 'I have attained to so great grace as to be deemed worthy of the prophecy which foretold of my life on earth in the words "I am the voice of one crying . . ." and "Behold I send my messenger . . ." '

Ibid. VI.49 (30): (When Mary conceived she stayed with Elizabeth) 'when the one child who was being formed [the unborn Jesus] graciously bestowed [ἐχαρίζετο] on the other [John] with some exactness His own likeness, and caused him to be conformed to His glory. That is why later John was supposed to be Christ, from the similarity of appearance, and Jesus was thought to be John raised from the dead, by those who were not capable of distinguishing the image from its own likeness.'

—of Mary's divine and unique privilege of bearing Jesus—

Hom. Lk. VII on 1^{42}: ' "Blessed art thou among women." For no woman has been or ever can be a partaker in such grace. There has been but one divine conception, one divine birth, one bearer of the God-man.'

Ibid. VIII: (Mary reflects) 'Since I have been deemed worthy of such great and wondrous grace from God . . . I above all women must glorify the One who is working such miracles in me.'

D

—of Jesus' God-given equipment for saving mankind: e.g. sinlessness, wisdom, divine power to overcome His enemies and to work miracles for the saving and betterment of mankind—

Hom. Lk. XIX on 2^{40}: ' "And the grace of God was on Him." Not only when He grew to adolescence, nor when He openly taught, but when He was still a little boy, He had the grace of God.' [N.B. The context makes it clear that the grace-gifts of sinlessness and wisdom are meant.]

Comm. Jn. X.25 (16) (on the historical difficulties of the temple-cleaning: if the story is taken literally, Jesus was at least badly outnumbered!): '(Of course) there is one resource left by which the literal interpreter could meet this objection —the more divine power of Jesus, who could at will quench the rising wrath of His enemies, and get the better of thousands by divine grace.'

Cels. III.31 (Celsus has scouted the claim that the miracles of Jesus suggest His divinity, and quoted typical pagan miracle-workers whom nobody has suggested to be gods. Origen in reply points to the moral and spiritual purpose and effects of the miracles of Jesus, and contrasts these e.g. with the pagan story of Abaris and the arrow):[22] 'What was the purpose of the divinity that graciously granted [χαρισαμένη] that Abaris should be carried along by an arrow, in bestowing on him such a gift? Was it that the human race should receive some benefit? Or did Abaris himself gain any advantage? . . . [Assume, for argument's sake, that the story was true and the agent was a demon.] But if my Jesus is said to be taken up "in glory" (1 Tim 3^{16}), I see God's gracious providence [οἰκονομία].' (His purpose being the spiritual empowering and amelioration of the spectators.)[23]

—Of God's forbearance; of His restoring to the human soul what had

---

[22] Chadwick (*Celsus*, p. 148, note 2) points out that the original story of Herodotus IV.36, that Abaris carried an arrow over the whole world without taking food, had become in later writers the legend that the arrow carried him.

[23] Origen's point is that the miracles of Jesus *do* suggest His 'quite exceptional divinity' not merely because of their miraculousness, which might be demon-inspired, but because of their moral and spiritual purpose. χαρίζεσθαι is used, not without irony, of the 'gracious endowment' of miraculous power granted Abaris, if at all, by a demon: *sensu proprio* it would be used of God's endowment of Jesus with the power to work miracles for the good of mankind.

been lost from the created state; of His power that arouses the souls of sinners to faith—

Hom. Ezek. X.2 on 16⁵²ᶠ: 'To the sinful Jerusalem the word is spoken—"Bear your disgrace". . . . But if one has fulfilled this injunction—"Be ashamed" . . . "Bear your disgrace", he may thereafter see the grace by which forbearance takes the place of shaming.'

Comm. Song Songs II, pp. 147f (Is the 'substance' of the human soul the same as that of the angels, seeing that both are 'rational'?): 'Even if the human soul is not the same in substance but becomes so by grace, if it has proved worthy,[24] is it not still true that the possibility of being made wholly akin to the angels implies that such kinship has already been received by a like common nature? If a thing has been lost it cannot be restored; but that can never be conferred which the Creator did not give from the beginning.' (Cf. ibid. IV. p. 227 and the other extracts below, pp. 37f.)

Comm. Jn. Frag. 50 on 3³⁵ ('The Father loves the Son and has given all things into His hand'): 'For if "all things were made by Him", all things—according to the purpose of creation and providence—come under His hand. But they had wandered away through sin and left the shelter of that hand. It is, then, for their own salvation that the father puts them (back) into the hand of His Son, the point of the gracious bestowal [χαριζόμενος] being not His Son's advancement but their own betterment. For He gives them to His Son as their teacher and doctor, to free them from ignorance and disease—i.e. from sin—and so keep them under His protection and kingly rule.'

Comm. Ser. Mt. 139 on 27⁵¹⁻³: 'The tombs in question . . . are the bodies of the souls which were sinful, i.e. dead to God. But when through the grace of God such souls have been aroused to faith, their bodies . . . . are made the bodies of the holy. . . .'

—all this through the death of Jesus, who by grace wrought for us justification and forgiveness—in a word, salvation.

Comm. Jn. I.35 (40) on Hebrews 2⁹ [where Origen discusses

24 See p. 20, note 5 above.

the variants χωρὶς Θεοῦ and χάριτι Θεοῦ.[25] Origen is unwilling to rule out χάριτι, though he prefers χωρίς. He would not
(that is) deny that the death of Jesus for everyone was con-
sonant with God's grace].

Comm. Rom. (Gk), § 18 on 3[28] (*JTS*, XIII.222): 'That the law
of faith suffices for justification in the complete absence of any
works on our part, is shown by the robber who was crucified
along with Jesus and by the sinful woman in Luke (7[37ff]).
For her sins were remitted, not because of any work of hers,
but from faith. . . . But that after the recognition of this,
unrighteous behaviour can bring to nothing the grace of
the One who has justified, (Paul) himself will make clear at a
later point. My own view is that even such works as appear
good, if done before the coming of faith, cannot justify the
agent, because they are not "built on the fair foundation of
faith" (1 Cor 3[11f]).'

Comm. Rom. IV.2: 'He does not say that the faith of the
righteous is counted to them for righteousness. If it were, what
grace would appear to be counted to the righteous? Righteousness for righteousness?'

Ibid. VIII.7 on 11[6]: 'The works which Paul repudiates . . .
are not the works of righteousness which are laid down in the
law, but those in which the observers of the law according to
the flesh make their glory, i.e. circumcision, the sacrificial rites,
the observation of the sabbath and new moons. . . . if a man
is justified by such as these he is not justified freely [Latin,
'*gratis*']; for such works are least of all expected from one justified by grace—*his* care is to watch that the grace he has received does not become of none effect in him (cf. 1 Cor 15[10]).
Now there is no danger of this, and no ingratitude to the grace
of God, in harnessing to that grace works worthy of it; but a
man who receives that grace and then sins becomes guilty of
ingratitude to the One who made the grace available for him.
But if you have *not* made the grace of none effect, you will
have it multiplied to you, and receive a multitude of graces,
as it were for a reward of good works (and quotes 2 Pet 1[2],
1 Pet 4[10]).'

Sel. Ps. 45[2B]: 'Grace is poured out on the lips of the imitator
of Christ and of Christ Himself, not only in respect of the

[25] See Moffatt's 'Hebrews' (*I.C.C.*), pp. 25ff, where Origen's discussion is translated.

words of grace that proceed from His mouth, but in respect of the forgiveness of sins, when He says "Thy sins be forgiven Thee" (Mt 9⁵).'

Comm. Ser. Mt. 126 (refers to a tradition that Adam was buried in the same place that Christ was crucified, and in that place) 'found resurrection through the resurrection of the Saviour. . . . For it was unfitting that while the many sprung from him should receive remission of sins and the blessing of resurrection, he—the father of mankind—should not all the more attain to grace of this kind.'

Comm. Jn. Frag. 9 on 1¹⁴: 'He, the only-begotten Son of the Father, is said to be wholly filled with grace and truth—and He is none other than the things with which He is said to be filled. [Cf. John 14⁶—"I am the truth": Origen points out that the truth cannot be "filled" by *other* truth.] . . . And so with grace.' [Origen then notes as the gracious work of Christ 'not the punishment but the offer of remission of sins', 'the offer of remission of all sins to those who flee to Him in repentance'; and Origen insists that the offer is to all. . . .] For if He granted His grace to some and not to others He would not be filled with grace—any more than He would be filled with truth if He banished some shadows (of ignorance) but not others.'

Ibid. 12 on 1¹⁷: 'Grace forestalls, by the remission of sins, the punishment of the sinners laid down by the law.'

Comm. Jn. Frag. 50 (p. *35*) (for 'salvation').

By grace we were created and are preserved by God;

Comm. Rom. IV.5 (p. *19*).

—by grace—by the enabling of Christ—we die with Him and rise in Him to a restored life; and with this gift of regeneration through Christ the original image of God is recovered:

(On dying with Christ, cf. *Comm. Jn. Frag.* 79. p. *23*.)

Comm. Jn. XX.25 (21) (Origen paraphrases Romans 6⁴ in the form—): 'But we by the grace of God have been buried with Christ and risen with Him—if indeed we have become formed in the likeness of His resurrection—and we walk with Him in newness of life.'²⁶

---

²⁶ Origen's excellent gloss, 'χάριτι Θεου', shows how broad is the scope of grace for him.

Hom. Josh. XIV.1: 'Before the advent of our Lord and Saviour all the demons reigned in men's minds and bodies, in undisturbed possession of their spirits. But when the grace and mercy of our Saviour God appeared on earth to teach us how each man's spirit should regain the liberty and image of God in which it was created . . .'

Comm. Song Songs IV, p. 227: 'Every soul has the power and choice to do everything that is good. But because this good feature in human nature had been betrayed when a chance of sin offered . . . the "fragrance it gives forth" (Song 2^{13}), when it is redeemed by grace and restored by the teaching of the Word of God, is that very fragrance which the creator had bestowed at the first and sin had taken away. . . . The grace which [the soul] had first received from the Creator, lost, and now recovered . . . [etc.].'[27]

and our Christian vocation is initiated and sustained by grace.

Excerpta Procopiana in Cant. Cant. 7^2: 'The "lilies" (of Song 7^2) are the flowers of the grace of God, which He collected from the midst of the world's thorns.'[28]

Hom. Isa. VI.2: 'Isaiah's wish, when he had once received grace from God, was not to receive it to no purpose, but to use it for what lay before him' [Latin, '*necessaria*'].

Hom. Jer. III: 'When (God) rejected Israel . . . grace was poured out on the Gentiles'; ibid. IV.2: 'The calling of the Gentiles took its start from the fall of Israel.' [Hence Origen himself, a Gentile, can converse about the promises of God— can have faith in the God of Israel,] 'and by the grace of God can accept Jesus Christ, who was heralded aforetimes by the prophets.'[29]

Comm. Rom. I.7 on 1^5: 'He says that he has received grace and apostleship through Christ, in His capacity of mediator between God and men. The reference in "grace" is to Paul's patient labouring, and in "apostleship" to his authority as a preacher, just as Christ too was called an "apostle" (Heb 3^1)

[27] Cf. ibid. II, pp. 147f (p. 35), and the other passages there quoted, to which the present passage adds the (implied) point that grace is at once the means of regeneration and the content of the regenerate life.

[28] Presumably the reference is to those who are called of God and make response.

[29] Cf. *Comm. Jn.* XIX.5 (p. 25), where the grace of Jesus Christ is His calling to the world (not the Hebrews) to recognize God as their Father. This theme of the call to the Gentiles is illustrated below, pp. 46, 83ff, 150ff.

(i.e. sent from the Father . . .). All then that Christ has He gives to His disciples—e.g. the "grace" which is said (Ps 44^2) to be poured out on His lips . . . so that with it in times of labouring they can say "By the grace . . ." (1 Cor 15^{10}).'

Ibid. I.2 (p. *23*), (where grace = the offer of divine power to fulfil our various Christian callings).

Throughout the Christian life the grace of Christ is our protecting shade (cf. the guardian angels).

Sel. Lament. 4^{20}: 'We live under the shadow of the grace of Christ.'

Comm. *Jn.* VI.57 (of the divers grace-gifts brought back by the ascended Christ to His apostles): 'The cloven tongues as of fire, and the holy angels who would stand by and save the apostles in all their doings.'[30]

The ethical qualities of this life are (in part) (cf. pp. 25ff) the gifts of God's grace—

See the passages given above, pp. *25*ff.

Comm. *Song Songs* III, p. 176 (speaks of God's grace in connection with the 'bodily' virtues of chastity, continence, etc.—i.e. it is not confined to the more recondite 'spiritual' virtues of the soul).

—to be received with humility, otherwise a different gift of grace (e.g. Paul's 'thorn in the flesh') will come to forestall pride—

Sel. Ps. 131^1 ('O Lord, my heart is not lifted up'): 'These are the words of a righteous man, endowed with great and wonderful grace-gifts, who does not preen himself on them . . . but remains humble.'

[On Paul's 'thorn in the flesh' 'by way of a grace-gift' see Hom. *Jer.* XII.8 (above, p. *21*, note 7).]

—and such grace, with its offer of spiritual maturity even in our childhood, rises through that justification that issues in good works, and is thereby multiplied to the grateful believer, to the crown of perfection.

Hom. *Jer.* I.13 on 1^{6f}: (It is possible to be a child in the outer man but a man in the inner.) 'Such was Jeremiah, who

---

[30] On Origen's doctrine of guardian angels see the references given by Chadwick, *Celsus*, p. 56, note 1. Cf. *Cels.* VIII.27, p. 57.

already possessed grace from God when he was still physically in the age of childhood.'

Comm. Rom. VIII.7 (p. *36*) [on justification and good works].

Comm. Song Songs II, p. 163 (the 'grace of justification' is given to certain men . . . this perfection comes 'by faith'); p. 172 (perfection is characterized [in a context allegorizing the spices and scents of Song 1¹²ᶠᶠ] as 'drawing in the grace of a divine savour').³¹

Through the grace of Christ we receive revelation of the mysteries of divine truth, and from His treasury the gifts of wisdom and faith—which are indeed graded (wisdom ranking higher than faith) and primarily spiritual; but God also gives e.g. healing of the body, and Jesus bestows physical as well as spiritual sight.

(For Christ's revelation of the mysteries of divine truth see *Comm. Jn.* VI.3 (2), pp. *24*f.)

Hom. Jer. VIII.5 on 10¹³ ('he maketh lightnings . . . treasures'): 'What treasures? Compare the words "in Him are hidden all the treasures of wisdom and knowledge" (Col 2³). These treasures are in Christ. From that source come forth these winds, these spirits, so that one man becomes wise, another faithful, another has knowledge, and others receive whatever grace-gift of God it may be (and quotes 1 Cor 12⁸ᶠ).'³²

Comm. Jn. XIII.53 (52) on 4⁴²: 'It is better to walk by sight than by faith (cf. 2 Cor 5⁷). For this reason those who walk as it were by sight might be said to live by the higher grace-gifts—the "word of knowledge through the same spirit" (1 Cor 12⁸). But those who walk by faith—if indeed that faith is a grace-gift³³ (after the fashion of "to another, faith in the same spirit" (1 Cor 12⁹))—are inferior in rank to the former.'

Ibid. XX.32 (26) on 8⁴⁶ᴮ: 'The grace-gift of believing [Christ] —ranked third in the Pauline list . . . (cf. Phil 1²⁹). . . . But it is no commonplace gift of God, when so many different articles

---

³¹ Cf., however, *Comm. Eph.*, § 37 on 6²⁴ (*JTS*, III.576), where Origen suggests that 'those who love the Lord in incorruption'='those who are free from all sin'. To say that Grace is with such would thus implicitly exclude from Grace those who love the Lord, but not in incorruption. Origen never leaves us clear as to whether perfection issues from Grace or is a condition of its bestowal.

³² On the 'grace-gift of faith' see pp. *22*ff, *25*ff.

³³ I.e. their faith *might* be of the human variety (see pp. *26*f above). But we note uneasily the suggestion of 'intellectualism' and a 'double standard' for Christians. Cf. next passage.

of belief are preached by so many who profess to teach the truth, to be able to withhold credence from all except the truth.'

Prayer XVI.2: 'Everyone who asks of God "earthly" and "small" things (Jn 3¹², Mt 6³³, Lk 12³¹) disobeys Him that bids us seek "heavenly" and "great" things from the God who knows not how to bestow of His grace [χαρίζεσθαι] anything earthly or small; and to the objection that bodily gifts were granted to the saints [sc. in Bible-stories] through prayer, and the Gospel expressly teaches that "earthly" and "small" things are added unto us, the reply is that just as we do not say, when someone gives us a body of some sort, that he has given us the shadow of the body [because the latter automatically accompanies the real gift] . . . even so if on a higher level of thought we consider the gifts that are made to us of set purpose by God, we shall agree that the bodily gifts are the most suitable accompaniment of the great and heavenly grace-gifts, and are given "to each" of the saints "for their profit", according to the "measure of their faith", or "as the giver wills".'³⁴

Comm. Jn. Frag. 61 on 5² (pool of Bethesda): 'They descended (into the water) and were cured—many not immediately (although the first to descend did profit straightway from grace) lest the (too) easily available cure should diminish the wonder.'

Ibid. *Frag.* 92 on 12³⁹ᶠ (where Origen maintains that the 'blinder' is the evil one, the 'healer' is Jesus): 'But as for "they could not believe", we must say that the case is similar to that of congenital physical blindness, later cured by the Saviour: to say "I cannot see because I am blind" would not be to deny that the blind man would ever be able to see. Indeed later he could, when Jesus opened the eyes of the blind and graciously bestowed [χαριζομένου] the gift of sight. . . . In the same way those who once could not believe because their eyes had been blinded by the evil one were still able to come to believe by coming to Jesus . . . and seeking the gift of (spiritual) sight.'

Nor is the grace of God idle in life's institutions, whether private—marriage as well as celibacy—or public: ethical standards or public laws and

³⁴ The same collocation of Scripture passages as at *Comm. Rom.* IX.3 (p. 20). Origen expands his shadow-analogy at *Prayer* XVII.1 where see Jay, p. 134, note 2: 'The point of Origen's elaborate analogy here is that just as we are given bodies, and the shadow thereof varies or even disappears at times, so God's spiritual gifts to us may or may not be accompanied by material gifts.'

*institutions, or even the ordinary spheres of educated knowledge (although
elsewhere Origen contrasts God's grace—the source of progress in ethics,
natural science, and contemplative philosophy—with human arts).*

Comm. Mt. XIV.16 on 19³⁻¹²: 'Since God has joined together
(a man and woman in marriage), for this reason there is a
grace-gift for those joined together by God. Paul knew this,
and declares that equally with the purity of the unmarried
state is a marriage according to the word of God a grace-gift
(Origen quotes 1 Cor 7⁷). Those who are joined together by
God obey in thought and deed the command "husbands, love
your wives" [etc.] (Eph 5²⁵).'³⁵

Comm. Rom. IX.24: '(Paul in Romans 12) ties up with the
gifts of graces moral precepts, to show that to Christians these
too are given by the grace of God. For there are many Gentiles whose moral standards are orderly and whose institutions
are honourable, who never ascribe the merit of these to God
or confess that they have received grace from Him; they lay
them to the credit of their own industry, or preen themselves
on their masters and legislators. But the apostle makes clear
to us that everything that is good comes from God and is
given through the Holy Spirit (and Origen quotes James 1¹⁷,
1 Cor 1³¹).'

Comm. Song Songs II, p. 149: (Origen's thoughts on a soul's self-
knowledge are not for the benefit of everyone, but for a chosen
few, who while capable of thought and understanding in general,
need prompting on the duty of *self*-knowledge.) 'Who, although
they have been given by God the grace of thinking on and understanding many things,³⁶ neglect other spheres of knowledge
and give no heed to self-knowledge.'

Ibid. Prol., pp. 78f: 'This . . . threefold division of divine
philosophy (moral, natural, contemplative) was, I think, pre-
visaged in [Abraham, Isaac and Jacob]. . . . For Abraham
shows forth, by his obedience, moral philosophy . . . , Isaac,
who digs wells and searches the mysteries of nature, represents
natural philosophy . . . , Jacob is the contemplative, and was

---

³⁵ Cf. *Comm. 1 Cor.*, § 34 on 7⁷ (*JTS*, IX.503), where Origen refutes from this verse
the Marcionite notion that marriage is merely an ordinance of the 'demiurge', whereas virginity is commanded by the Supreme God. One and the same God ordained
both.
³⁶ From the context this must mean the ordinary spheres of educated knowledge—
which are, N.B., 'under grace'.

named "Israel" because of his meditating on divine things (cf. his visions). . . . Hence we are not surprised to find that these three blessed men built altars to God—i.e. consecrated to Him the progress of their philosophy, that they might teach that these things should come under the heading not of human arts but of God's grace.'

Grace, in short, is the gift of God that begins and ends the Christian pilgrimage, the power of God fighting evil in man and counteracting the effects of unbelief; for it is grace that mediates the presence of God to the believer, and is the source of all human good. Grace is the unshakable promise of God to the believer.

Hom. 1 Sam. 5 on 1[1ff] [Helchana had two wives, Anna (the 'nobler' wife) and Fennana; but he had children at first by the latter only]: 'This Helchana—which means "the possession of God"—is first made a father by his second wife . . . and it is only after she has had several children that the womb of Anna is opened in response to her prayers and she becomes the mother of that son whom he "offered to God". . . . "Fennana" means "conversion", and "Anna" means "grace". Hence each of us who wishes to become "the possession of God" should marry those two wives . . . : the first . . . which is the nobler and higher-born, "grace", and is first joined to us through faith (cf. Eph 2[8]) . . . ; union to Fennana (i.e. "conversion") should come second, because it is only after the grace of belief that one experiences betterment of conduct and conversion of life. But the order of procreation is different from that of marriage. The first wife . . . to bear us children is Fennana, because the first fruits that we bring forth are those of conversion. . . . For our first work of righteousness is to be converted from sins, since unless we are first converted . . . from evil, we cannot become fathers by Anna and bear children by grace. Note . . . the difference: Fennana has sons who do not wait on God—nor can the "sons of conversion" be such as can wait on and cling to God. They are not indeed useless, or completely alien from divine things, for they receive "portions" (1 Sam 1[4]) from the divine sacrifices. . . . Each of us, then, is first converted from sin and by his conversion brings forth works of righteousness; later "Anna" is stirred up in us . . . "pours forth her prayer to God" and herself bears sons . . . (and the sons of grace) are such as wait upon God. Now "grace and truth came through Jesus Christ". He then is a son of grace who gives his time to God and to God's word.' Cf. *Hom. Gen.* XI.2: 'If therefore a son of grace is of such greatness and quality, let us also hasten to marry "Anna"; but let us be patient, that our first sons may be of conversion—that we should first give satisfaction by our good works, and only thereafter breed a son of grace and the "gift of the Spirit" (Acts 2^{38}) . . . (namely) "Samuel" . . . which means "God is there". \ . . For where the "spirit of grace" is, there is said to be God Himself.'[37]

Hom. 1 Sam. 10: 'When the grace of God has driven out the evil spirit (cf. Rom 5^{20}) it brings in the Holy Spirit, and the soul which was filled with an evil spirit is now filled with the Holy Spirit.'

Hom. Lk. IX on 1^{56ff}: ' "John" means "the grace of God". Hence when Zacharias wrote on the tablet that the name was John, immediately his mouth was opened by the grace of God . . . and his tongue, no longer bound by unbelief, was restored to him.'

Frag. on *1 Sam.* 16^{18}: (David is 'of handsome appearance',

---

[37] I have translated these passages at length as a fair sample of the lengths to which Origen pursues his allegoristic hares. Here is a simple Old Testament story of a man with two wives metamorphosed into a striking doctrinal scheme: (1) prevenient grace, (2) conversion, (3) good works, the fruit of conversion, (4) communion with God, the fruit of grace. The scheme itself poses one or two obvious questions: are not the good works which issue from conversion also the fruit of grace? Or is grace, as it were, suspended at that point to allow human merit to prove itself? (Cf. continuation of the *Hom. Gen.* passage: 'For unless the works of conversion come first, we shall not merit the grace of the spirit'; cf. also *Comm. Mt.* XII.31, where every 'son of grace', like Samuel, must seek the weightier food of the gospel, as contrasted with 'milk for babes' [1 Cor 3^2]—grace appertaining to the maturity of the Christian life, as distinct from its beginnings.) And again, how far is the marriage and childbearing analogy to be pressed? Does it imply synergism and anticipate the Pelagian heresy?

On such points as these, however, we should remember that Origen brings his doctrines to his scriptural passage, rather than educes them from it. Such questionable implications of his allegories as the above may therefore witness merely to the defective ingenuity of the allegorizer (inevitably defective, even when the allegory is invented—cf. Macaulay on Bunyan: 'It is not easy to make a simile go on all-fours. But we believe that no human ingenuity could produce such a centipede as a long allegory in which the correspondence between the outward sign and the thing signified should be exactly preserved.'). Origen's doctrines on such points as post-conversion good works and synergism must first be found in his deliberate expositions of such themes (if any); we can then illustrate the expositions from the allegories—not vice-versa.

For our present purpose it seems safe to see in the passages the idea of *grace as that which begins and ends the Christian pilgrimage.*

'the Lord is with him'—the first, says Origen, is 'by nature', the second 'by grace'.)[38]

Comm. Rom. IX.24 (p. *42*) [on grace as the source of all human good].

Ibid. IV.5 on 4^{16} (q.v.): 'Here he [Paul] is seeking to show that if the promise were of the law and not of grace, it would not be "firm". . . . His idea, I suppose, is somewhat as follows: things covered by the law are external to us, but things which come of grace are within us. We may put it thus: the law is written with the pen-and-ink on parchment or paper, but things which come of grace are inscribed by the Spirit of God on our heart (cf. 2 Cor 3^3), . . . (hence the greater "firmness"). With such . . . letters of the promise the soul is inscribed which has offered its faith to God like wax tablets made ready for the grace of God to be worthily written thereon; and such a faith is counted for righteousness which has shown itself able to receive divine grace.'

This Christian life is initiated by the grace of baptism, lived out as grace-given adoptive sonship of God, and may be rewarded by God's gifts of pre-eminence in His Kingdom, of resurrection, and of eternal life.

Comm. Jn. VI.33 (17) (p. *22*), *Comm. Rom.* II.1 (below, p. *51*), and *passim* in Origen—the 'grace of baptism'.

Comm. Jn. XIX.5 (p. *25*) on adoptive sonship.

Comm. Mt. XVI.5 on $20^{20\text{ff}}$: 'The mother did not know who are the pre-eminent, and that such a gift is grace from the One God who is over all, who breathes with and works with and establishes in such pre-eminence those whom He has seen to be fitted for it.'[39]

Comm. Ser. Mt. 126 (p. *37*) on the grace of resurrection.

Comm. Rom. (Gk), § 22 (*JTS*, XIII.358): 'The apostle said that "death" is the "wages of sin". But he did not say that eternal life is "wages", as if God owed it to us, but rather His gift of grace (Rom $6^{23\text{b}}$).'

Ibid. § 34 (ibid. p. 368) on 6^{23}: '(Paul) does not assess the

---

[38] I.e. grace mediating the presence of God to the believer.
[39] Again the note of doubt! God 'breathes with and works with' the successful candidates, whom He has already seen to be suitable! Pre-eminence may be a free gift, but you have to work for it.

"grace-gift" of God as "eternal life" *simpliciter*, for eternal life is not conceived as accomplished unless it is "in Jesus Christ our Lord".'

Grace is especially associated with the world-wide mission of Christ— with the divine, universal, converting power of His teaching, the Gentiles now having become the chosen recipients of God's grace in place of the Jews, and the forgiveness and calling of Christ being now offered to the world.

Princ. IV.1.5 on Ps 44^{2B} ('grace has been poured out on thy lips') (where to Origen of course the reference is to Christ). 'Evidence of this grace poured out on His lips lies in the speed with which the world has been filled with His teaching and Christian worship. For we Gentiles have been captured, worsted and conquered by the grace of His word.'

Hom. Jer. I.12: 'Christ received "grace from God poured out on His lips", so that not only when He was present in the body but now also when He is present in power and the Spirit He may prophesy "to all the nations", thus making good that prophecy and drawing men to salvation from all the nations.'

Comm. Mt. X.22: 'Thanks be to God, that although the grace of prophecy was confined to Israel, now a still greater grace than all they had has been poured out on the Gentiles through our Saviour Jesus.'

Cels. V.50: 'We Christian say that although (the Jews) "enjoyed the favour of God"[40] and were loved by Him more than any others, yet this dispensation and grace changed over to us when Jesus transferred the power at work among the Jews to the Gentile believers.'

Hom. Jer. III and IV.2 (p. *38*).
Comm. Jn. XIX.5 (p. *25*).
Ibid. *Frag.* 9 (p. *37*).

(D) THE WHOLE TRINITY IS ACTIVE IN THE PROVISION OF GRACE, AND ONCE RECEIVED IT IS TRANSMISSIBLE FROM BELIEVER TO BELIEVER.

For the Trinity, cf.—

Comm. Lam. Frag. 116 (pp. *31*f).

[40] The phrase is Celsus', who denies this 'favour' even to the Jews.

Comm. Jn. II.10 (6): 'In my view the Holy Spirit makes available, as it were, the raw material of God's grace-gifts to those who, because of that Spirit and their participation in it, are known as "holy ones". The "raw material" of the grace-gifts is made active by God, and tended by Christ, but owes its actual existence to the Holy Spirit.'

For the Transmission of Grace, cf.—

Cels. VIII.47: 'It is not credible that the apostles of Jesus, uneducated and ignorant men (Acts 4[13]) should have dared to proclaim Christianity to mankind in reliance on anything but the power which was given them and the grace in speech of making the matter clear' [i.e. the converting power of the word given by *God to the apostles*].

Sel. Deut. 1[9t] (p. *31*) [i.e. the grace of prophecy and leadership in which *Joshua succeeds Moses*].

(Gk.) *Hom. 1 Sam.* 28 (pp. *32f*) [i.e. *prophet to prophet*].

Sel. Ps. 119[79] (the Psalmist cries 'Let them that fear Thee turn to me'): 'He asks that such people should turn to him . . . that he might give them of the grace within him.' [i.e. *Psalmist to believer*.]

Comm. Rom. I.7 (pp. *38f*). [i.e. the commission and equipment to labour for the Gospel, given by *God to Christ and Christ to His disciples*.]

Comm. Rom. I.12 (p. *26*). [i.e. God's gift of a strengthened faith, transmissible from *apostle to believer*.]

SUMMARY AND DEFINITION

Grace, then, is throughout a matter of divine giving; it is especially operative in Scripture, both in the inspiration and power of the writings and in the insight given to understand them; it is operative throughout the whole of every man's salvation; in its provision the whole Trinity is engaged.

One or two observations may be made before we seek to extract from these hundred-or-so passages a formal definition.

(1) Although once or twice Origen seems to rise to the height

of the great argument and directly identify grace with Christ,[41] he normally thinks of it as diffused in its innumerable ways to meet (and transcend) every human need, and in this fashion revealing every facet of God's providence and salvation.

(2) In general Origen seems to link grace rather with divine *power* than with the other attributes.[42] This may be a mere matter of emphasis, or the accidental result of 'selective quotation'; but at any rate one could hardly define grace in Origen with the words in which Dr Manson begins his definition for Paul: 'Grace . . . signifies the generous love . . . of God . . .'

(3) χάρις in Origen has almost[43] lost its classical connotation of 'beauty'.[44] This alone should warn us, against dismissing Origen as a 'mere Hellenist'.

Bearing all this in mind, we may suggest that if Origen had been required to offer a formal definition of grace, he would have responded somewhat as follows:

GRACE IS THE POWER OF GOD FREELY BUT NOT UNCONDITIONALLY PLACED AT MAN'S DISPOSAL, WHEREBY HE APPROPRIATES THROUGH THE HOLY SPIRIT THE OFFER OF SALVATION TO A NEW AND ULTIMATELY ETERNAL LIFE REVEALED AND ENACTED IN SCRIPTURE BY THE INCARNATE JESUS CHRIST AND NOW MADE AVAILABLE BY HIM TO THE WORLD.

[41] Cf. *Comm. Jn. Frag.* 9 (p. *37*); *Comm. Lam. Frag.* 116 (pp. *31*f): ('the prophetic grace-gift is Christ, i.e. comes from Christ'); *Hom. Josh.* XVII.3 (where the partaking of the 'wisdom and knowledge' of God, His 'truth' and His 'Word' is summarized as 'partaking of the divine grace'; since the words in quotation marks are all scriptural designations of Christ, Origen is coming near to identifying grace with Him); *Comm. Jn.* I.10 (11): 'To say that the apostles bring good tidings of the Saviour and that they bring good tidings of "good things" is one and the same. For it is He who secured from the Father that there should be "good things", in order that every man, receiving through Jesus what his capacity or capacities allow, should enjoy "good things" . . . " good things" are none other than Jesus Himself' (where N.B. 'good things' is clearly synonymous with grace); cf. also *Hom. Gen.* XI.2 (p. *44*) ('For where the Spirit of grace is, there is said to be God Himself').

[42] Cf. *Cels.* II.50 (where grace = the miraculous power of Moses, contrasted with the mere trickery of the Egyptian magicians); ibid. VI.2 (p. *28*); *Hom. 1 Sam.* 10 (p. *44*); *Comm. Mt.* X.17 (p. *28*); *Comm. Ser. Mt.* 139 (p. *35*); *Hom. Lk.* IX (p. *44*); *Comm. Jn.* X.25 (16) (p. *34*); *Comm. Rom.* I.12 (p. *26*); *Cels.* III.31 (p. *34*); etc.

[43] Cf. p. *28*, note 15.

[44] Cf. e.g. Manson, *The Doctrine of Grace*, 34: '*Charis* in classical Greek has as its original sense "beauty", "attractiveness", "loveliness", literally "that which delights or charms" '; Torrance, *The Doctrine of Grace in the Apostolic Fathers*, 1: 'The classical word χάρις . . . in its original and fundamental sense is applied to what awakens pleasure or secures joy. It is the quality giving pleasure or thrilling the aesthetic sensibility.'

§ 2. SYNONYMS

If, as maintained above (p. *17*), Origen was not conscious of a technical theological problem in χάρις, and did not therefore feel it necessary to guard himself by definition, etc., in his use of it, we should expect that he will often use the *idea* of grace without affixing its official label—*die Sache* and *das Wort*, that is, will not always correspond.[45] Keeping the above definition in mind, we must therefore look for other expressions of the idea— and in a writer as copious as Origen we shall be prepared for a wide range of such 'synonyms'.

They seem to fall into four groups, and I shall give a representative selection of passages for each, taking the groups in the order of frequency of occurrence (and therefore probably of importance), and following as far as possible, in each group, the order of subject-matter as set out for χάρις itself in § 1.

(A) Δωρεά, δωρεῖσθαι, μεγαλόδωρος (**Latin: *donum, dare, munus, praesto, (dis)tribuo*[46])—which bear the root-meaning of GIFT.**

> *Comm. Rom.* II.14 on 2²: 'One thing only have I found that it was fitting for me to offer to God—namely, my conviction that He can receive nothing from man, only give (*dare*).'
>
> Ibid. IV.1 on 4⁴ᶠ: 'I cannot really persuade myself that any human work can demand a reward from God as its due, when the very fact that we can do anything, think anything, say anything, is entirely due to God's gift and largess (*dono et largitione*).'
>
> *Prayer* XVI.2 (p. *41*) (where δωροῦμαι is used throughout synonymously with χαρίζομαι of God's gifts to men in general, primarily spiritual, but not exclusive of material).
>
> *Martyrd.* 2 (p. *18*) (where δωροῦμαι, μεγαλόδωρος ['bounteous'] are used of the abundant grace of God).
>
> *Comm. Mt.* XV.37 (p. *30*) (where the δωρεά of insight into a difficult passage of Scripture is equated with a χάρισμα).

---

[45] It is the neglect of this principle that makes, for example, even the great work of Torrance on the Apostolic Fathers somewhat unsatisfactorily narrow in its scope.

[46] *Hom. Lk.* XXXIX (pp. *19f*), where Jerome translates αἰτεῖ δὲ παρ' ἡμῶν . . . ἵνα ἡμῖν ἀντιχαρίσηται τὰ αὑτοῦ by . . . (*ut*) *postquam si dederimus, nobis id ipsum* **tribuat** *in salutem.*

E

Sel. Lam. 4²⁰: 'Christ, who has given us [δωρησάμενον] the Spirit of prophecy.'

Comm. Jn. VI.3. (2) (pp. *24*f) (where δωρεά = χάρις = the vision of divine truth revealed by Christ).

Hom. Josh. VI.2 (where *munus = caelestis gratia* = baptism).

Comm. Ser. Mt. 3 (where God's *'maximae gratiae'* [above all the 'word of wisdom, knowledge'] are summed up as 'his omnibus *donis*').

Sel. Ps. 4⁶: 'Even he who has been made perfect will fall from grace if he should exalt himself because of his goodness, and ascribe to himself responsibility for it, instead of giving the due glory to Him who has made by far the greater contribution [πολλῷ πλεῖον δωρησαμένῳ] to his continuing possession of it. It is possible that the holy apostle has in mind that our own choice is by far the lesser factor in the gaining of blessings, as compared with the power of God, when he says (Rom 9¹⁶) "it is not of him that willeth nor of him that runneth but of God that hath mercy". He does not mean that God's mercy has nothing to do with our willing or running, but that the latter are as nothing compared with the former.'

Hom. Josh. I.6 on 1³: 'Joshua of course is speaking of the expulsion of the Canaanites, etc., and the occupation of their land; but to us⁴⁷ (Christians) there are certain devilish breeds of hostile powers against which we struggle. . . . The territories, . . . provinces, kingdoms of such of these powers as we can "tread beneath our feet" and conquer, we shall take into our possession—and Jesus our Lord will apportion (*distribuente*) them to us.'

Ibid. XII.3: '(Marcion, Basilides, Valentinus, etc., object to the violence of the Old Testament battle-stories and bring in the Creator-Redeemer theory.⁴⁸ But Origen's prayer is that) Jesus the Son of God, my Lord, may grant and order me to tread beneath my feet the "spirit of fornication", to tread on the neck of the spirit of wrath and anger, the demon of avarice (etc.) . . . and then when I have done this to fix the glory of my achieve-

---

⁴⁷ The identity of the Hebrew 'Joshua' and the Greek 'Jesus' is of course a godsend to the allegorizing Alexandrian.

⁴⁸ I.e. the Gnostic attempt to meet the difficulties of reconciling Old Testament and New Testament by postulating a 'demiurge', creator, as the author of the former, different from and even alien to the true God, the God of the New Testament, the Redeemer.

ment not on myself but on His Cross. . . . (After such victorious expulsion of these spirits) even so shall we at length be able to receive their places and kingdoms as an inheritance from Jesus . . . , our own Lord and Saviour making them available (*praestante*) to us.'

Sel. Ps. 61⁶ᴮ: 'He is saying that "being rich, Thou makest available great gifts" (δωρεάς), or rather "granting of Thy grace (χαριζόμενος) to the perfect that they should become Thy sons, Thou hast given them the heritage".'

Hom. Jer. XII.8 (p. *21*, note 7) (where δωροῦμαι is explained by ἐν χαρίσματος μοίρᾳ 'by way of a grace-gift'—of Paul's thorn in the flesh).

Comm. Rom. II.1 on 2²: 'We may ask if God appears to serve judgement "according to the truth" on those whose sins have been remitted through the grace of baptism, or covered through their penitence (Ps 32¹ᶠ), or to whom sin is not to be imputed because they have won the glory of martyrdom. Judgement, "according to the truth", indeed, demands that a bad man should be punished and a good man rewarded; and although the gifts and largess (*dona et largitio*) of God are not such as can be submitted to human inquiry, yet even here let us seek to show the range of facts that determine His judgement.'⁴⁹

Comm. Mt. XVI.5 (p. *45*) (of the δωρεά of pre-eminence in the Kingdom, which is χάρις).

Cels. III.81 (on the life after death. We agree with some pagan philosophers on the *fact*, but on little else. This is clear from a comparison of the pagan doctrine with the Christian view of) 'the blessed end with God in Christ . . . which will be the experience of those who have lived in irreproachable purity and have recovered their undivided and unbroken love for the God of all things—and which will come to them by God's gift (δωρεᾷ)'.

---

⁴⁹ It is particularly significant that God's judgement itself—just, but merciful—comes under the heading of such 'grace-words' as 'gifts and largess'. Cf. p. *61*.

(**B**) Εὐεργεσία, εὐεργετεῖν; εὐποιΐα, ἀγαθοποιΐα (**Latin: bene-ficium**)—**which bear the root-meaning of BLESSING.**
(For the identity of *Beneficium* with *Gratia* cf. *Hom. Isa.* VI.2
where the 'grace' received by Isaiah at his calling is described
by both words within a few lines; *Comm. Ser. Mt.* 2, where
'*beneficia eius et gratiam*' = God's continued blessings on the Christian throughout life; ibid. 126 (p. *37*) where again both words
are used—of forgiveness and resurrection; *Comm. Rom.* IV.5
(p. *19*) where *gratia* = '*benevolentiae beneficium*', and as such contrasted with '*merces*').

Martyrdom 28: 'The saint, who is an honourably scrupulous
man and determined to repay the benefits (εὐεργεσίας) conferred on him by God, seeks for something he can do for the
Lord in return for all he has received. And he finds that there
is nothing a man of proper intentions can give to God in return—as it were to counterbalance (οἱονεὶ ἰσόρροπον) the
benefits—as fittingly as a martyr's death.'[50]
Comm. Mt. XVI.6 on 20[20ff]: (What is this 'cup'? One
answer is 'martyrdom'—cf. Mt 26[39] and Ps 116[12f, 15, 18]). 'For
we can give no greater return to the Lord for the benefits
we have received (ἐφ' οἷς εὐηργετήθημεν) than to take up
whole-heartedly the cup of salvation and call upon the name
of the Lord.'
Cels. VIII.57: ('We owe the demons no gratitude) but we
eschew ingratitude to God, filled as we are with His kindly
acts (εὐεργεσιῶν)—being His creatures, the objects of His
providence, judged according to our condition, and with hopeful
expectations from Him beyond this life.'[51]
Princ. II.9.2 (on 'rational beings'): 'Whatever goodness
existed in their being was there not by nature but by the
beneficence (*beneficium*) of their Creator . . . the Creator

[50] εὐεργεσίαι is a general term for God's blessings. Here is the fateful suggestion
that they can be 'repaid', 'counterbalanced' by the human offering of martyrdom—
but Origen, who can be so eloquent in the same work (c.2, p. *18*) on 'grace abounding', shows perhaps here his uneasiness about the equivalence of martyrdom by his
οἱονεί ('as it were'), and by the form of the last sentence ('*nothing is as good a repayment as* martyrdom').
[On the question of martyrdom in Origen see pp. *164*ff.] Cf. next extract; *Comm.
Rom.* II.1 (p. *51*).
[51] N.B. the *list* of εὐεργεσίαι, from creation to eternal life.

granted (*indulsit*) to the minds He had created the faculty of free and voluntary movement, in order that the good that was in them might become their own, since it was preserved by their own free will.'[52]

Hom. Jer. I.1: 'God is swift to deeds of kindness (ἀγαθοποιΐα) but slow to punish those who deserve it. Although He could silently administer punishment to those He has condemned and give them no warning, He does no such thing, but even if He condemns He speaks—when speech is opportune to turn from condemnation the man about to be condemned.' [Origen quotes Jonah 3⁴, Gen 19¹², adding in this latter case] 'it was not that the angels were ignorant that [Lot's relatives] would not follow him, but rather that they were expressing the kindness (χρηστότης) and love of God to men (φιλανθρωπία)'.
Ibid. 3: 'God passed judgement on Jerusalem because of its sins, and its inhabitants were condemned to be delivered into captivity. Even so God in His kindness (φιλάνθρωπος) sent at the eleventh hour Jeremiah . . . to give those who would a chance to hear and repent.'

Comm. Jn. II.26 (21): 'Just as the Father "alone hath immortality" (1 Tim 6¹⁶)—our Lord having, for love of us (φιλανθρωπία), taken on Himself the burden of death on our behalf—by the same showing to the Father alone belong the words "in Him there is no darkness"—Christ having, for man's benefit (εὐεργεσία), taken on Himself our darkness, that by His power He might bring our death to nought and disperse the darkness in our souls.'[53]

Ibid. VI.57: 'It was only Jesus who had such love for man (φιλανθρωπία) as to eat and drink with sinners and publicans, and to offer His feet to the tears of the repentant woman who

---

[52] For this thought cf. ibid. I.2.4: 'Some of those who were created would prove unable, in consequence of the good being within them by accident and not by nature, i.e. not essentially, to remain strong, steadfast, unchanging, and to persist to the end in the fair and temperate use of these self-same blessings.'

[53] This passage should be set alongside those quoted by Butterworth, *Origen on First Principles*, p. 20, note 1, as giving a context in the setting of which their orthodoxy becomes less questionable. (*Origen ap. Jerome ad Avit.* 2: 'The Son, who is the image of the invisible Father, is not the truth when compared with the Father; but in relation to us, who are unable to receive the truth of God Almighty, He is a shadow and semblance of the truth'; *Origen ap. anon. ap. Photium Bibl. Cod.* 117: 'The image of God, considered in relation to God . . . and in so far as He is image, is not truth.' At the Council of Alexandria, A.D. 400, where Origenism was condemned, the charge becomes 'The Son compared with us is truth, but compared with the Father He is falsehood.')

had sinned, and to go as low as death for the ungodly. . . .
He grants His benefits (εὐεργετῶν) to the whole world—
since it is the world which God in Christ reconciles to Himself. . . . (2 Cor 5¹⁹)—but He bestows His benefits (τὰ
εὐεργετούμενα εὐεργετεῖ) with order and method, not
making all His enemies in one swoop the footstool of His
feet, . . . (but taking them one by one until He reaches the last
one—death).'

Hom. Lk. XVII on 2³⁴ ('for the falling and the rising up of
many'): 'The first blessing (εὐεργεσία) is that he who stands
in sin should fall and die to sin: the second that he should rise
and live in righteousness. Faith in Christ graciously bestows
(χαριζομένης) both these blessings.'

Sel. Ps. 2⁹: '(repentant sinners) who take refuge in . . .
the kindness (χρηστότης) of God, who is alone able to
benefit (εὐεργετῆσαι) them.'

Princ. III.1.12 (on Isa 63¹⁷ᵗ: 'why didst Thou harden our
heart, that we should not fear Thy name?'), i.e. says Origen:
' "Why didst Thou spare us so long, not visiting us for our
sins, but leaving us until our transgressions have grown great?"
For God abandons most men, leaving them unpunished, that
the character of each may be laid bare by the tests at our own
disposal, and the better ones may become manifest by the test
applied to them, while the others . . . may find the way of
healing later: for they could not have known the benefit
(εὐεργεσία) unless they had already condemned themselves.
Now this is of advantage to each, because it allows him to
realize his own character and the grace of God. He who does
not realize his own weakness and the divine grace, even if he
receives a benefit (εὐεργετῆται) before he has come to know
himself and condemn himself, will count as his own achievement
what has actually been freely supplied him (ἐπιχορηγῆθεν)
from the heavenly grace. This produces pride and conceit,
and will be a cause of his downfall.'

Ibid. 1.14: '(God in His dealings with us works slowly but
surely. Just as the wise farmer will not value rocky ground
and quick results that won't last) even so the great Farmer
of all nature delays the blessing (εὐποιΐα) which might be expected sooner, for fear it prove superficial.'

Prayer XIII.3: (Origen gives examples of effective prayer

from the life of Jesus and other Scriptural characters) 'and how many things has each of us to tell of his own experience, if he remembers with gratitude ($\epsilon \dot{v} \chi \alpha \rho \iota \sigma \tau \omega s$)[54] benefits ($\epsilon \dot{v} \epsilon \rho \gamma \epsilon \sigma \iota \tilde{\omega} \nu$) he has himself received and is willing to praise God for them'.

Cels. I.61: (Herod slew the infants, intending that among his victims should be 'He who was born king of the Jews'. But Jesus) 'was to be king not in the way Herod imagined, but in the way in which it was fitting for God to give a kingdom—for the benefit ($\epsilon \dot{v} \epsilon \rho \gamma \epsilon \sigma \iota \alpha$) of the subjects, and on One who would not bestow a moderate and, so to speak, indifferent benefit ($\epsilon \dot{v} \epsilon \rho \gamma \epsilon \sigma \iota \alpha \nu \ \epsilon \dot{v} \epsilon \rho \gamma \epsilon \tau \eta \sigma o \nu \tau \iota$) on His subjects, but would educate and guide them by the genuine laws of God.'

---

[54] The adverb of course stamps by implication $\epsilon \dot{v} \epsilon \rho \gamma \epsilon \sigma \iota \alpha$ as a 'grace-word'.

(C) Φιλάνθρωπος, φιλανθρωπία **with such other words as** χρηστότης, εὐμένεια, ἐπισκοπή, βοήθεια, ὠφέλεια **and the adjective** ἵλεως. **Cf. also** φωτισμός (*fons*, *lux*). **The root-meaning is PROVIDENTIAL HELP, KINDNESS, LOVE.**

Cels. VII.44: (Celsus supposes that we gain knowledge of God by the methods of 'synthesis with other things', 'analytical distinction' from other things, or 'analogy'.) 'But' [replies Origen] 'when the Word of God says that "No man has known the Father save the Son, and he to whom the Son may reveal Him" (Mt 11²⁷, Lk 10²²), He shows that God is known by a certain divine grace which does not come into the soul without God's working (ἀθεεί) but with a sort of inspiration [or "God-possession": ἐνθουσιασμοῦ]. Indeed it is likely that the knowledge of God is beyond the reach of human nature—hence the great blunders men make about God—but that by God's kindness (χρηστότητι) and love toward man (φιλανθρωπίᾳ) and by a miraculous and divine grace the knowledge of God reaches those who have been determined in advance by God's foreknowledge, because they would live worthily of Him when He was made known to them.'

Ibid. 46: 'Out of love to man (φιλάνθρωπος) God manifested the truth and that which may be known of Himself (Rom 1¹⁸f) not only to those who are devoted to Him but also to some who know nothing of pure worship and piety toward Him.'

Hom. 1 Sam. 11 on 2²: ' "There is none holy like the Lord": However great a man's growth in holiness and his attainments in purity and sincerity, yet none can be as holy as the Lord, because He is the bestower (*largitor*) of holiness, while man receives it; He is the fountain (*fons*) of holiness . . . while man . . . drinks it; He is the light (*lux*) of holiness while man looks on it.'⁵⁵

⁵⁵ Cf. *Comm. Jn.* XX.12, where Origen in using Hebrews 6⁴ᶠᶠ speaks of 'enlightenment' (φωτισμόν) and the other blessings (εὐεργεσίας) to him from God'. Cf. Moffatt, 'Hebrews', *I.C.C.*, p. 78: in Hebrews 6⁴ 'enlightened' corresponds to λαβεῖν τὴν ἐπίγνωσιν τῆς ἀληθείας at 10²⁶—i.e. 'enlightened' in the sense of 'having their eyes opened (Eph. 1¹⁸) to the Christian God'. For this significance in Origen cf. *Comm. Jn. Frag.* 73 on 9³⁷: 'The man has seen Him properly in whose case God Himself has enlightened the eyes of his soul.'

Cels. VIII.34: 'He to whom we render our firstfruits is also the One to whom we send up our prayers . . . and we "hold fast the confession" (Heb 4¹⁴) as long as we live, obtaining as we do the love of God for man (φιλανθρώπου τυγχάνοντες τοῦ Θεοῦ) and the love of His only-begotten Son who is manifested to us in Jesus.'

Ibid. 64: 'We must then seek the favour of (ἐξευμενιστέον) the one God over all and pray that He may be gracious (ἵλεω), seeking His favour by piety and every virtue.'

Sel. Ps. 2⁹ (p. *54*) (χρηστότης = God's undeserved kindness to the sinner).

Hom. Jer. I.1 (p. *53*) (χρηστότης, φιλανθρωπία of God's merciful loving-kindness, seeking even at the last to save His people from judgement).

Comm. Jn. VI.53 (55): (Christ went to His atoning death) 'in accordance with the Father's love for man' (φιλανθρωπίαν).

Ibid. 57 (pp. *53*f) (φιλανθρωπία is the motive, just as εὐεργετῶν is the whole range of blessings won by, the atoning death of Christ for the world).

Ibid. II.26 (21) (p. *53*) (φιλανθρωπία = the motive which impelled Christ to rescue us from sin and death).

Cels. VIII.27: (Christians need have no fear of demons) 'For even if the demons were not kindly-disposed (εὐμενεῖς) to them, they could still suffer no harm from them, being under the guardianship of the supreme God who is kindly-disposed to them because of their piety, and who makes His divine angels stand over those worthy to be so guarded that they suffer not from the demons. But the man to whom the supreme God is kindly-disposed because of His piety toward Him, and because he has accepted . . . the Lord Jesus, is satisfied with the kindly goodwill of God through Christ Jesus, and may say with boldness, as one who will suffer nothing from the whole army of demons: "The Lord is my light . . ." (Ps 26¹, ³).'⁵⁶

Ibid. VII.41 (Celsus commends to us the authority of the ancient Greek poets and philosophers in place of the Bible); 'He would have us leave . . . Moses and the prophets . . . and

---

⁵⁶ Cf. c.36, where in the same connexion we hear of God's 'help'—'who alone can help (βοηθεῖν) all who are worthy'—and where again we note the qualifying of the recipient (cf. in the text—'because of their piety', 'those worthy to be so guarded'). For βοήθεια cf. *Comm. Mt.* XV.17 (p. *58*) and note 58.

Him who enlightened mankind and showed how to worship God and, as far as He could, left none without some taste of His mysteries, but who because of His exceeding great love for man was able to give the more educated a conception of God which could lift their soul from earthly things and yet who came down even to the level of the more common-place capacities of ordinary men and simple women and slaves. . . .'

Ibid. 42 (where Celsus has quoted some famous words of Plato [*Timaeus* 28 C]): 'To find the Maker and Father of the universe is difficult, and when one has found Him it is impossible to declare Him to all men'—words which Origen admits are 'noble and impressive'[57]—'but see if the divine Scripture does not show more love for mankind when it introduces (φιλανθρωπότερον . . . εἰσάγει) the Divine Word, who was "in the beginning with God", becoming flesh, that the Word, of whom Plato says that after finding Him it is impossible to declare Him to all men, may be able to reach all men.'

Comm. Mt. XV.17 on 19[16ff] (growth to ethical perfection): 'It is not necessary to suppose that (perfection) will accrue on the self-same day to the man who gives away his possessions and sells them to the poor: rather from that day the oversight (ἐπισκοπή) of God will begin to lead him toward it. . . . Advancing . . . because of the help (βοήθεια)[58] God gives him in Christ, he will grow (in all virtue, etc.). . . .'

Prayer II.3 (The Holy Spirit helps those who recognize their own insufficiencies in prayer): 'The Spirit that cries in the hearts of the blessed, "Abba, Father" . . . makes intercession for us to God with groanings beyond utterance (Rom 8[26]), taking on Himself our groanings because of His great love and pity for men (φιλανθρωπίαν καὶ συμπάθειαν).'

[57] Cf. p. *28*, note 16.
[58] βοήθεια, cf. p. *57*, note 56; cf. ὠφέλεια—*Comm. Jn.* VI.33 (17), (p. *22*) of the divine 'benefits' of baptism: ibid. X.6 (4) of the blessings made available for mankind by the incarnation of Christ.

(D) (᾿Επι)χορηγεῖν, χορηγία **with the Latin** *largior, indulgere.* **Cf.** κοσμεῖν, **etc. The root-meaning here is 'FURNISH IN ABUNDANCE'.**

Comm. Rom. IV.1 (p. *49*) (*largitio* of God's grace which makes human thought and action possible).

Hom. Num. IX.8 on 17⁵: (Origen notes that while God promised only the budding of the rod, the fulfilment included leaves, blossoms, nuts) 'just as in this case God fulfilled His promise fourfold, and abundantly bestowed (*largitus est*) far more and far more precious gifts than He promised, even so—but far more so—in all the passages of Scripture which contain a promise of God, a fulfilment many times greater is laid up for any who deserves to attain it'.

Hom. 1 Sam. 11 (p. *56*) (*largitor* of God as the source of holiness and purity).

Comm. Jn. VI.36 (20) (κ ο σ μ ε ῖ ν of God's furnishing the beneficiary with fitness to receive His grace).

Princ. II.9.2 (pp. *52*f) (*indulgere* of God's gift of free-will to created beings).

Ibid. III.1.12 (p. *54*) (ἐπιχορηγεῖν = χαρίζεσθαι, of God's εὐεργεσία in the special sense of healing of sin).

Cels. V.1 (beginning a new book of his reply to Celsus, Origen prays for divine help) 'that He who gives "the word to those who preach with great power" (Ps 68¹¹) may furnish (ἐ π ι χ ο ρ η γ ε ῖ ν) this also to us, and bestow on us this great power, so that by the word and power of God faith may be born in my readers'.⁵⁹

Comm. Jn. VI.2 (in pursuing his commentary, Origen says): 'We have faith . . . in God, who enriches us in all utterance and knowledge (1 Cor 1⁵), that He will enrich us as we strive to observe the spiritual laws, and that, progressing in our construction on the strength of His bounties (ἐκ τῶν ἐπιχορηγουμένων ὑπ᾿ αὐτοῦ), we shall attain to the crown of the edifice.'

---

⁵⁹ On (ἐπι)χορηγεῖν, with reference to Scripture, cf. *Prophetic Fragments* (Klostermann, Vol. III, GSDEJ) No. 15—of God τοῦ χορηγοῦντος εἰπεῖν καὶ φωτίζοντος 'who furnished abundantly their speaking and enlightening (the prophets)'.
Comm. Lam. Frag. 116 (pp. *31*f) (where Origen, perhaps quoting from memory, replaces διαιροῦν at 1 Cor 12¹¹ by χορηγοῦν—'dividing' by 'furnishing abundantly').
Comm. Mt. XIV.6 (where ἐπιχορηγούμενος similarly replaces the δίδοται of 1 Cor 12⁸—'furnished abundantly' in place of 'is given').

(N.B. ἐπιχορηγέω here paraphrases the Pauline πλουτίζω, 'enrich'.)

Hom. Num. XII.3: 'When we have offered to Him gifts from our own store, we then go on to receive gifts from Him. For when we have offered Him our faith and love, then He freely bestows on us (*largitur*) the various gifts of the Holy Spirit.'

Ibid. XXIV.2: 'God's desire is first to receive something from us, and then to give us (*largiri*) of His own, that His gifts and bounties may be seen to be bestowed on the deserving.'

Sel. Ps. 119[131] (naïvely misinterpreted by Origen as 'I opened my mouth and drew down the Spirit'): 'The price of the bestowal (χορηγία) of the Spirit is the recital and fulfilment of the laws of God.'

Comm. Rom. II.1 (p. *51*) (*largitio* of God's judgement, just yet merciful).

———

It is clear, I think, that in the mind of Origen these four groups of words, if our analysis is correct, bring out four necessary aspects of the grace of God—grace as God's gift, as His blessing, as His lovingkindness, and 'grace abounding'. The link of each group with χάρις can usually be inferred from the contents of the extracts, and is sometimes (as shown) made explicit by Origen himself.

The content and range of grace, which we set out above (pp. *18*ff), will be seen, as regards much of its substance, to be further illustrated by the use of these 'synonyms'. Grace is God's free giving, generous and abundant (*Hom. Num.* IX.8 [p. *59*]); grace gives the insight to understand and comment on Scripture (and to write Christian apologetic!) (*Comm. Jn.* VI.2 [pp. *59*f], *Cels.* V.1 [p. *59*)]; the spirit of prophecy is granted us by Christ (*Sel. Lam.* IV.20 [p. *50*]); the grace of baptism is a gift of God (*Hom. Josh.* VI.2 [p. *50*]); it is to the blessings wrought by Jesus that we owe our education and guidance in the laws of God (*Cels.* I.61 [p. *55*]); it is to God's undeserved kindness that we owe the healing of our sin (*Princ.* III.1.12 [p. *54*], *Sel. Ps.* 2[9] [p. *54*]); it is to Christ that we owe our victory over hostile spiritual powers (*Hom. Josh.* I.6 [p. *50*], XII.3 [pp. *50*f], *Cels.* VIII.27 [p. *57*]); it is through the help and oversight of God in Christ that we gradually attain perfection [from which, again, self-glorification can cause our fall—*Sel. Ps.* 4⁶ (p. *50*)] (*Comm. Mt.* XV.17 [p. *58*]), and a blessed end beyond the grave (*Cels.* III.81, VIII.57 [pp. *51*, *52*]). There are also interesting side-lights on the superiority of the revelation of God's saving love in Christ to the highest flights of the Greek poets and philosophers (*Cels* VII.41f [pp. *57*f]).

At other points the range of grace is seen to be enlarged, or at least looked at from a fresh viewpoint. There is an almost Barthian insistence (not forgetting the favourite Barthian cita-tion of Mt 11²⁷, Lk 10²²) that the knowledge of God comes only through God's own grace, kindness, love (*Cels.* VII.44 [p. *56*]), and that God's holiness is the source of, and as such in a different category from, our own (*Hom. 1 Sam.* 11 [p. *56*]). Again, human action, thought and speech are only possible by God's gift and largess (*Comm. Rom.* IV.1 [p. *49*]), and free will itself (on which, of course, Origen is famous for his insistence) is a faculty which we owe to God (*Princ.* II.9.2 [pp. *52*f]). There are new sidelights on the place of prayer in the scheme of grace (*Prayer* XIII.3 (pp. *54*f), *Cels.* VIII.34, 64 [p. *57*]), on the method by which grace makes forgiveness effective (*Princ.* III.1.12, 14 [p. *54*]), and on the love of God in Christ for man as the motivating force which led Christ to His Cross (*Comm. Jn.* II.26 (21), VI.57 [pp. *53*f]; VI.53 (55) [p. *57*]; *Hom. Jer.* I.1 [p. *53*]). Nay, judgement itself is now seen to come within the range of the grace of a merciful God (*Comm. Rom.* II.1 [p. *51*], *Cels.* VIII.57 [p. *52*], *Hom. Jer.* I.1 [p. *53*]).

Certain uneasy doubts and questionings, however, to which expression was given in the footnotes as we reviewed the χάρις passages, appear to be rather reinforced than removed by some of these new extracts.

There was, for example, a hint of 'dual standards' of rank and achievement for Christians, with what may possibly be the intel-lectual snobbery of the Professor at its root (p. *40*, note 33; cf. *Comm. Jn.* VI.4 [p. *25* with note 11]). We are not now re-assured to find the 'word of wisdom' and the 'word of knowledge' described as God's 'greatest graces' (*Comm. Ser. Mt.* 3 [p. *50*]).

But the great query concerns what seemed Origen's uncer-tainty about the status of faith and virtue—whether they are 'of merit' or 'of grace'. Alongside such passages as *Comm. Rom.* IV.5 (p. *19*), where grace is the very opposite of a reward, and the impressive array of assertions (p. *19*, note 4) that everything mankind has it receives from God, that man's offerings to God are a giving back rather than a giving away, that man's victory in the battle of life should be laid not to his own credit but to that of the Cross of Christ—in short, that the response we make to God's grace is itself prompted and empowered by that grace (pp. *22*ff), we noted elsewhere that grace and merit are, as it were, correlatives; that human virtue and faith are split into the part we owe to God and the part we have achieved ourselves and out of our own resources, and where grace becomes something very like a reward of human deserving (pp. *25*ff). This inconsistency is, to say the least, not removed by the new extracts. Alongside what is practically a definition of pure grace (*Comm. Rom.* II.14 [p. *49*]), the almost Barthian insistence on the sovereignty of grace (ibid. IV.1 [p. *49*], *Cels.* VIII.57 [p. *52*], VII.44 [p. *56*], *Hom. 1 Sam.* 11 [p. *56*]), and the reminders that it is God who furnishes the beneficiary with fitness to receive His grace (*Comm. Jn.* VI.36 [20] [p. *59*]), and that our free-will itself is a faculty which we owe to God (*Princ.* II.9.2 [pp. *52*f]), we find other hints and assertions of a different tenor. God makes 'by far the greater contribution' to our continuing possession of grace (*Sel. Ps.* 4[6] [p. *50*]); it is the already perfect whom God makes His sons and heirs (*Sel. Ps.* 61[6B] [p. *51*]); it is to those who have lived in 'irreproachable purity' who will receive the 'blessed end with God in Christ'—by God's free gift! (*Cels.* III.81 [p. *51*]); it is 'gifts from our own store' of faith and love that occasion God's gifts through the Holy Spirit—indeed, the 'price' of the latter's bestowal is our fulfilment of God's law; we must give something to God first, that His gifts may be bestowed on 'the deserving' (*Hom. Num.* XII.3, XXIV.2; *Sel. Ps.* 119[131] [p. *60*]). Origen goes so far as to suggest that martyrdom can 'repay', 'counterbalance' God's blessings to us—although possibly with misgivings (p. *52*, note 50).

§ 3. SUMMARY

What have we so far achieved? A suggested definition of grace in Origen, formulated apart from any presuppositions of our own, and based on a hundred examples of his use of χάρις, χαρίζομαι, χάρισμά; further insight into his meaning by the investigation of four groups of synonyms or 'grace-words'; a conviction of a range and richness of thought in Origen which stamp him, beyond all question, as a Christian theologian of high quality and insight; and some unhappy doubts about one or two rather vital features and implications of his doctrine.

On the credit side we must note with real appreciation that the definition itself bears comparison with that of Dr Manson with which we started. We should have preferred a more prominent emphasis on the love of God rather than His power; we are not too happy about the conditions of the bestowal of grace. But we do not miss the recognition of the work of the whole Trinity, the emphatic placing of Scripture in the centre of the stage, the close linking—almost the identification—of the determinative enactment of grace with Jesus Christ, the universal offer of salvation, the eternal dimensions of the new life available to the believer through grace. For all his Alexandrine provenance, Origen knows from the start that the New Testament χάρις is something new and unique—there is hardly a hint of the Hellenistic significance of the word. Indeed, he opens a new era in his understanding of the 'apostle to the Gentiles'— much of the ground lost by the Apostolic Fathers is here reoccupied, and one could wish that in this great and salutary achievement he had carried the Church of the next centuries with him.

The 'doubts and questionings' which we cannot but feel are indeed serious. It would be a revealing inquiry to trace through to the Reformation (and even beyond) the course of Christian thought on these issues. We are not suggesting that Origen was the first man to go off the rails—far from it. Indeed, he seems rather to be succumbing to temptations which are perpetual and inevitable to the human mind when it seeks to 'fathom the eternal thought'.

The sovereign freedom of grace is emphatically vindicated by our own author; but is he not compromising or even under-mining it by the conditions he represents God as demanding? Can man in any sense earn—and thus compel—the grace of God? In being conditional does grace degenerate from Gospel to Law? Does it really cover every aspect of human life? Or does Origen lessen the total and exclusive responsibility of God for our salvation and leave however modest a degree of the credit to us?[60]

The same question in another form is posed by the respective standing Origen gives to grace and nature.[61] Origen never makes things easy for himself; and his loyal determination to bring all life's institutions, its ethical standards, culture and philosophy within the realm of grace[62] sharpens the problem. What, in any case, is the relation of Origen's own philosophical inheritance to his finished theology? We suggested above (p. *19*, note 4) the category of question and answer; but it would still be possible that the innocent function of philosophy in posing questions for theology to answer becomes unintentionally compromising by the form and implications of the questions themselves, as in some degree limiting and prescribing the answers that can be given.[63]

A disturbing misgiving is aroused by Origen's grading of God's 'grace-gifts' and the ranking of wisdom and knowledge higher than faith.[64] We must remember, of course, Origen's dichotomy of faith into the divine and the human—also, possibly, the equa-tion in some passages of faith with intellectual belief.[65] But we must watch for any trace of 'intellectualism' as such, involving as it does a 'dual standard' of Christianity based on intellectual achievement.

Finally, the interpretation of the Bible. True theology has been known to issue from false exegesis, and our own concern is not with Origen's allegorism or his 'atomistic inspirationalism' (p. *28*, note 14) as such, but his conclusions. The real question is—Has he or has he not made up his mind about doctrine be-fore ever he reaches the biblical text?[66] Or does he formulate

[60] Cf. *Martyrd.* 2 (p. *18*); *Hom. Lk.* XXXIX (p. *19* and note 4); *Comm. Rom.* IX.3 (p. *20* and note 5); *Comm. Jn.* I.20 (22) (p. *21*); *Hom. Lk.* III (p. *22*); passages quoted pp. *25*ff and notes; *Comm. Mt.* XIV.11ff (pp. *30*f); *Comm. Jn.* XIII.53 (52) and XX.32 (26) (pp. *40*f); *Hom. 1 Sam.* 5, *Hom. Gen.* XI.2 (pp. *43*f); *Comm. Mt.* XVI.5 (p. *45*); and the 'synonym'-passages above, pp. *50*f.
[61] Cf. *Comm. Jn. Frag.* 11 (p. *26*); *Comm. Song Songs* II.147f (p. *35*); *Frag. 1 Sam.* 16[18] (pp. *44*f).
[62] Cf. pp. *41*ff.   [63] Cf. p. *19*, note 4, and *Cels.* VII.41f (pp. *57*f).
[64] Cf. p. *61*.   [65] Cf. *Comm. Jn.* XX.32 (26) (pp. *40*f).
[66] Cf. *Comm. Jn. Frag.* 11 (p. *26* and note 12).

his theology from a more-or-less correct interpretation of *Scripture-as-a-whole*, his guilt lying merely in its application to particular passages—in which case his excursions into the intricate by-ways of allegorism will be of value for the doctrines rather than the texts that they illustrate?[67] The first alternative would impugn his very claim to be a Christian theologian; the second merely his exegetical soundness and consistency. We venture to think that his determination to find Christ—the revealed and incarnate Word of God—in every passage of Scripture would count heavily here to him for righteousness.

What seems to be at stake in the ground we have so far covered is not so much a radical misapprehension of the Christian revelation as a failure to absorb the whole intractable area of human life into the sovereign χάρις of God. Origen's failure, should this be true, is at least a gallant one. We have already noted the freshness and hospitality of his mind: like Plato he was never afraid to follow 'wherever the argument leads' (above, p. 2). The real question is how far and how compromisingly it leads him from Grace—whether it is true that for him Christ in the end has lost, in whole or part, the Name that is above every name, and is no longer 'all in all'.

<hr />

[67] Cf. *Hom. I Sam.* 5, etc. (pp. *43*f, and p*44*, note 37).

F

CHAPTER TWO

THE GRACE OF THE FATHER, GOD THE SON, GOD THE HOLY SPIRIT

W E HAVE FOUND by analysis the meaning of χάρις in Origen; we have traced numerous expressions of the *idea* of grace, in whole or part, in a wide range of other words; we have given a preliminary appreciation and criticism of the doctrine that has emerged. What we must now do is to look at the whole question from a different point of view. If grace for Origen is God's power at work for and in mankind—the offer and substance of salvation, wrought for us by Jesus Christ and appropriated through the Holy Spirit—we can only understand at all adequately the range, the content, the *modus operandi* of grace if we look in turn at the specific work of each Person of the Trinity in the whole scheme of creation and redemption. The landscape is enormously broad: I can only select a few of the decisive landmarks, trusting that they are adequate pointers to the nature of the terrain as a whole. Origen has at least, by the generous range of his χάρις-theology, given us leave to look at every point beyond the *word* and seek the fullness of his doctrine in the *theme*.

It is worth adding that we are not called upon to contribute yet another discussion of Origen's Trinitarianism. Origen, indeed—like ourselves—does not always write with the Trinitarian *problem* uppermost in his mind. Often no specific Person of the Trinity is mentioned:[1] often the noun (ὁ) θεός[2] or the adjective θεῖος[3] merely point the reference to God as against man not 'Father' as against 'Son' or 'Holy Spirit'. Prophecy, for example, is normally represented as given χάριτι Θεοῦ,[4] but is at one passage subjected to a specific 'division of labour' between the Persons.[5] Nor, even when such a division is indicated, should

---

[1] E.g. *Cels*. VIII.47 (p. *47*), where of course Origen could have supplied the reference without difficulty.

[2] Especially in the stock χάριτι Θεοῦ, e.g. *Cels*. VI.57 (p. *29*).

[3] E.g. *Princ*. IV.1.6 (p. *28*), *Hom. 1 Sam*. 2 (p. *29*).

[4] E.g. *Cels*. VIII.46 (p. *31*).

[5] *Comm. Lam. Frag*. 116 (pp. *31*f): The source is God the Father, the inspiration is the Holy Spirit, the target or object is Christ.

we expect perfect consistency. The doctrine of the Trinity was as yet far from authoritative definition by the Church—even if later orthodoxy (some would add heresy!) owes much in the matter to Origen himself.

What we are seeking is, in broad outline and with a necessary measure of selection, the contributions of the Father, the Son and the Holy Spirit to the whole scheme of grace as envisaged by Origen.

§ 1. THE GRACE OF GOD THE FATHER

(A) CREATION

God the Father created all things and all beings.

Princ. Pref. 4 (first in Origen's list of 'doctrines which are believed in plain terms through the apostolic preaching' is) 'God is One, who created and set in order all things, and who, when nothing existed, caused everything to be'.

Ibid. *Frag.* 7 (Koetschau) at I.3.3: 'Everything whatever except the Father and God of the universe is created.' Ibid. *Frag.* 9: 'The God and Father, who holds the universe together, is superior to every being that exists, for He imparts to each one from His own existence that which each one is.'

Hom. 1 Sam. 11: 'Nothing that exists owes its existence to itself: Thou alone hast been granted Thy existence from no other. We all—i.e. the whole creation—did not exist before we were created: our existence is due to the will of the Creator.'

Comm. Rom. IV[5]: 'The fact that we exist cannot possibly be a reward of our works but is due to the grace of our Creator.'

Sel. Ezek. 16[8]: 'He is maker of all.'

The agent of creation was Christ, who in His various attributes foreshadowed, pervades and thus explains the universe.

Cels. II.9: 'We say that it was to Him (Jesus) that the Father gave the command, in the Mosaic story of creation, when He said "Let there be light" [etc.] . . . and all the other things that God commanded to come into being. It was to Him too that He said "Let us make men according to our image and likeness". Thus commanded the Word made everything that the Father enjoined Him. . . . Who . . . could be . . . capable of fulfilling so great an injunction from the Father except He who was what I may call the living Word and Truth?'

Princ. II.6.3: 'The only-begotten Son of God . . . through whom . . . "all things visible and invisible were made" (Col 1[16]), according to the teaching of Scripture both made all things and "loves what He made" (Wisdom 11[24]). For since

He is the invisible "image of the invisible God" (Col 1^{15}), He granted invisibly to all rational creatures participation in Himself . . .'.

Ibid. II.9.4: 'Everything which had been made is said to have been made through Christ and in Christ (quotes Col 1^{16}, Jn 1^{1}, Ps 104^{24}). . . . Since, then, Christ, as He is the Word and wisdom, is also righteousness (1 Cor 1^{30}), it will . . . follow that those things that have been made in the Word and in wisdom, may also be said to have been made in that righteousness which is Christ . . . [i.e.] in everything that was made there was nothing unrighteous, nothing without a purpose.'

Ibid. I.2.2 (one of Christ's titles is 'the Wisdom of God' (1 Cor 1^{24}). Origen quotes Proverbs 8$^{22-5}$ and applies the words to Christ): 'Wisdom therefore must be believed to have been begotten beyond the limits of any beginning that can be spoken of or comprehended. Hence because in this very subsistence of Wisdom there was contained every capacity and form of the future creation, . . . pre-formed and arranged by the power of foreknowledge, Wisdom says (through the mouth of Solomon) that she was created as a "beginning of the ways" of God, the references being to just those creatures who had been (so to speak) sketched and prefigured in herself; she means that she contains within herself the beginnings, the *raisons-d'être* (Latin: *rationes*), the types of the whole creation.'

Ibid. I.4.4: 'In this Wisdom . . . which ever existed with the Father, the sketch and fashion of the Creation was always present, and there never was a time when the prefiguration of what was to be was not present in Wisdom.'

Ibid. I.2.4: 'This Son . . . is . . . "the Truth and the Life" (Jn 14^{6}) of everything that exists, and rightly so. For how could the things that were made live, unless from "Life" as the source? Or how could the things that exist do so in true reality, unless they had been derived from the "Truth"? Or how could rational beings exist, unless the "Word" or "Reason" had existed before? Or how could they be wise, unless "Wisdom" existed?'

Hom. Gen. I.1: ' "In the beginning God made heaven and earth." What is the "beginning" of all things except our Lord and Saviour of all, Jesus Christ, the "first-born of all creation" (Col 1^{15})? *This*, then, was the "beginning"—i.e. His

Word—in which God made heaven and earth (cf. Jn 1¹ᶠᶠ). Hence the meaning is not some "beginning" in time, but "in the beginning" in the sense of "in the Saviour". . . . Time did not exist before the world, but only began with the days that followed the Creation.'[6]

Comm. Jn. VI.38 (22): 'The Son of God, the Word, through whom all things were made, subsists in the underlying essence of things, and is the same as Wisdom. For He pervades the whole of creation, and hence things that come to be are always made through Him, and the sayings "All things were made by Him", "In Wisdom hast Thou made them all" (Jn 1³, Ps 103²⁴) are true of everything whatsoever.'

The purpose of Creation was to punish and remedy the Fall of pre-existent souls.

Princ. I.8.1 (*Frag.* 15 [Koetschau]): 'Before the ages minds were all pure—demons, souls and angels—offering service to God and keeping His commandments. But the devil, who was one of them, since he possessed freewill, desired to resist God, and God banished him. All the other powers revolted with him. Those whose sin was grave become demons; the lesser sinners angels; the least, archangels. Thus each in turn received the reward of his own sin. But some souls were left who had not sinned sufficiently to become demons, or again so lightly as to become angels. God therefore created the present world and bound the soul to the body as a punishment. . . . For if this were not so, and souls had not pre-existed, why do we find some new-born babies to be blind, when they have committed no sin, while others are born with nothing defective at all? But it is clear that certain sins pre-existed in the souls, because of which each soul receives a return according to its deserts. They are sent forth from God as a punishment, that here on earth they may undergo a first judgement. That is why the body is called a "frame", because the soul is "framed", "bound" within it.' [δέμας ('person', 'body') suggests δέω ('bind').]

---

[6] Origen of course is playing on the shifting senses of ἀρχή, *principium*—beginning, basis, principle, cause. So did Philo before him (*de opif. mundi* 26: 'understanding the beginning not, as some do, in the temporal sense'); and the thought of time beginning with creation (Philo, ibid.: 'for time did not exist before the creation') goes back at least to Plato [*Timaeus* 38B: 'Now time began with the (creation of the) heaven'], and was not, as Brunner seems to suppose, an invention of St Augustine (*Scottish Journal of Theology*, IV.1.1).

Ibid. II.1.1 (*Frag.* 18 [K]): 'Since the world is so very rich in variety and embraces so many different types of rational being . . . what other cause must we give for its coming into existence . . . except the different degrees of Fall of those who decline from (the original) unity in different ways?'

Ibid. III.5.4 (excerpt *ap. Jerome Avit.* 9) (Origen notes that the scriptural word καταβολή ['foundation' of the world, cf. Eph 1[4], etc.] means literally a 'descent', 'casting down'. He compares Romans 8[20], 'the creation was subjected to vanity'): 'I think we must understand that the beings above have a more divine dwelling-place and a true rest, in which rational creatures used to dwell together in enjoyment of their original blessedness, before their descent to these lower regions and their migration from the invisible to the visible and their Fall to the earth caused them to require gross bodies. Hence God the Creator made for them bodies suited to these lowly places and fashioned this visible world and sent into it ministers for the saving and correction of those who had fallen. (These ministers are not only the angels but also the sun, moon, stars, etc.). . . . This "creation has been subjected to vanity" in the sense that it has been clothed with gross bodies and made visible. Nevertheless it was subjected to vanity not of its own will, but by the will of Him who subjected it "in hope" ' (i.e. of being delivered from the bondage of corruption, when the children of God have been gathered into one [Rom 8[21], Jn 11[52]]).

We are not here concerned with the origin and affinities of the doctrine of a pre-mundane Fall. Nor can we set out here the total structure of speculation in the *Principiis* of which it forms a part—the pre-existence and transmigration of the human soul, the succession of worlds, the '*apocatastasis*' (or ultimate salvation of all free moral creatures). As Origen says (*Jerome Avit.* 4), he offers them 'not as dogmas', but as 'inquiries and conjectures intended to show that the problems have not been completely overlooked'. The overall problem is of course the reconciliation of God's overlordship of the universe with the fact of evil. Rejecting with finality Gnostic speculations which would cut the knot by ascribing the world to another and lesser creator, Origen holds firmly to the biblical doctrine of creation by the Supreme God. He equally rejects any form of fatalism, and his insistence on human freewill safeguards the essentially moral tone and purpose of all his thought. What does, however, leap to notice is his failure to think out the doctrine of a pre-mundane Fall in terms of his own Christology. There is little or no room for Christ in these speculations.

The consequences are serious. The universe *may* be an expression of the divine wisdom, truth, righteousness and life which is Christ. It *may* be a punishment for pre-mundane sin, an expression in its diversity of the varying human declensions from perfection. It cannot very well be both. One conception must in all consistency give way to or be radically reinterpreted by the other.[7]

Again: if creation is the granting to us of participation in Christ, it is throughout 'of grace'. But the whole structure of Origen's doctrines of pre-existence, Fall, succession of worlds, etc., is built on merit.[8] No window of divine grace is flung open to refresh

---

[7] Cf. too such passages as *Comm. Jn. Frag.* 50 (above, p. *35*) implying only sin *after* creation.

[8] Cf. Butterworth's summary of Origen's teaching at this point: 'God is entirely just and has no favourites; souls are the masters of their own destinies and each obtains what he deserves' (*Princ.*, p. xxxiii). See, for example, *Princ.* II.9.5-6 (The Marcionites, Valentinians, etc., object to our doctrine that the world, with all its variety, was created by the 'good, righteous and absolutely fair God', pointing among other things to the differences that exist between the sorts and conditions of men): 'Some, for example, receive at birth a happier lot . . . like [Jacob] who while still in the womb supplants his brother and before he is born is said to be "loved by God" (Rom 9¹³, Mal 1²ᶠ, Gen 25); and, in general, one man is born among the Hebrews, among whom he finds knowledge of the divine law, another among the Greeks, the men of wisdom and extensive learning; another however is born among the Ethiopians, whose custom is to feed on human flesh, others among the Scythians, among whom parricide is as it were legalized, and others among the Taurians, where visitors are offered in sacrifice. This, then, is the objection [the Marcionites, etc.] raise: If this great diversity of things and these so various and diverse conditions of birth—in which clearly the faculty of freewill has no place (for a man does not choose for himself where or among whom or in what condition he is to be born)— if, they say, the responsibility for all this lies not with diversity in the nature of souls, i.e. an evil-natured soul being destined for an evil nation and a good one for good nations, what else is there but the assumption that it is all due to blind chance? (which would exclude the creation, providence, and judgement of the supreme God).'
[Origen's reply]: 'God the creator of the universe is good, just, omnipotent. When in the beginning He created what He wished to create, i.e. rational natures, He had no other reason for creating them except Himself i.e. His goodness. Since therefore He Himself was the cause of everything that was to be created, and in Him there was neither variation nor change nor limits to His power, He created everyone equal and alike. . . . But since the rational creatures themselves . . . were endowed with the faculty of freewill, this freedom induced each one either to progress through the imitation of God or to deterioration through negligence. This . . . was the cause of diversity among rational creatures. . . . But God, to whom it seemed just to

this dreary atmosphere of rewards and punishments. What, then, is his true and final position—'The fact that we exist cannot possibly be a reward of our works but is due to the grace of our Creator' (*Comm. Rom.* IV.5 (above, p. *68*) or 'God . . . made the present world and bound the soul to the body as a punishment' (*Princ.* I.8.1 (above, p. *70*))?

Every Christian cosmology is confronted at the outset with the antinomy of divine creation and human evil. It is to the credit of Origen that he looks both these facts in the face. No Christian cosmology has really eliminated the 'surd': but Origen hardly tries. He gives little evidence that he is even aware of the need. Here is a cardinal instance of what we called (p. *65*) 'a failure to absorb the whole intractable area of human life into the sovereign χάρις of God'. There are only one or two hints of the way his mind would have been led had he attempted to do so.

> *Princ.* I.3.8: 'Thus the working of the Father, which confers on all their existence, is found more glorious and splendid, when each one, through participation in Christ as "Wisdom", "Knowledge", "Sanctification", advances and comes to higher degrees of progress; and when each, through participation in the Holy Spirit, has been sanctified and made purer and of higher integrity, and thus more worthy to receive the grace of wisdom and knowledge, in order that all stains of pollution and ignorance may be removed and that he may receive such advancement in integrity and purity that the life which he received from God may be worthy of God, whose purpose in giving it was that it should be pure and perfect: that the creature should be as worthy as the Creator. For in this way also shall the man, who is such as his Creator wished him to

arrange His creation according to merit, brought the diversities of minds together into the harmony of one world . . . , and these were the reasons, I think, for the diversity of this world, where divine providence arranges everyone according to the varieties of their movements and intentions. That is why the Creator will not seem unjust when for the above reasons He distributed each one of His creatures according to merit; nor will the happiness or unhappiness of anyone at birth, or any condition that may fall to his lot, be thought fortuitous; nor will there be any grounds for belief in different creators or rational diversities of souls.' (I have quoted this passage at length to show the kind of questions Origen was seeking to answer. It is to his credit that, once he had seen it, he never shirked a difficulty, and these Gnostic criticisms of the Christian doctrine of Creation are uncomfortably up-to-date.)

be, receive from God the power to exist for ever and to abide for eternity.'[9]

No Christian system can be at heart pessimistic, and in this passage we see due recognition of human sin swallowed up into the 'optimism of grace'. This, we make bold to believe, was the ultimate intention of Origen.

---

[9] Cf. *Princ.* III.6.1 (Origen gives the familiar patristic exegesis of Genesis 1[27] ['He made him in the image of God'] as excluding 'in the likeness'—in spite of 1[26]—i.e.): ' "Man received the honour of God's image" in his first creation, but the perfection of God's "likeness" was reserved for him at the consummation.' The exegesis is wretched enough: but the doctrine is a welcome corrective e.g. of *Princ.* I.8.1: 'God . . . made the present world and bound the soul to the body as a punishment.' Cf. also the chink in the iron-curtain of merit-reward set out in the long passage quoted above (p. *72*, note 8), when a little later Origen says (ibid. 7): 'Some beings οι higher merit are ordained to suffer with the rest and offer a service to those who are inferior, for the sake of ameliorating the condition of the world, and that in this way they themselves may become participants in the suffering (or "endurance") of the Creator. . . .' Cf. also COMM. EPH. p. 2. (*JTS*, III, 235): 'If a man who has been granted participation in existence forgets this and ascribes to himself the cause of his being, instead of offering all his gratitude to the One who graciously made him from nothingness to be "like" Him and "in His image" . . .' (where note in the one sentence καταχαρίσηται, εὐχαριστίαν, χαρισάμενον).

(B) PROVIDENCE

God's providential care embraces throughout all ages the whole creation—the universe, the nations, man in all his needs and doings—and is not absent even from animals.

Comm. Jn. II.3 (it is only atheism—destructive and immoral—that is blind to the fact of) 'providence (πρόνοιά), evident and almost visible'.

Hom. Gen. III.2: 'We confess, as a certain and unshakable dogma, that God cares for mortal things, and that nothing is done apart from His providence (*providentia*)—in heaven or on earth.'

Cels. VI.71: 'The oversight (ἐπισκοπή) and providence (πρόνοιά) of God pervades all things—but not like the spirit of the Stoics. It embraces all things that are subject to its providential care (τὰ προνοούμενά) and contains them—but not as a containing *substance* . . . rather as a divine power.'

Ibid. IV.74: 'Providence (πρόνοιά) primarily cares for rational beings, but it has resulted that the irrational animals also profit from what is designed for man.'

Ibid. 99: 'All things have been created primarily for the benefit of the rational being. . . . God does not take care (μέλει δὲ τῷ Θεῷ οὐχ), as Celsus thinks, only of the universe as a whole, but besides this of every rational being in particular.[10] And providence will never desert the universe. For even if some part of it degenerates because of the sin of the rational being, God sees to (οἰκονομεῖ) its purification and to the subsequent turning back of the universe to Himself.'

Sel. Ps. 144[1]: 'We are His debtors on many grounds: He created us out of nothing; He made us to be such as we

---

[10] Origen at times emphasizes the Stoic point that the world comes first: e.g. *Hom. Jer.* XII.5: 'God does not care in His providence (οἰκονομεῖ) just for one man, but for the whole world. . . . He considers what is expedient for the whole world and everything that is; so far as is possible he considers also what is expedient for the individual man, but not so that what is expedient for the individual causes loss to the world.'

are; having made us He has dominion over us, His providence cares for us (προνοεῖ) every day—in public and in private, secretly and openly, even when we know it not.'[11]

Princ. II.11.5: '. . . the things that happen to men . . . do not do so by chance or accident, but for a purpose so carefully calculated, so lofty, that not even the number of the "hairs of our head" (Mt 10[30]) is outside it—and that not only of the saints but (one may say)[12] of all men; this providence (*providentia*) extends even to "two sparrows" which are sold for a penny (Mt 10[29]), whether "sparrows" is meant spiritually or literally.'

Cels. VIII.70: 'To such a degree has divine providence (πρόνοια) embraced everything that not even the hairs of our head have escaped being numbered by Him.'

Ibid. IV.69: 'Nothing has been or will be neglected by God, who at every point does what is fitting that He should do in a shifting and changing world. Just as at the different seasons of the year a farmer does different agricultural works on the earth and its crops, so God cares for (οἰκονομεῖ) whole ages as if they were just years (so to speak); in each age He does what the interests of the universe suggest—a matter which is most clearly understood in its real truth, and thus brought to fulfilment, by God alone.'

Hom. Jer. III: '(God) cares for (οἰκονομῶν) the soul [i.e. the seat of the faculties] of every man, that he may be rational, that he may attain to knowledge, that his intelligence may find exercise in (the life of) the body, that his senses (Heb 5[14]) may be in good fettle.'

Comm. Rom. I.2 (above, p. *23*) (human 'callings' are in accordance with the 'providence and choice' of God).[13]

Hom. Jer. XII.8 (above, p. *21*, note 7) (Paul's thorn in the flesh is a gift of God's providence [οἰκονομία] to forestall his pride).

Comm. Ser. Mt. 126 (Greek fragment): Simon of Cyrene was

[11] Cf. *Cels.* VIII.57 (above, p. *52*): 'We are His creatures, the objects of His providence (προνοούμενοι); *Sel. Ezek.* XVI.9 (above, p. *21*): 'The acts of His providence (αἱ πρόνοιαι) are as various as are those whom His providence rules (τῶν οἰκονομουμένων). . . . His spiritual servants receive dispensations (οἰκονομίας) of His grace, glory and splendour.'
[12] Latin *fortassis*, possibly hinting at the idea above (p. *75*, note 10).
[13] *Secundum id quod in eo* praevidet . . . *Deus.*

pressed into service not fortuitously 'but predetermined (προ-
ορισθέντα) by God to serve the Cross of Christ'.

Cels. VIII.67: 'Whatever we receive that is right and good
we have from God and His providence[14] (πρόνοια), such as
cultivated crops and bread . . . the pleasant vine . . . the
fruits of the olive "to make the face shine with olive oil"
(Ps 104[15]).'

Sel. Ps. 145[3]: 'Since the greatness of God is there to be seen
in Christ and in the created things, and there is no limit to
His greatness, perhaps we may see from the same sources His
providence (πρόνοια) toward the beings of His creation, lasting from infinity to infinity.'

Cels. III.5: 'The ancient Egyptians . . . as men who had
wronged strangers and suppliants . . . suffered the fate which
through divine providence (πρόνοια) the whole nation had
to endure.'

*God's providential care guides men to salvation, to perfection—and watches
over them to all eternity.*

Princ. II.9.7: 'All things were created by the Word of God
and His wisdom, and set in order through His just disposal.
But through the grace of His mercy He provides for (*providet*)
all and exhorts them to be cured by the several available
remedies, and calls them to salvation.'

Hom. Jer. VI.2 (quotes the third clause of Jeremiah 5[3] (LXX)
as 'Thou didst perfect them, but they would not accept the
training'): 'When God, who exercises providence (προνοῶν)
over all things, purges the soul for its salvation, He has "brought
it to perfection". . . . When therefore providence has done
its all for our maturing and perfecting, and we do not accept
the guidance of that providence that draws us to perfection
(the words of Jeremiah 5[3] become applicable).'

Princ. III.1.13: 'In the case of some sinners, God is longsuffering, and not without reason, for it will be to their advantage, having in mind the immortality of the soul and the eternal
world, that they should not be helped to a quick salvation, but

---

[14] Cf. the emphatic 'no benefit comes to mankind without God's action', and the
example of physicians healing our bodies (*Cels.* I.9—p. *80*, below).

brought more slowly to it after undergoing many ills. [Origen illustrates this by the practice of doctors to administer a slow remedy to ensure a permanent cure of a "hidden poison in the body".] In the same way God, who knows the hidden places of the heart and foreknows the future, in His longsuffering may permit the hidden evil to remain, even while He draws it out by means of external happenings, the purpose being to purify him who through heedlessness has allowed entry into himself of the seeds of sin; when these latter come to the surface the sinner may then vomit them out, and even if he is far gone in evil may later be able to obtain purification, i.e. be formed anew after his evil life. For God has dealings with (οἰκονομεῖ) souls not with a view to the fifty years, so to speak, of our life here, but to the boundlessness of eternity. For He has made our intellectual nature deathless, akin to Himself, and the rational soul is not, as it were, shut out from healing by being confined to this life.'

God's providence ordained and disposed the writing of Scripture and bestowed it on mankind for salvation.[15]

Princ. IV.2.4: 'Scripture, which has been ordained (οἰκονο-μηθεῖσα) by God to be given for man's salvation.'

Frag. Prov. 1[6] (above, p. *28*): 'The grace which disposed (οἰκονομούσης) the word of God.'

Comm. Ps. 1[4] (*Philocalia*, ed. Robinson, p. 39): 'This is our understanding of everything that was written under the inspiration of the Holy Spirit: that through the writings holy Providence (πρόνοια) was granting superhuman wisdom to mankind, sowing (as it were) oracles of salvation in every writing possible, to show the way to wisdom! . . .'

Comm. Gen. III (*Philocalia*, p. 188): 'All the divine dispensation (οἰκονομία) through the law and the prophets.'

Providence ordained the Bible-story itself: the Old Testament—

Cels. IV.41: 'Is it not wonderful that the survivors of every species were brought inside [the Ark] by the providence (προνοίᾳ) of God in order that once more the earth might

---

[15] On the 'accommodating' (οἰκονομεῖν) of Scripture by God to human receptive capacity, cf. *Cels.* IV.71 (below, pp. *87f*).

possess the seeds of all the living creatures, and that God used a most righteous man to be the father of all that should be born after the flood?'

Ibid. VII.7 '(The Jewish prophets) were chosen by providence (προνοίας) to be entrusted with the divine Spirit and with the words proceeding from Him, because of their quite exceptional qualities—courage, independence, fearlessness in face of death and danger.'

Ibid. VIII.53 (Celsus is inconsistent: he respects e.g. pagan philosophers like Empedocles without reflecting that) 'it was likely that the [Jewish] people also, who served the God of the universe, and for the sake of the honour which is His due and the dispensation of the Law He was believed to have given often risked countless dangers and deaths, were not overlooked by God, but that some revelation (ἐπιφάνειαν) was made to them? They despised the images produced by human handiwork, and essayed to ascend by their reason to the God of the universe Himself; and [Celsus] ought to have reflected that the common Father and Creator of all—the "all-seeing and all-hearing"[16]—the righteous judge of the sincerity of all who seek Him and aspire to piety, assigns to [the Jews] also some fruit of His protection (προστασία), in order that they may grow in the knowledge of Him that they have already received.'

Ibid. IV.42: 'When Jesus said to the Jews, "the Kingdom of God shall be taken from you and given to a nation bringing forth the fruits thereof" (Mt 21⁴³), what other dispensation was He giving than (τί ἄλλο ᾠκονόμει ἤ) to bring forth to light by divine power the whole Jewish Scripture, which contains the mysteries of the Kingdom of God?'

—and, supremely, the Person and Work, the Incarnation, Passion, Ascension, and lasting presence of Jesus Christ.

Cels. IV.14: '... what the Scriptures call God's "descent" into human affairs. For this He does not have to be "changed", as Celsus thinks we say ...; He remains unchanged in essence and comes down in His providence and dispensing care (προνοίᾳ, οἰκονομίᾳ) to the world of humanity.'

Ibid. 19: 'This act of providence (οἰκονομίαν, i.e. the

[16] The Homeric tag—here of course an *argumentum ad hominem*.

advent of Jesus to men) took place . . . for the sake of those who because of sickness in the soul and distraction of the natural reason are still enemies of God, so that they may become His friends. For Jesus is clearly said to have endured everything on behalf of sinners, that He might free them from sin and make them righteous' (Mt 9¹³, etc.).

Ibid. I.9: 'A religious man will not believe that even a physician of the body, who restores many sick people to health, comes to live in cities and among peoples without divine providence (ἀθεεί). For no good thing takes place among men apart from God.[17] . . . how much more true must this be of Him who cured, converted, bettered so many *souls*, attaching them to the God of the universe, teaching them to refer every action to the standard of what pleases Him, and to avoid everything that is displeasing to Him—down to the most trivial words, deeds, and thoughts?'

Ibid. III.14: 'God . . . taught men by the prophets to hope for the advent of Christ, who would save them.'

Ibid. II.9: 'After the Incarnation (οἰκονομίαν) the soul and body of Jesus become one with the Word of God.'[18]

Sel. Ps. 2⁸ (applied to Jesus): 'He is represented . . . as a man who inherits all by divine dispensation (οἰκονομικῶς) for the purpose of redeeming that portion which by right belongs to Him, i.e. those on earth who have been corrupted and scattered abroad by the devil and his evil powers. When He has fulfilled this task He says to His Father about us "I have manifested Thy name to the men whom Thou gavest me out of the world" . . . (Jn 17⁶).'

Comm. Jn. II.11 (6): (Does the Holy Spirit rank higher than Christ because of e.g. Isa 48¹⁶—[the Spirit sends Christ, and not vice-versa]? No, it is) 'not as if the Spirit were naturally higher than Christ, but because the Saviour was made less than the Spirit through the divine plan (οἰκονομία) of the Incarnation of the Son of God'.

Ibid. VI.53 (35): 'The divine plan (οἰκονομία) of the

---

[17] οὐδὲν γὰρ χρηστὸν ἐν ἀνθρώποις ἀθεεὶ γίνεται—this emphatic assertion might be made a text for the whole doctrine of grace in Origen.

[18] οἰκονομία, as often, practically a technical term for the Incarnation. Cf. *Cels.* II.26: 'Jesus said such things during His οἰκονομία'; ibid. 65: 'after He had accomplished the work of His οἰκονομία His divinity was more brilliant'; *Hom. Josh.* III.2: 'The dispensation of the flesh' (*dispensatio carnis*) 'fulfilled in Christ.'
For similar quasi-technical use in connexion with the Cross, see below, p. *82*.

bodily coming of the Son of God into the life of men.'

Frag. in Lk. 1[1] (quoted by Macarius Chrysocephalus): 'He said "the facts" (πραγμάτων), because the incarnate presence of Jesus was not an act that He played in make-believe; but He who was Himself the Truth carried through His divine assignment (οἰκονομία) in true reality.'

Cels. V.12: 'God in His kindness comes down to men not in the local but the providential sense (προνοητικῶς), and the Son of God is with His own disciples not only at that time but at all times.'

Ibid. VI.78 (Celsus criticizes the doctrine of the Incarnation: why did God wait until *then*? Why only *there* [in Palestine]? Why only *one* Son of God?): 'It was not [Origen replies] as if God had awakened from a long sleep to send Jesus to the human race; although now—for good reasons—He has fulfilled the dispensation (οἰκονομίαν) of His Incarnation, He has always been working for the good of mankind. For nothing good has happened among men without the working of the Divine Word, visiting the souls of those who have been able for however short a time to receive His operations.

'Again, although the advent of Jesus gives the impression of being "in one corner" (Celsus' words), there was a reason for it; for it was necessary that the One prophesied should visit those who had come to know the One God and were reading His prophets and learning of the Christ they heralded, and that He should come at the critical moment when His word could be poured out from "one corner" over all the world.'

Ibid. 79: 'For this reason too it was not necessary for there to be many bodies and many spirits like Jesus in all places, for the whole world to be enlightened by the word of God. The One Word sufficed, which arose like a "sun of righteousness" (Mal 4[2]) to send out from Judaea those rays which reach the souls of those willing to receive Him. . . . Let the Word, that comprehends the sleepless nature of God, teach us that in His own good time God is administering (οἰκονομεῖ) the affairs of the world, as one would reasonably expect. It is not, indeed, surprising if, because the judgements of God are mighty and mysterious, "uneducated souls" (Wisdom 17[1]) go wrong about it, and Celsus among them. The truth is that the Son of God's being sent among the Jews—among whom were the

G

prophets—was in no way ridiculous; the point was that He could begin from there in bodily form, and rise in power and spirit upon the world, which was unwilling to be any longer apart from God.'

Ibid. 80: '(Celsus is blind to) all the providential care (οἰκονομίαν) of God for the Jews and for their venerable and sacred society, and sees not that because of their fall salvation has come to the Gentiles—that their fall is the riches of the world and their loss the riches of the Gentiles, until the fulness of the Gentiles comes in, that after this "all Israel" . . . "may be saved" ' (Rom 11).

Comm. Ser. Mt. 47: 'The dispensation (οἰκονομία) of the Passion of Jesus.' Ibid. 126: 'The Cross, divinely ordained' (τὸν τῆς οἰκονομίας σταυρόν).

Comm. Jn. XXXII.8: 'Notice that, wishing to wash the feet of His disciples, He chose the very time when the devil had just been cast into the heart of Judas, that Judas might betray Him . . . , and when the divine plan (οἰκονομία, i.e. the Cross) for man was about to find fulfilment. Before this the time was not ripe . . . , nor at the moment of the Passion . . . nor after the divine event (οἰκονομία) was completed. For by then the hour had come for the advent of the Holy Spirit to the disciples—cleansed, as they were, and with feet washed, and holding themselves fit and ready to spread the good news of the Gospel by the Holy Spirit.'

Ibid. 25 (17) on John 13³¹ᶠ: 'He glorified . . . God by His death also. . . . When the divine plan (οἰκονομία) for the approaching death of Jesus was being set in motion (Judas went out).'

Ibid. *Frag.* 89 on John 12³¹: 'The passion of (Jesus) on the Cross was the judgement of the whole of this world. . . . Since the divine event (οἰκονομία) on the Cross entailed the judgement on all existing things, He could say when the moment of the Passion drew near—"Now is the judgement of this world".'

Cels. III.31 (above, p. *34*): 'But if my Jesus is said to be taken up "in glory", I see God's gracious providence (οἰκονομία)' [i.e. the spiritual empowering and amelioration of the spectators].

Ibid. VIII.43: (Celsus) 'The men who tortured and punished

your "present God" suffered nothing for doing it; . . . what new thing has happened since which might convince one that he was not a sorcerer but a son of God?') Ibid. 43: (Origen) 'This . . . is the "new thing" that has happened since Jesus suffered—the fate of the city and the whole nation,[19] and the sudden birth of the race of Christians. . . . And it was also a "new thing" that those who were strangers to the covenants of God and alien to the promises (Eph 2[11]), who were far from the truth, accepted it by some divine miracle. These were not the achievements of a sorcerer but of God, who sent His own Word in Jesus to bear His messages—that Jesus who was so savagely punished that the savagery of the unjust men who punished Him, which He bore so bravely and so meekly, is now held against them. His punishment did not destroy God's messages, but (one may dare to suggest) promulgated them. This is what Jesus taught, in the words, "Except a corn of wheat . . ." (Jn 12[24]). Jesus was the grain of wheat who died and bore much fruit, and the Father is always caring in His providence ($\dot{a}\epsilon\grave{\iota}\ \pi\rho o\nu o\epsilon\hat{\iota}$) for the fruits—past, present and future—of the death of that grain of wheat. The Father of Jesus, then, is a holy Father; for He "spared not His own Son but delivered Him up for us all" (Rom 8[32]) as His lamb, the "lamb of God" who died for all that He might "take away the sin of the world" (Jn 1[29]). Not that His Father compelled Him, but He willingly bore the inflictions of those who outraged Him.'

Comm. Jn. VI.57 (on Lk 12[50]: after the Resurrection and Ascension Christ received His 'baptism' in heaven and returns bringing) 'all kinds of grace-gifts—cloven tongues as of fire for the apostles, and holy angels who should stand by them and save them in all their doings. For before these events of God's providence ($o\grave{\iota}\kappa o\nu o\mu\iota\hat{\omega}\nu$) the apostles (could not and perhaps would not have received the angels).'

It was through Providence that the Gentiles succeeded the Jews as God's people and were called to a world-wide mission for Jesus.

Cels. II.8: 'It is clear that although the Jews saw Jesus they did not know who He was, and although they heard Him they did not understand from His sayings the divinity within

---

[19] I.e. the subsequent fall of Jerusalem and the Dispersion of the Jews.

Him, which was transferring God's care (ἐπισκοπήν) of the Jews to those Gentiles who believe in Him. Hence we may see how after the advent of Jesus the Jews have been entirely forsaken, and retain none of their traditionally sacred possessions, nor even a hint of the divine presence among them.'[20]

Ibid. 78: '(Jesus) did not come with the purpose of producing unbelief among the Jews, but by His foreknowledge He predicted that unbelief would befall them, and He used the unbelief of the Jews to call the Gentiles. . . . God's providence (πρόνοια) has been wonderful: it has used the sin of the Jews to call the Gentiles into the Kingdom of God by Jesus, strangers though they were to the covenants and alien to the promises' (Eph 2¹²).

Ibid. IV.32: 'Since nothing in human nature abides unchanged, even that [traditional Jewish] society had to be gradually broken down and replaced. Providence (πρόνοια) changed their venerable doctrine where change was necessary to make its application universal, and gave instead the noble religion of Jesus to believers everywhere.'

Ibid. VII.26: 'Providence (πρόνοια) which of old gave the Law but has now given the Gospel of Jesus Christ, did not wish that the ordinances of the Jews should survive, and so destroyed their city and temple, and the service to God in the temple with its sacrifices and prescribed worship. Just as Providence did not desire them to be offered any longer and destroyed them, in the same way it made the Christian ordinances grow and daily (Acts 2⁴⁷) granted increase and boldness of speech to the multitude. . . .'

Hom. Judg. VIII.4 on 6³⁶⁻⁸ (Origen asks the meaning of the twin signs obtained by Gideon): 'I remember one of our predecessors[21] saying in his commentaries that the fleece of wool was the people of Israel, while the rest of the ground was the rest of the nations, and the dew which fell on the fleece was the Word of God, because divine indulgence was shown (*coelitus fuisset indultum*) to that people alone. . . . But the second sign, the opposite of the first, is understood like this: observe the whole people of the Gentiles, gathered throughout all the

---

[20] Cf. ibid. V.50 (p. *46* above) of the transfer of 'this dispensation and grace' (ταύτην τὴν οἰκονομίαν . . . καὶ τὴν χάριν) 'from Jews to Gentiles'.
[21] Unknown: perhaps a Jewish Christian (Hanson, *Allegory and Event*, p. 134, note 4).

world, possessing now within itself the divine dew—see it
sprinkled with the dew of Moses, bedewed with the writings
of the prophets; see it green with the watering of the Gospel
and the apostolic (writings); while the fleece, the people of
the Jews, is left to suffer in dryness, barren of the Word of
God.'[22]

Providence guided and guarded the early Christian Church.

Cels. VIII.41, *Comm. Jn.* VI.57 (above, pp. *82*f).

Cels. III.8: '(God) always fought for (the early Christians)
and at critical moments stopped their adversaries who wished
to kill them. It is true that from time to time a few . . . have
died for the Christian religion by way of a reminder to the
others and a prompting, when they see a few striving for piety,
to stand fast and defy death. But God did not allow the extinc-
tion of the whole race, because He wished it to become estab-
lished and the whole world filled with this saving teaching of
religion. And again, that the weaker among them might conquer their fear of death, God has providentially cared for the
believers (προυνοεῖτο); by His will alone He has scattered
every conspiracy against them, that kings and local rulers and
the common people should not be able to burst into too violent
a flame against them.'

Hom. Num. IX.2 on 16[41-3] (q.v.): 'Let us learn from this
passage what great advantage accrues through the Christian
persecutions, how great a grace is bestowed, how God becomes
the champion of the Christians, how abundantly the Holy
Spirit is poured on them. For the grace of God is then most
mightily at hand when the savagery of men is stirred up; and
then do we have peace with God when we are in suffering
from men because of the justice of war. . . . Although Moses
and Aaron stand high through the achievements of their lives,
although in natural attainments they are pre-eminent, nevertheless the glory of God could never have shone on them unless
they had come to be persecuted, in tribulation and danger,
nay almost at the point of being killed. And you (my hearers)

---

[22] Providence is implicit, though not mentioned. N.B. however the 'grace-word'
coelitus indultum; and cf. Theodoret, *Qu. in Jud.* 15 (quoted by Baehrens), with explicit use of χάρις. 'This passage means that aforetimes Israel had the benefit of
divine χάρις, as the fleece had of the dew; but later all humanity was granted
spiritual gifts.'

—you too must not suppose that the glory of God can shine upon you if you are idle or asleep.'[23]

Cels. VII.26 (above, p. *84*): the passage continues): '(Providence) granted increase and boldness of speech to the multitude in spite of the fact that there were countless obstacles to the spread of the teaching of Jesus in the world. But since it was God who wished the Gentiles also to be helped by the teaching of Jesus Christ, every human plot against the Christians has been thwarted, and the more kings and local rulers and peoples everywhere have humiliated them, the more they have grown in numbers and strength.'

God in His Providence prepares men to know Him, and accommodates Himself to the capacity of weak and sinful men to know Him and be guided by Him.

Cels. VII.33: 'The organ which knows God is not the eye of the body but the mind, for it sees that which is in the image of the Creator, and it has received by the providence ($\pi \rho \acute{o} \nu o \iota a$) of God the faculty of knowing Him.'

Ibid. 46: ' "The invisible things of God", i.e. the things conceived by the mind, "are understood by the things that are made", and "are clearly seen from the creation of the world" by the process of thought. And [the disciples of Jesus], in their ascent from the created things of the world, do not halt in the invisible things of God; but after sufficient mental exercise among them to produce understanding of them, they ascend to the eternal power of God and (quite simply) to His divinity. They know that out of love to man ($\phi \iota \lambda \acute{a} \nu \theta \rho \omega \pi o s$) God revealed His truth and that which may be known of Himself—and this not only to those devoted to Him, but also to some who know nothing of pure worship and piety toward Him. But some of those who by God's providence ($\pi \rho o \nu o \acute{\iota} \alpha$) have ascended to the knowledge of such great truths do not act worthily of the knowledge, and impiously hold down the truth in unrighteousness; and just because of this knowledge

[23] Note the complementary reconciliations of the persecutions with God's Providence: they were in themselves a mighty means of grace to the Christians (sufferers and non-sufferers)—and Providence ensured that more were not lost through death than the Church could afford. (On the general question of suffering cf. *Comm. Inéd. des Psaumes* p. 95 (CVIII.3b): 'To be attacked and hated for Christ Jesus' sake is—a free gift of God.')

. . . they can no longer plead an excuse before God.' (Cf. throughout, Rom 1¹⁸ᶠᶠ.)

Hom. Jer. XVIII.6 on 18⁸ (Origen asks how God can be said to 'repent'. He notes that sometimes, e.g. Numbers 23¹⁹, God speaks or acts 'not as a man', while elsewhere, e.g. Deuteronomy 8⁵, 1³¹, as if He were a man). 'That is: when the Scriptures speak of God in Himself, and do not weave His providence (οἰκονομία) into human affairs, they say He is not as a man. . . . But when divine providence is woven into human affairs, He assumes the human mind, manner, and diction. When we talk to a two-year-old child we use baby-talk for his sake. . . . Such is the situation you must imagine when God exercises His providence (οἰκονομῇ) on the human race, especially on the "infants" thereof. . . . Again, since *we* repent, God when talking to us says "I repent"; and when He threatens us He does not presume to have knowledge of the future, but threatens us as if He were talking to children. . . . (E.g.) "Speak to the children of Israel—perhaps they will hear and repent" (Jer 33²ᶠ). This "perhaps" does not indicate any uncertainty on God's part . . . but is designed to leave open your freedom of choice, and to prevent your saying: "If He foreknew my destruction I must perish: if He foresaw my salvation I must certainly be saved." . . . You will find thousands of other such statements about God accommodating Himself (τροποφοροῦντος) to man. If you hear of God's wrath and anger, you must not suppose that wrath and anger are passions in God. They are accommodations in the use of language,²⁴ in order to correct and improve the child. We too put on a fearful frown for children, not because such is our disposition but as a means of managing them.'²⁵

Cels. IV.71: '. . . because Celsus has not understood them, he pours scorn on passages in the Scriptures which speak of God as subject to human passions—"angry words" uttered by God against the impious and "threats" against sinners. He must be reminded that just as when we are talking to very small children we do not aim to speak in the finest language

---

²⁴ So Hanson, *Allegory and Event*, p. 228, for οἰκονομίαι χρήσεως λέξεων: literally, 'instances of Providence manipulating words'.

²⁵ κατ' οἰκονομίαν: 'for an ulterior motive' (Hanson).

possible to us,[26] but use language fitted to the weakness of
our charges, and suit our actions also to what seems useful for
the correction and guidance of children as such, even so does
the Word of God seem to have disposed (ᾠκονομηκέναι) the
Scriptures, determining what style of narrative is suitable by
the capacity of his hearers and their real needs.'

Frag. on *1 Sam.* 15⁹⁻¹¹ (q.v.): 'The "repentance" of God is
actually the change of His providence (οἰκονομία) from one
dispensation to another. (Why use the term? . . .) Because
the prophets had to use the more down-to-earth form of expression in speaking of God to the slowest-witted, to give it
a chance of being understood. . . . We must not impute to
God the mercurial character of the human mind; for we in-
tend to impute to the essence of divine providence the changes
of dispensation it rightly makes when dealing with us.'

Hom. Ezek. I.2: 'If it was not of use toward the conversion
of sinners to put them to torment, a merciful and kindly God
would never have visited crime with punishment. But like a
most indulgent father He "chastens" (Prov 3¹¹) His son to
teach him, and like a most far-seeing (*providentissimus*) master
He reproves an unruly pupil with a look of severity, lest the
latter, secure of being loved, should perish. Some of you may
be so outraged by the very word "anger" that you condemn
it even in God. Our reply will be that the "anger" of God is
not so much "anger" as a necessary dispensation. The speaker
(of Ps 6¹) knows that the "wrath" of God is a means to human
healthfulness, and is applied to the task of healing the sick,
of curing those who have scorned to hear His word. . . . Everything that comes from God is good, and we deserve our "chas-
tening". . . . Everything that comes from God and seems
harsh is actually of avail for teaching and healing. God is
doctor, father, master—and not severe, but lenient. . . . When
you find people, according to the accounts of Scripture,
punished, you should "compare Scripture with Scripture" (cf.
1 Cor 2¹³) . . . and you will see that what appears the harshest
is actually the sweetest.'

---

[26] So Chadwick: Hanson (*Allegory and Event*, p. 226)—'We do not assume as the
object of our instruction any strong understanding in them.' The Greek is οὐ τοῦ
ἑαυτῶν ἐν τῷ λέγειν στοχαζόμεθα δυνατοῦ. Hanson's rendering (I think) gives less
force to the emphatic ἑαυτῶν and separates δυνατοῦ from its more natural link with
the defining ἐν τῷ λέγειν.

Comm. Mt. XVII.17-20 on 22¹ (where the Greek is actually
'the Kingdom of heaven is likened to a man [who was] a king'.
Origen asks: Why liken God to 'a man'?): 'In so far as we are
men, to whom it is not salutary to behold the riches of God's
goodness (Rom 2⁴) . . . , the Kingdom of heaven was of necessity likened to a king who was a man, who could speak as a
man to men and manage (οἰκονομήσῃ) men who have not
the capacity to be managed by God—although God remains
wholly God both in His speaking through the prophets and
in His management (οἰκονομεῖν) of men. . . . (1 Jn 3² should
be understood in the same way). For now, even if we are
deemed worthy of seeing God with our mind and heart, we
do not see Him as He is but as He becomes to us in order to
bring His providence to bear on us.²⁷ . . . (Hence also the title
"Son of Man".) The Saviour is first and foremost the "Son
of God" and "God" and "Son of His Love" and the "Image
of the invisible God". But He does not remain in this
state, but becomes "Son of Man" . . . to accommodate His
providence to us.'²⁸

Providence allows man's freewill full scope in his co-operation with God.

(Cf. *Cels.* IV.3—'If you take away the element of freewill from
virtue you destroy its essence'—[This conviction is one of the
pillars of Origen's ethics and theology].)
   Cels. IV.82: '. . . man, who has the power to think everything out and arrange everything in order, seeing that he is
co-operating with providence (προνοίᾳ) . . . and doing works
which are not only the product of God's foresight (προνοίας)
but of His own.'
   Sel. Ps. 4⁶ (on Ps 127¹, 'Except the Lord build the house'):
'Such a blessing would be beyond the range of our choosing,
that the strength of the Lord should lay hold on the work of
the builder and co-operate with him in the task of finishing
it, which he could not do himself. . . . Just as I should say
good husbandry, which brings forth a good crop, is compounded of what is under the husbandman's control—his skill
at his work, and what is not under his control but depends on

²⁷ διὰ τὴν ἡμετέραν οἰκονομίαν, which includes a hint of God's self-accommodation
to us.
²⁸ κατ᾽ οἰκονομίαν. The meaning is shifting from 'providence' as such to the 'principle of accommodation' as such.

providence (παρὰ τῆς προνοίας)—a favourable climate and
a sufficient supply of rain: even so the good which a rational
being seeks is compounded of the effects of his own choice and
of the divine power which co-operates with a man who chooses
the highest as his aim. And it is not only for the achievement
of honour and goodness that we need both our own choice
and the divine co-operation which is independent of it; we
need both also for the continued possession of these virtues.'
(See the continuation of this passage at p. *50* above.)

Cels. V.21: 'We [Christians] say that the universe is administered (οἰκονομεῖσθαι) by God in accordance with the conditions of the freewill of each man, and that as far as possible
it is always being improved . . . and that the nature of our
freewill is to admit various possibilities, for it cannot attain
to the utter unchangeability of God.'

Hom. Gen. III.2 (following the extract above, p. *75*): 'Note
that we say nothing is done apart from His *providence* (*providentia*)—not His *will*. Many things take place against His will,
but nothing apart from His providence. For providence is that
with which He cares for, dispenses, provides for (*procurat, dis-
pensat, providet*), the things that are done: His will is that with
which He wills something or does not will it.'

Sel. Ex. 15²⁵: 'God . . . is not ignorant of the future, but permits man to do what he wishes through his faculty of free-will.'

Providence—and belief therein—are the source of the good life.

Cels. III.27, 28 (Origen argues that the difference between
such pagan miracle-workers as Aristeas [Herodotus IV.14f]
and Jesus lies in the ethical and religious fruits of their work):
'Look impartially at the story of Aristeas and that told of
Jesus. See whether, in view of their effects in helping to reform
the character and promote devotion to the Supreme God, we
may not say that the story of Jesus cannot be dissociated from
divine providence (οὐκ ἀθεεί) whereas the reverse is true of
the story of . . . Aristeas. For why should providence have
contrived the miracles of Aristeas, and why—if its intention
is to benefit the human race—should it have displayed such
"great events" . . . ? You cannot tell. But in our case, when
we recount the stories of Jesus, we offer a weighty defence of
their historicity—namely, that God wished to establish the

Word that came through Jesus as bringing salvation to men, confirmed as it was through the apostles who were (so to speak) foundations of the incipient edifice of Christianity, and spreading as it is in recent times, when many cures are performed in the name of Jesus, along with other far from negligible manifestations.'

Ibid. IV.53: 'Let anyone dare to deny that the source and origin of every blessing (ὠφελείας) is to believe in the supreme God and to do everything with reference to His pleasure—absolutely everything—and not even to desire anything unpleasing to Him, since not only words and deeds but even thoughts will be subject to His judgement. What other teaching could more effectively lead human nature towards the good life than the belief or the conviction that the supreme God watches over (ἐφορᾶν) everything that we say, do, and even think?'

Evil, while not created by God, is a by-product of His providence, and permitted to continue as a foil and challenge to goodness, and to purge and purify mankind, only until its work is done.

Comm. Jn. Frag. 50 (above, p. 35): (Creation and Providence (πρόνοια) did not envisage sin, which necessitated further measures—the healing and teaching work of Jesus Christ).

Princ. III.2.5: 'I do not think that human nature can of its own resources hold the fort against "angels" and "heights and depths" and "any other creature" (Rom 8³⁸f); but when it has felt the presence of the indwelling Lord, it will say, confident of receiving the divine help, "The Lord is my light. . . ." (Ps 27¹⁻³.)'

Cels. VIII.58: '. . . the God who alone is worshipped and splendidly honoured is capable of granting the man who honours Him, because of that worship, a power which prevents the attacks of demons against the righteous man . . . the invocation "in the name of Jesus", pronounced by true believers, has healed many from diseases and demonic possession and other distresses.'

Comm. Song Songs II, p. 133: '[The soul] which has been converted to God and come to have faith suffers . . . the mental attacks and wrestlings of the demons who strive to recall that soul to the allurements of its former life. . . . But to forestall this . . . divine providence (*providentia*) has looked ahead and arranged to provide angels as the champions and defenders . . . of such as are "infants" (1 Cor 3¹) and such as cannot from their own resources withstand in battle "wiles of the devil" (Eph 6¹¹) and the attacks of the demons.'

Comm. Jn. I.14: 'The angels are not merely entrusted with one small service for the gospel. . . . But the angel "flying" on duty "in mid-air" (Rev 14⁶) has a gospel wherewith to evangelize all nations—for the good Father has in no wise deserted those who have fallen from Him.'

Princ. III.2.7: '. . . all the events which happen in this world which are counted "indifferent",²⁹ whether tragedies (e.g. in the story of Job) . . . or whatever else, are not God's doing: yet are they not without Him. For God not only refrains from preventing but even gives permission to evil and hostile powers wishing to bring such things about—but only at certain times and to certain persons. E.g. in the case of Job, it is said that at a certain time he was made ready to fall into the power of others and his house to be plundered by evil men. Hence divine Scripture teaches us to accept all things that happen to us as from the hand of God, knowing as we do that nothing happens without Him.'

Cels. IV.69: 'When God purifies the world by a flood or conflagration, He is not rectifying defects in it like a faulty builder or an unskilful creator; His real aim is to prevent the flood of evil spreading further—and (as I should conjecture) in an orderly way He is making evil disappear entirely, for the benefit of all. . . . Even though at the creation of the universe everything had been arranged by Him in most sure and orderly beauty, He has yet had to administer medicinal treatment to people sick with sin and to the whole world which that sin has, as it were, defiled.' (See the continuation of this at p. 76 above.)

Ibid. VI.44: 'It was not possible for that which is good by chance and circumstance to be good in the same way as that which is good in its essence.³⁰ The former can be secured to a man if he takes to himself what I may call the "living bread" (Jn 6⁵¹) for his preservation. If he loses it, it is through

---

²⁹ Latin *media*, which translates μέσα or ἀδιάφορα. The Stoics believed that all 'external' things (life, death, glory, disgrace, pain, pleasure, riches, health, disease) are 'indifferent', whereas virtues are 'good', vices 'evil'. (Butterworth, p. 221, note 4.)

³⁰ For this thought cf. *Princ.* II.9.2 and I.2.4 (above pp. 52f and 53 note 52).

his own fault in neglecting to partake of the "living bread" and the true drink. . . . Now it was necessary for God, who knows how to use for a needful purpose even the consequences of sin, to station those who became evil in this way at a certain place in the universe and to make available a school of virtue for those who wish to strive "lawfully" (2 Tim 2⁵) to achieve it. His purpose was that when they had been tested by the evil on this earth like gold in the fire, and done everything to ensure that no impurity had entered their rational nature, they might show their worthiness to ascend to the divine realm, and be drawn up by the Word to the loftiest of all blessed states and what I may call the mountain-peak of goodness.'

Ibid. VII.68: (Origen criticizes Celsus' statements that "all things are administered (διοικεῖται) according to the mind of God' and 'all providence (πρόνοια) is derived from Him' as too facile.) '[The former statement] requires examination, to see if the "administration" extends to sins which are committed. . . . This would imply that not only the sins but their consequences are administered according to the mind of God; and this is a very different thing from their happening because God does not prevent them. Indeed, if we were to interpret "administered" strictly, it would imply that even the consequences of evil are subject to the control of God's administration . . . , and that no sinner offends against it.

'A similar distinction must be drawn concerning providence. There is some truth in the statement that "all providence is derived from Him", when the "providence" in question signifies something good. But if we mean that every single happening follows the guidance of [God's] providence, including evil, the statement is false . . . , unless indeed one meant that even the accidental consequences of the providence of God are caused by that providence.'³¹

---

³¹ This possibility is expressed in other words at VI.53: 'Be the truth what it may about evil—whether God made it or whether, if He did not, it has come into being as a by-product in relation to the primary (creations). . . .'; cf. VI.55: 'God has not made evils, if "evils" is meant strictly. But the primary works of His creation have given rise to consequences—few in comparison with the orderly arrangement of the whole—which resemble the spiral shavings and sawdust which are a consequence of the primarily intended work of a carpenter. . . .' These distinctions and even the illustration are from Stoic philosophers. Whether they really succeed in rationalizing the presence of evil in a divinely created universe is another matter. (See for the source of the distinctions, etc., Chadwick's *Celsus*, pp. 370, note 3; 372, note 1.)

Ibid. VIII.72: 'We [Christians, as contrasted with the Stoics]
believe that the time will come when the Word will have
mastered the whole of rational nature and transformed every
soul to His own perfection, when everyone will choose what
the Word wills by the unaided use of his own powers and remain in the condition he chooses. We believe that just as it is
unlikely that any of the consequences of physical diseases and
wounds will in the end prove beyond the resources of medi-
cine, even so in the case of souls it is unlikely that any of the
consequences of sin will be beyond curing by the supreme,
rational God. For the Word and the power of healing within
Him are stronger than all the evils of the soul, and He brings
this power to bear on each, as God wills, and the end of the
matter is the destruction of the sin.'

Hom. Num. XIV.2: 'By a certain dispensation (*dispensatione*)
and wisdom of God everything in this world is so arranged
that nothing is wholly useless to God, whether it be evil or
good. . . . God did not create evil, nor when others have contrived it does He stop it (although He could do) but uses it
for necessary ends. For by means of those in whom is evil,
He makes those who are working towards the achievement of
goodness famous and praiseworthy. For if evil disappeared
there would be nothing to stand over against goodness, and
goodness, having no opposite, would not shine out with its
greater brightness and proved superiority. For goodness is not
goodness unless it is proved and tested. (Origen compares
Joseph and his brethren, the sin of the latter being necessary for
the whole story of Exodus to Deuteronomy; Balak; Judas Iscariot
—even the devil, for if he were suppressed) this would entail
the simultaneous disappearance of our struggle against his wiles,
and he who had struggled "lawfully" (2 Tim 2⁵) could no
longer expect the crown of victory.'

Cels. V.16: 'The Word says that only those who have been
utterly purified in doctrine, morals and mind will be granted
no taste of fire and punishment; but the others, who need the
dispensation (οἰκονομία) of punishment by fire according to
their merits, will suffer the punishment which God fittingly
administers to those who, although made in His image, have
lived contrary to the intention of that nature which is in His
image—and this punishment will go on until a fixed end.'

Ibid. VIII. 31ff: 'Our view is that the earth bears the things said to be administered (διοικεῖσθαι) by nature because of what is in reality the tending (προστασίας) of unseen husbandmen, as I may call them' (i.e. certain angels of God) 'and other ministers (οἰκονόμων), and that this applies not only to the things that grow on the earth but also to all flowing water and the atmosphere. . . . If we may be so bold as to say what are the functions of demons, we may suggest famines, barren vines and fruit-trees, droughts, pollution of the atmosphere which damages the crops and sometimes even kills animals and brings pestilence to men. All these things are the work of demons, who like executioners have received authority by divine appointment (κρίσει τινι θείᾳ) to bring about these things at certain times, either for the recalling of men who are drifting towards the flood of sin, or for the schooling of rational beings (to virtue). The purpose is that those who remain God-fearing even in times like these and do not degenerate, may stand out in their true colours before the spectators—visible and invisible—who hitherto have not seen their quality; but those who react the opposite way, while hiding the evidence of their sin, may be shown up by what comes to them both in their own eyes and in those of the ones we have called the "spectators".'

Ibid. 32: 'The psalmist (Ps 78[49]) is witness that the more dreadful calamities are, by divine appointment (κρίσει) caused by certain evil angels. . . .'

Ibid. 33: 'We are not under the control of demons but of the God of the universe, through Jesus Christ who brings us to Him. According to the laws of God no demon has inherited control of things on the earth; but one may suggest that through their own defiance of the law they divided among themselves those places where there is no knowledge of God and the life according to His will, or where there are many enemies of His divinity. Another suggestion would be that because the demons were fitted to govern and punish the wicked, they were appointed (ἐτάχθησαν) by the Word that administers (διοικοῦντος) the universe, to rule those who have subjected themselves to sin and not to God.'

Along with incidental synonyms, such as ἐπισκοπή ('oversight'), προστασία ('patronage', 'protection'), ἐφορᾶν ('oversee'), μέλει τῷ Θεῷ ('it is a concern to God'), οὐκ ἀθεεί ('not without God'), and the words signifying God's appointings (τάσσω, θεῖα κρίσις), the two great words of Providence are πρόνοια (providentia) and οἰκονομία (dispensatio). The former emphasizes God's divine foreseeing and planning, the latter His actual administration and care—in certain contexts with the specialized reference of God's 'self-accommodation' to mankind. The pervasive importance of the whole theme in the mind of Origen is shown not only by the very wide range of aspects of the working of Providence in his writings but by the way it dovetails, so to speak, into other theological issues—often implicitly: in some of the above extracts the words themselves are not used.

What is the relationship of πρόνοια, οἰκόνομία to χάρις? Formally (but still significantly) the words are on occasion brought together. Princ. II.9.7 (above, p. 77): 'through the grace of His mercy He provides (providet) for all'; Frag. Prov. 1[6] (above p. 78): 'the grace which disposed (τῆς οἰκονομούσης χάριτος) the Word of God'; Comm. Jn. VI.57 (above, p. 83): 'the events of God's providence' (οἰκονομίαι), i.e. the Resurrection and Ascension of Christ) made possible the 'grace-gifts' (χαρίσματα) of 'cloven tongues and holy angels' to the apostles; Cels. V.50 (above, p. 46): 'this dispensation and grace' (οἰκονομίαν καὶ χάριν)—i.e. God's calling—'were transferred from Jews to Gentiles'; Sel. Ezek. XVI.8 (above, p. 21): 'the acts of His providence' (πρόνοιαι) are exemplified by 'dispensations of His grace' (οἰκονομίαι χάριτος); Cels. VII.46 (above, p. 86)—the motive for God's self-manifestation is equally His love for man (φιλάνθρωπος) and His πρόνοια.

More significant, however, is the unity of range and content between the words and the balance of emphasis within each. Grace is God's free self-giving to mankind; it is especially operative in Scripture; supremely in Christ, and through Him in the whole of every man's salvation. A peculiar feature of Grace is the calling first of the Jews and then, in their place, of the Gentiles. Providence, likewise, is God's planning and care for all creation; Providence ordained and disposed the Bible—the Old Testament and (supremely) the Person and Work of Christ for all mankind: it was through Providence that the Gentiles succeeded the as Jews God's chosen people. Both Grace (cf. p. 48

and note 42) and Providence (cf. e.g. *Cels*. VI.71 (above, p. 75), IV.42 (above, p. 79)) are suggestive above all of divine *power*.

It will be illuminating to look also at the doubts and questionings aroused by some implications of Origen's doctrine of Grace, to find if they are also suggested by what he says of Providence.

(1) What is the status, in the scheme of Providence, of human merit? Origen, we recall, was not consistent on the question of merit and grace—sometimes the latter was absolute, sometimes it was conditioned by or even complementary to man's own achievements. Now *prima facie*, at any rate, Origen's doctrine of providence is absolute enough. There is no corner of the universe, no aspect of human life, no tract of time, that is beyond the pervasive power of the foresight and care of God. Providence, indeed, is not a kind of 'substance' (Stoic-wise) that works by a quasi-physical automation—it is not in any way compulsive. It is throughout a matter of personal relations—God at work in a world of sinners, God's self-accommodation to the limits of human capacity. Providence opens God to human search; it guides and saves without ever destroying—nay, by confirming—man's freewill. It never wearies in its dispensations: man's greatest sin is met by the greatest dispensation of all—the Incarnation and Passion of Christ. It is satisfied with nothing less than the mountain-peak of perfection; and none will in the end be able to refuse its healing and ameliorating beneficence.

In detail, a number of emphatic assertions suggest an uncompromising theocentricism. *Hom. Gen.* III.2 (p. 90): 'Nothing is done apart from God's providence'; *Cels*. VIII.67 (p. 77): 'Whatever we receive that is right and good we have from God and His providence'; ibid. I.9 (p. 80): 'No good thing takes place among men apart from God'; ibid. VI.78 (p. 81): 'Nothing good has happened among men without the working of the divine Word'; ibid. IV.53 (p. 91): 'The source and origin of every blessing is to believe in the supreme God.' *Princ*. II.11.5 (p. 76) (Providence is all-embracing, even to the hairs of our head); *Sel. Ps* 144[1] (p. 76) (we are His debtors for creation—for making us out of nothing to be such as we are; and His Providence cares for us every day, whether we know it or not); *Princ*. III.2.5 (p. 91): 'human nature of its own resources cannot hold the fort' (against demons, etc., but conscious of the presence of the indwelling Lord it can) (and so *Comm. Song Songs* II, p. 133 (pp. 91f).

The real test comes when Origen seeks to relate this providence to man, and above all in the questions of God's self-accommodation and of human freewill. We summarized the first question: 'God in His Providence prepares men to know Him, and accommodates Himself to the capacity of weak and sinful man to know Him and be guided by Him' (p. *86*). *Cels.* VI.78 (p. *81*): 'He visits the souls of those who have been *able to receive* His operations'; ibid. 79 (pp. *81*f): 'The One Word . . . sent out the rays which reach the souls of those *willing to receive Him*': *Comm. Mt.* XVII.17ff (p. *89*): 'Even if we are *deemed worthy of seeing* God, . . . we do not see Him as He is, but as He (accommodates Himself to us). 'Able', 'willing', 'worthy',—but it is by God's providence that His believers 'ascend to the knowledge of great truths' (*Cels.* VII.46 [p. *86*]), for the mind has received from providence the very 'faculty of knowing Him' (ibid. 33 [p. *86*]). So too with ethical qualities; *Cels.* VII.7 (p. *79*) (The Jewish prophets were chosen by providence 'because of their quite exceptional qualities'); ibid. VI.44 (pp. *92*f) (God's 'school of virtue' for those who wish to strive 'lawfully', which will 'test them like gold in the fire', that they might *'show their worthiness'* to ascend to the divine realm—it is none the less the Word that 'draws them up'); ibid. V.16 (p. *94*) ('fire and punishment' await the defaulters, who *'according to their merits'* will suffer fitting penalties—but it is because they have ignored the 'intention' of their own nature, which is in God's image, and the punishment itself will be an οἰκονομία [cf. above, p. *51*, note *49*]).—It seems fair to comment that in these passages the characteristic ethical conditioning is seen in a theocentric context, and the 'sovereignty of providential grace' is not compromised.

The freewill passages, however, raise an acuter problem. Origen was just as notoriously the champion of human freedom as was Luther of human bondage. I am not aware that any adequate attempt has been made to compare—on a basis of first-hand knowledge—the positions of these two great doctors of theology. I suspect they would be found rather nearer to each other than might be expected.

'Providence', said our summary of Origen at this point (p. *89*), 'allows man's freewill full scope in his co-operation with God.' *Cels.* IV.82 (p. *89*): (man *co-operates with* providence; he has the power to 'think and to arrange'); *Sel. Ps* 4[6] (p. *89*): (the Lord *co-operates with* the builder, otherwise the building could never be completed; husbandry is *compounded of* human skill and providential climate and rain; rational good in general is *compounded of* man's choice and the *co-operating divine* power.); *Cels.* V.21 (the universe is administered by God '*in accordance with the conditions of*' human freewill); *Hom. Gen.* III.2 (God's providence is to be distinguished from God's will; much happens contrary to the latter, but the former is rather that 'caring, dispensing, providing' for all things—good or bad); *Sel. Ex.* 15²⁵ (God 'permits man to do what he wishes' (although Himself not ignorant of the future).

'Co-operation', 'compound', 'conditions'—ominous words; but is Origen doing more than to insist on the validity of man's response to God's call? Is he saying that man is in any sense and to any degree responsible for his own salvation?[32] If we put the freewill passages alongside the 'uncompromising theocentricism' of the passages quoted on pp. 97f, is it not clear that Origen would never deny the 'prevenient, concomitant, subsequent' grace that is presupposed by every bit of good in humanity? Had he been able to foresee the Pelagian controversies, would he not have been more careful to insert his 'For it is God that worketh in you. . . .' (Phil 2¹³) after every vindication of the place and value of human choice?

Such at any rate is suggested by another passage (*Cels.* VIII.72 [p. *94*]) where Origen looks towards the end. 'The time will come when the Word will have mastered the whole of rational nature and transformed every soul to His own perfection, when everyone will choose what the Word wills by the unaided exercise of own powers. . . .'

(2) The kindred problems of the interpretation and valuation of the Bible, and of the source of Origen's finished theology and its relation to his philosophical inheritance may be dealt with together.

The reader will have observed the preponderance of the *Celsus* as a source-book for Providence, as contrasted e.g. with χάρις itself. This, of course, is because in the *Celsus* Origen is entering the field of natural theology—the arguments and rejoinders of

---

[32] Cf. *Comm. Rom.* (Gk), § 22 (*JTS*, XIII.358): 'We must not suppose that the Gospel saying "With what measure ye mete, it shall be meted back to you" (Luke 6³⁸) was meant for the matters of greater moment (ἐπὶ τῶν κρειττόνων ἔργων). For "we are *saved* by grace . . .". What we *must* suppose is that punishment is inflicted according to the measure of our sins.'

Stoics and Platonists—in which one major battleground was the Stoic doctrine of πρόνοια. The *Celsus* 'helps us to see', says Dr Chadwick (*Cels.*, p. ix), 'both the arguments Origen would have used when engaged in disputation with learned pagans at Alexandria or Caesarea, and the way in which he himself in his own mind could be satisfied that Christianity was not an irrational credulity but a profound philosophy'.

This explains from the start the absence of allegorism from the providence-passages (the twin-signs of Gideon [pp. *84*f] is an exception, and it is not from the *Celsus*). Allegory is for the initiated Christian—theologian or sermon-taster—and would mean nothing to the public at which the *Celsus* was aimed. Formally, indeed, the Bible has little enough to do with Origen's doctrine of providence at all. Only three or four passages are cited as direct authorities for it: the obvious ones about care of the sparrows and numbering of the hairs of our head (Mt 10^{29f} (above, p. *76*)), and a couple of sentences from the Psalms (Ps 126^1, 'Except the Lord build . . .' (p. *89*) and Ps 27^{1-3}, 'The Lord is my light . . .' (p. *91*)). The doctrine is *illustrated* by several Biblical stories: Noah and the Ark (with the excellent point that new human race after the flood was given a first-rate start by the providential provision of a supremely righteous man as its father (*Cels.* IV.41 [pp. *78*f]); the persecution of Moses and Aaron, which gave the opportunity for the 'glory of God' to 'shine' on them (*Hom. Num.* IX.2 [pp. *85*f]); the twin-signs of Gideon (*Hom. Jud.* VIII.4 [pp. *84*f]): and (from the New Testament) the timing of the feet-washing (*Comm. Jn.* XXXII.8 [p. *82*]); 'Now is the judgement of this world' (ibid. *Frag.* 89 [p. *82*]); 'Except a corn of wheat . . .' (*Cels.* VIII.41 [pp. *82*f]); and the interpretative paraphrase of Rom. 1^{18ff} (ibid. VII.46 [pp. *86*f]).

But most of Origen's discussions on providence show him entering (zestfully enough) on controversies that the Bible hardly envisages. 'In truth', says Chadwick (ibid. p. X), 'the Stoa and the Academy had provided arguments and counterarguments on a wide range of subjects, with the result that we frequently find that where Celsus shows affinity with the Academy, Origen has only to fall back on the traditional refutation provided by the Stoics, and vice-versa.' Even so, of course, this does not necessarily compromise Origen's claim to be a *Christian* philosopher. To stand aloof from the controversies of this world would be a denial of the Incarnation, and Christianity is not necessarily impartial as between the rival philosophies of mankind. The real question is whether Origen in stepping into the dialectical arena of Stoa and Academy allows the prescribed questions to limit or contaminate the faith in which he seeks to answer them—whether he sails too far from the harbour of the Christian revelation.[33]

Let us seek to answer this question by looking at some of Origen's 'problems of providence'.

(a) *The attempted rationalizing of evil, sin, suffering.* (Above, pp. 91ff, and *Princ.* III.1.13 [pp. 77f] and *Cels.* II.78 [p. 84]). The rise of evil, says Origen, has been a by-product, an accidental consequence, of the workings of divine providence, like the shavings and sawdust that litter the carpenter's bench. (In the *Princ.* passages quoted above pp. 70ff, the direct responsibility for evil is traced to the freewill of pre-existent souls, and first and foremost the devil.) God, who could have prevented it, did not do so—indeed, it may be said to exist with His permission; we can still accept everything that befalls us as from His hand, for nothing happens without Him. Evil, in truth, has its uses: if it vanished there would be nothing to stand over against goodness, that the latter might prove itself, and stand out in its true colours. Evil makes possible God's school of virtue, by testing and purifying the aspirants to the good life, like gold in the fire. The persecutions were the occasion of the shining of God's glory on the sufferers, who could not have known or appreciated it otherwise. Providence used the sin of the Jews as a means of calling the Gentiles into the Kingdom. If God's cure of sin is often slow, it is because the cure must be permanent—like the physical cure of hidden poisons in the body. Finally, God only gives a limited range to evil—it never runs beyond the ultimately victorious power of His providence, which in the end will make it disappear entirely, for none of its consequences will be beyond curing by the supreme, rational God.

There is a surprisingly modern ring about these speculations, in spite of their Stoic ancestry. As a rationalizing of evil, indeed,

[33] An instance from the extracts I have given of Origen's impartiality toward the philosophers would be the comparison of *Cels.* VI.71 (p. 75). (The Stoics are wrong in regarding providence as a quasi-physical substance) with *Hom. Jer.* XII.5 (p. 75, note 10) (The Stoics are right to claim that God's care is first for the world as a whole.)

they are no more successful than any other such essays. The
illustration of the carpenter's shavings (and the 'mess that lies
beside buildings—the dirt, for example, that falls off the stones
and plaster'—another Stoic illustration given at *Cels.* VI.55) is
an admirable one, if God's creation is looked at as no more than
a piece of carpentry or bricklaying. *Creatio ex nihilo*, however,
and still more that creation which is an expression of the righteousness and wisdom of Christ, bears little or no analogy to such
human enterprises—and leaves no room for such 'by-products'
or 'accidental consequences'. What is more, the shavings and
the dirt are presumably removed at convenience to a rubbish-
dump or tipped into the nearest canal—a poor analogy to the
testing and purifying of the aspirants to virtue and the means
of calling the Gentiles. Freewill is indeed a necessary presupposition of sin—but freewill in those created in God's image
should have meant freedom to will as does the 'great Original'
from the start. The origin of evil remains to this day the great
'surd' with which the Christian theologian wrestles in vain.

What really matters, however, is the firm preservation by
Origen in all this speculation of the genuinely biblical insights
and presuppositions of the Christian theologian. There is the
consistent determination to 'give God the glory', and providence
the priority, in the whole sinful story of humanity. There is the
strong ethical emphasis. There is the keen sense of history and
progress. There is the underlying recognition of the super-human
and the sub-human tensions that seem to be generated by powers
—good and bad—beyond the range of our own human reason
and will, and turn man alternately into an angel and a demon
(for such is the permanent truth of the curious doctrine of the
premundane fall and the angelic and demonic powers). There is
behind Origen's eschatology (which brought him into such dis-
repute in later generations) a keen conviction of the 'optimism of
grace', which some of his detractors might have done better to
emulate.

(*b*) *The answers to Celsus' criticisms of the Incarnation.* (*Cels.*
VI.78ff, above, pp. *81*f.) Why only *then*? Why only *there*? Why
only *one* Son of God? To the first question Origen replies that
the Incarnation was not a reversal of God's previous policy of
inactivity: He has always worked for the good of mankind. To
the second he suggests that historical consideration that the

advent of Jesus required a people prepared for Him by knowledge of the true God and understanding of His purpose to redeem mankind, so that when Jesus came His Word could be poured out from this 'one corner' to the world. To the third he replies that more than one Jesus was unnecessary: He was capable of filling the world with the 'rays' of the sun of righteousness—and His inspired followers and teachers themselves serve the purpose of the other 'Christs' that Celsus would look for.[34]

The 'scandal of particularity' is a very old one, and it is not easy in principle to improve on Origen's answers to this day. That they are not convincing to the rationalist is inevitable, because the ultimate rationale of the Incarnation lies deep in the counsels of God. As Origen well knows (see below, p. *159*), the Incarnation conceals as well as reveals the divine mystery. But he does all we can reasonably ask of the Christian theologian— he is not shirking the questions of this world; he is showing that God's οἰκονομία does not fall below human reason, even if it rises far above it; and he is not compromising the essentials of the κήρυγμα by rationalizing its 'scandal' away.

(*c*) *The doctrine of 'Accommodation'*. (See the passages quoted above, pp. *86*ff.) God, says Origen, revealed in His Providence and love that which may be known of Him and gave men the eyes of the mind to know it. But the distance between man and God remains, and so when Providence weaves itself into human affairs God must assume the human mind, manner, and diction, and say and imply things which are not true of Him in His divine essence. This is especially true of His profession of human emotions such as anger, and of His implied disclaiming of foreknowledge of the future; the former is for the correction and improvement of man, and spoken in the only language he will understand, while the latter leaves you full freedom of choice, and avoids cutting the ethical nerve by the suggestion that the future is already foreknown and determined. The 'repentance' of God—a blasphemous notion!—is the expression in human terms of His change from one dispensation to another. This

---

[34] Chadwick (p. 391, note 4) points out (from Geffcken) that Celsus is adopting the Epicurean argument against the Stoic notion of the making of the world, and he compares the Epicurean in *Cicero De Nat. Deorum* I.9.21: 'Why did the builders of the world appear suddenly, after countless years of slumber?' Any doctrine of God which represents His providence as obtrusive as well as pervasive automatically provokes the same question.

'accommodation' is familiar to us in the human spheres of a doctor, a father, and a master. God indeed remains wholly God both in His speaking through the prophets and in His management of men; but even if we are deemed worthy of seeing Him with our mind and heart, we do not see Him as He is but as He becomes to us in order to bring His providence to bear on us.

Dr Hanson has given the doctrine of Accommodation full and most learned treatment in his recent book (*Allegory and Event*, pp. 210ff), from the point of view of Origen's biblical interpretation. He concludes that in his use of this principle Origen as an exegete is 'at his best and greatest. At times we feel that he is very near indeed to the doctrine of progressive revelation. . . . But he is always inhibited from seriously contemplating such a line of thought by his conviction—reached by *a priori* and arbitrary presupposition—that the immaturity and imperfection must lie in the audience to whom the biblical message was addressed and not in the agent' (i.e. the biblical writer) 'through whom the message was delivered. Still, when all has been said and done, this conception of accommodation was a noble principle nobly applied.' I do not wish in any way to dispute this authoritative verdict. Doubtless for his age and place Origen was taking a great step forward in biblical interpretation (not in the *invention* of the principle of accommodation, which was 'well-established in a rudimentary form in Philo' and may have been 'ultimately derived from Rabbinic exegesis' (Hanson, pp. 224f), but in its elevation to a leading rôle in the problems of scriptural exegesis). Doubtless, too, any conception of Providence which faithfully reflects the transcendence of God and the desperate state of erring and sinful man *must* be expressed in some such category as 'Accommodation'. It seems to me, indeed, that it is precisely this concern which is expressed in the 'Kenoticism' of theologians like Forsyth and Mackintosh, and many of us have welcomed the emphatic vindication of this type of thought in the recent *Person of Christ* by Vincent Taylor (1958). We remember, too, the idea of the Kenosis of the Holy Spirit worked out in Wheeler Robinson's *Christian Experience of the Holy Spirit* as long ago as 1928, which has had singularly little repercussion on subsequent theology, but of which (as we shall see) a suggestion may be found in Origen himself. Self-emptying, self-limitation, self-accommodation are essential forms of the self-revelation of the wholly supreme and transcendent God, and it is to Origen's credit that he takes this essentially Biblical insight so seriously and illustrates it so convincingly.

And yet there is something fundamentally wrong about Origen's whole presentation. He would rightly revolt from a god who is in any sense a reflection of humanity, fashioned in man's image. But by adopting, in common with much of the whole patristic and scholastic tradition, the presupposition of divine immutability and impassivity, he is allowing an invasion of the biblical picture by that *damnosa haereditas* of Greek Christian thought—the Stoic doctrine of apatheia. God is above feeling and change, for these are characteristic of man, whereas He transcends everything human. Therefore all the Biblical expressions which impute to Him emotions (wrath, repentance, etc.) are mere 'accommodations' and do not reflect anything in the inner life of God Himself. There is nothing in the divine essence corresponding to human suffering, or human indignation at injustice.

Now it is clear that if such be the truth of the matter, God cannot enter into any *real* relationship with man whatsoever, and this would deny not only the anthropomorphisms of the Old Testament but the whole structure of relevation in the Bible. 'God is Light' says the New Testament: and this *might* accord with a doctrine of God wholly removed from our darkness. But it also tells us that 'God is Love', and it is the essence of love to seek fellowship with the loveless. The one, pure, unoriginate Light of God must then likewise be conceived as broken up, as it were, through the lens of creation and redemption into the innumerable shades and colours to which sinful man can respond —and the vital point will be that the original Light is not a kind of divine abstraction from all colours (after the fashion of the *via negativa* of the scholastics) but something which mysteriously gathers them all into an infinitely pure and transcendent radiance —a *pleroma*, a divine harmony which while embracing all the themes and notes of providence is yet infinitely richer than them all. 'While there is suffering (for human sin) in the life of God, it is eternally swallowed up in victory and blessedness', in the now famous words of Donald Baillie (*God was in Christ*, p. 199).

That this position is difficult to state in such a way as to guard against the opposite errors of apatheia and anthropomorphism is true enough. The same difficulty besets the later controversies concerning the Trinity—and yet no Christian theology worth the name can rest satisfied with an 'economic' in place of an 'essential' Trinity, with 'modes of revelation' only, in place of 'modes of being'.[35] And this is why the language of Origen is ultimately so unconvincing—even, one may conjecture, to himself. There is a passage in *Hom. Ezek.* (VI.6)—in the Latin version of Jerome, whom one trusts far more than Rufinus—which recognizes this. 'The Father Himself, the God of the universe is "slow to anger and plenteous in mercy" (Ps 103[8]) and pitiful; has He then no feelings? Surely you must realize that when He intervenes in the world of humanity He shares human feelings. . . . The Father Himself is *not* impassible. If He asks, pities, shows sympathy, He "experiences"—and the experience is Love: He comes to be within those in whom He cannot be in the full majesty of His nature, and on our behalf He takes on Himself human feelings.' Cf. *Sel. Ezek.* 16[8]: 'God suffers with us by taking pity on us. For He is not without feeling.' (This flatly contradicts the earlier extract from the same passage [above, p. *21*], but such is Origen's way.) Here surely the biblical theologian is striving to exorcise, even if not with complete success, the spectre of the Stoic *apatheia*. It only remains to add that the 'full majesty' of God *is* His Love—just as, according to St John, the 'glory' of Christ *was* the Cross—and the exorcism is complete.

I have dealt at length with Origen's doctrine of Providence because it seems to me that for him πρόνοια and οἰκονομία are χάρις, when the work of God the Father is especially under consideration, and more particularly when Origen looks at the philosophical implications of his theology, or when he enters the lists as the champion against enlightened paganism of the Christian *Weltanschauung*. Only once—in this last matter of 'Accommodation'—have we found him really faltering; the identity of Providence and Grace is achieved, both positively and negatively, with remarkable consistency—and above all in the quasi-technical use of οἰκονομία for the Incarnation and Passion of

---

[35] Cf. Welch, *The Trinity in Contemporary Theology*, p. 277, Baillie, op. cit., p. 136, note 1. There is a good article on the whole question of Divine Impassibility by Pollard in the *Scottish Journal of Theology*, VIII.4.353ff.

Christ. A theologian who can rise to this is not in very grave danger of sundering his theology into wholly unrelated 'natural' and 'revealed' departments, or of surrendering in any vital measure the ultimate Lordship of Christ over all theology and all creation.

§ 2. THE GRACE OF GOD THE SON

Those who doubt the loyalty of Origen to the Lord Jesus Christ not so much in his life as in his theology should try, as I have, the experiment of collecting and classifying the countless references in his works to the Person and Work of the Saviour. Indeed, the real danger is that the necessary task of selection will force his superabundant luxuriance of exposition into a strait-jacket of our own construction. I have, as always, sought to let him speak for himself; and the paragraphs and sub-divisions have been, as it were, thrust at me once I had the range of references before my eyes.

(A) TITLES AND SUMMARIES

Origen is constantly playing, with all his rhetorical exuberance, on the *Names* of Jesus in which the New Testament (as well as, implicitly, for him, the Old Testament) abounds. The *locus classicus* is *Princ.* I.2, where the following titles are expounded and co-ordinated:

Wisdom of God (Prov 8[22ff])
Firstborn of All Creation (Col 1[15])
Power of God (1 Cor 1[24])
Word of God (Jn 1[1])
Way, Truth, Life (Jn 14[6])
Image of the Invisible God (Col 1[15])
Brightness of God's Glory, Express Image of His Substance (Heb 1[3]; cf. Wis 7[25f], breath of God's power, effluence—emanation—of His glory).
True Light that Lighteth Every Man (Jn 1[9]). The chapter ends as follows: 'It would be a large undertaking, demanding another work and another time, to collect all the titles of the Son of God, e.g. the true light, the door, righteousness, sanctification, redemption, countless others. . . .' The reference to 1 Cor 1[30] ('wisdom, righteousness, sanctification, redemption') is never far from Origen's mind. Here are examples of passages where the same theme is played:

Cels. IV.99: '. . . (God's) Son who is God, the Word, Wisdom,

Truth, Righteousness, and every other divine title that the holy Scriptures give to Him. . . .'

Hom. Jer. VIII.2 on 10¹²: 'God's "understanding", only to be sought for in Jesus Christ. For Christ is all such things as may be predicated of God; He is God's Wisdom, Power, Righteousness, Sanctification, Redemption. . . .'

Ibid. XVII.4 on 17¹³ (the 'endurance' of Israel, LXX): 'Just as the Saviour is Righteousness, Truth and Sanctification in person, even so is He "endurance" in person. It is impossible to be righteous or holy without Christ: and impossible to "endure" unless one possesses Him. For He is the "endurance" of Israel.'

Comm. Mt. XV.22 on 19²⁷: ' "We have followed Thee" means this: "Since the Father has given us the same range of revelations as He did to Peter, as to who Thou art—that (for example) Thou art Righteousness, we have followed Thee as Righteousness: and in the same way as Sanctification, Wisdom, Peace, Truth, the Way leading to God, the true Life.'

Comm. Jn. XXXII.31 (19): 'To seek Jesus is to seek the Word, Wisdom, Righteousness, Truth, the Power of the Father —for Christ is all these.'

Comm. Rom. I.1: 'What is . . . being a servant of Christ but being a servant of the Word of God, Wisdom, Righteousness, Truth, and every single one of the virtues—all of which are Christ?'

Ibid. V.6: 'Although Christ is one in essence, He has many titles to indicate His powers and His workings; for He is apprehended in His being as Grace, Righteousness . . . , Peace . . . , Life . . . , Truth . . . , the Word.'

There is one title, indeed, that Origen, with remarkable insight, adds to the biblical list[36]—Christ the αὐτοβασίλεια, the 'Kingdom in person'. The *locus classicus* for this is *Comm. Mt.*, where we can see the line of thought developing until it leads to the triumphant identification.

Comm. Mt. X.14 on 13⁵²: 'In the simpler sense of the words,

---

[36] Cf. also *Comm. Eph.*, § 1 (*JTS*, III.235), where Origen suggests that Christ may also be the 'Will of God' (Eph 1¹); ibid. § 9 (p. 398), the 'Glory of God'; ibid. § 4 (p. 238), 1⁶: 'The Saviour is called "The Beloved" without qualification: for although men can go wrong in their apprehension of "righteousness, truth, wisdom", they would all agree that they "love" these things.'

a scribe is trained for the Kingdom of heaven when he pro-
gresses from Judaism to the ecclesiastical teaching of Jesus.
In the deeper sense the words refer to the ascent from initiation into the letter of the Scriptures to their spiritual understanding, which is called the Kingdom of heaven. . . . In this
way you might allegorize the words "Repent, for the Kingdom of heaven is at hand": the scribes, i.e. those confining
themselves to the bare letter, "repent" from such an interpretation and become trained in the spiritual teaching that
comes through Jesus the Incarnate Word, such teaching being
called the "Kingdom of heaven". For this reason as long as
Jesus Christ, the divine Word that was in the beginning with
God, does not dwell in a soul, the Kingdom of heaven is not
in that soul. But when one is ready to receive that Word, the
Kingdom of heaven is nigh at his hand.'

Ibid. XII.14 (below, p. *143*) (the Kingdom of the heavens
is the totality of 'virtues', and Christ is each and every virtue).

Ibid. XIV.7 on 18²³ᶠᶠ: ' "The Kingdom of Heaven is likened
to a man who was a king": If it may be likened to such-and
such a king who has done such-and-such, what king can be
meant but the Son of God? For He is the King of the heavens,
and just as He is Wisdom, Righteousness and Truth in Person,
why should He not be the Kingdom in person? . . . If in
that case you ask what meaning the words "theirs is the Kingdom of heaven" (Mt 5³) can have, you may say that "theirs
is Christ, who as the *Kingdom in person* rules in His several
aspects over the man who is no longer subjected to the rule
of sin. . . . By "rules in His several aspects" I mean that He
rules as Righteousness, Wisdom, Truth. . . .'

Cf. *Hom. Lk.* XXXII on 10⁹: ('Heal the sick . . . and say . . .
"The Kingdom of God has come right to you".') 'He is here
speaking of Himself as the Kingdom of God, for He is King
and God.'

Along with these titles should be taken the passages where Origen
seeks to summarize the work of Jesus for mankind.[37] The following are examples:

---

[37] Cf. *Comm. Jn.* I.10 (11) (p. *47*, note 44 above), where Christ is identified with
'good things' in general; *Hom. Lk.* IV (p. *113* below), where the 'sojourn of the Saviour'
made available for us 'all good things'.

Princ. I.3.8 (above, pp. *73*f).

Cels. II.79 (refuting the Jewish charge that Jesus was a mere man): 'I do not know how a (mere) man could dare the attempt to spread His religion and teaching in all the world and achieve His intentions apart from God, and in so doing to show his superiority to everyone who attacked the spread of his teaching. . . . How could a mere man, in no way super-human, convert such a vast multitude? It would not have been remarkable if the conversion had extended only to some of the intelligent ones. But he converted also the most irrational, those most at the mercy of their passions, those who because of their lack of understanding are all the harder to convert to a better life. But because Christ was the Power of God and the Wisdom of the Father, He was able to achieve this and is still doing so. . . . (Therefore we Christians shall ignore charges that we "beguile" our converts.) A marvellous "beguiling", which results in self-control in the place of licence, or at least progress towards it, and righteousness in place of iniquity, or at least progress towards it, and wisdom instead of folly, or at least progress towards it; men changed from cowards, degenerates, effeminates into bravery and heroism— above all in their struggles for piety towards God. . . .'[38]

Ibid. V.33 (Celsus: Whence have the Christians come? Who made their laws? The truth is, from Judaism—and yet they rebelled against it!) 'We [Christians] have all come "in the last days",[39] when our Jesus came amongst us, to the "visible mountain of the Lord", to the Word "far above" every word, to the house of God which is "the Church of the living God, pillar and ground of the truth" (1 Tim 3[15]). We see how He built "on the tops of the mountains", which are all the sayings of the prophets, who are His foundation. This house is lifted "above the hills", which are those men who aspire to profess some exceptional ability in wisdom and truth. And "all nations" come to it, and many nations go, and we have speech with one another, encouraging each other to the worship

---

[38] Cf. ibid. III.27f (above, pp. *90*f), 31 (p. *34*), where the ethical and religious fruits of the work of Jesus are contrasted with those of a pagan miracle-worker like Aristeas. Cf. ibid. III.42: 'What work as great as His has been done by Asclepius, Dionysus, Heracles? What men can they show so reformed and strengthened in their morals as to support their own claim to be gods?'

[39] This whole passage is an application of Isa 2[2ff].

of God through Jesus Christ which has shone out "in the last days", saying "Come, let us go up . . . (etc.)". For there has come forth from those in Sion a spiritual law which has passed over to us. Moreover the "Word of the Lord" came forth from that Jerusalem to hold sway everywhere and judge "between the nations", choosing those He sees to be obedient, convicting "much people" who are disobedient.

'To those who ask whence we come or who is our Captain we reply that we have come in obedience to the behests of Jesus. . . . No longer do we take "the sword against a nation' . . . for we are become the "sons of peace" (Lk 10⁶) through Jesus who is our Captain . . . , and we receive a law for which we give thanks to Him who saved us from error. . . . Our "chorus-leader and teacher"[40] came forth from the Jews to administer the whole world by the word of His teaching.'

[40] Celsus' words.

(B) THE INCARNATION

There are full discussions in Origen—above all, *Princ.* II.6—on the rationale of the Incarnation, of the highest importance for the student of Christology. But our concern is rather its purpose and results—what God's grace achieved through it for mankind. Here we must seek the mind of Origen by a representative selection from the multitudinous hints and references in his writings.

Christ became like men that they might become like Him: He made available all good things—teaching the way to God, warning of judgement, exemplifying the good life, converting, reforming, purging from evil, gladdening His followers, sowing the seed of God's word, opening the Kingdom of God to all the world—to unworthy as well as worthy, even if not to the unwilling.

Comm. Mt. XII.29 on 16²⁷: ' "For the Son of Man has come already, but not in His glory" (quotes Isa 53²⁻⁵). He had to come in this way, that He might "bear our sins" and suffer "on our behalf"; for it was not fitting that the Christ in glory should "bear our sins" and suffer "for us". But He is coming again in glory after this preliminary preparing of His disciples through that appearing of His which had no "form nor comeliness". He became like them that they might become like Him, "conformed to the image" (Rom 8²⁹) of His glory: since at His first coming He became conformed to "the body of our humiliation" (Phil 3²¹) when He "emptied Himself and took the form of a servant", He restores men to the form of God and makes them like unto it.'

Hom. Lk. IV: 'The sojourning of the Saviour with us, which made available to us (as patron or host—πρόξενος) all good things.'

Princ. IV.1.1: 'Jesus Christ . . . who introduced the saving doctrines of Christianity. . . .'

Ibid. 2: 'God has in reality become man and delivered to men the doctrines of salvation.'

Cels. I.32: (God sent Christ into the world) 'to teach so many people and to convert many from the flood of evil.'

Ibid. 37: 'God wished to send a divine teacher to mankind.'

Ibid. 56: 'The prophecies tell of two advents of Christ, the

I

first subject to human passions and to humiliation, that by being among men Christ might teach the way that leads to God and leave no man on earth the excuse that he did not know of the coming judgement. The second will be His coming in glory and divinity alone, with no human passions mingling with His divinity.'

Ibid. II.38: 'It was not the aim of His first advent to judge mankind before He had taught them and shown them the things they should do; nor did He come to punish the bad and save the good, but to sow in His own wonderful way the seed of His word by a certain divine power among the whole human race.'

Comm. Jn. XIII.62 (60): (Origen suggests that the two visits of Jesus to Cana symbolize His two advents.)   'In the first, after washing, He gladdens us who make our lives with Him, giving us to drink of what by His power is wine. . . . For in reality before Jesus the Scripture was water, but since He came it has become wine to us. In the second [advent], He relieves from fever at the time of the judgement with which He has been entrusted by God, freeing from fever and completely healing the nobleman's son. . . . Thus at the first coming those who receive Him are gladdened; at the second those who were not willing before to drink of His wine are freed from all disease and the fiery darts of the enemy (Eph 6^{16}).'[41]

Cels. IV.3: (Celsus: 'What is the purpose of such a descent on the part of God?') '. . . originally to convert the "lost sheep of the house of Israel" (Mt 10^6), then because of their unbelief to take away from them what we call the Kingdom of God and give it to "other husbandmen" . . . , the Christians, who will "render" to God "the fruits" of the Kingdom in the due season for each fruit thereof—the fruits being their actions (Mt 21^{41ff}).

'(Celsus [sarcastically]: Did He descend to learn what was going on among men? Does not He know everything? If He does know everything, why doesn't He correct men by divine power?) None of us says that Christ came to this life in order to learn what was going on among men. . . . All

---

[41] The perverse but marvellous ingenuity of Origen's allegorism is shown here in his remarking that in the first visit Christ was actually at Cana: in the second the healing was from a distance (Jn 2 and 4^{46ff}).

[Celsus'] questions are silly. For God is always correcting those who hear what He says, and this is by His Word, which in every generation descends to holy souls and makes them "friends of God" (*Wis. Sol.* 727) and prophets; and by the coming of Christ He corrects through the word of Christianity not the unwilling but those who choose the better life, which is pleasing to God.' (Origen goes on to point out that overriding 'correction', e.g. by visions, which would take away evil altogether and implant virtue, would destroy freewill and thus be ethically worthless.)

Ibid. 9: 'After many prophets who administered correction to Israel, Christ came to correct the whole world.'

Hom. Josh. VI.1 on Josh 5 (Origen, N.B., identifies the 'uncircumcised' with those who disobey the commands of God): 'God does not wholly abandon either the circumcised or the uncircumcised, because He loves every soul. For He has sent Jesus to 'circumcise' everyone, worthy and unworthy: Jesus —*not* the son of Nun,[42] whose circumcision of the people was not the true and perfect one—but our Lord and Saviour. For it is He who has truly cut away the pollution in our flesh and purged the stains of our sins from our heart and soul.'

The one divine essence of Christ was revealed or imparted to men in many forms or aspects (ἐπίνοιαι), which applied not only to the nature of the divine Word but to the very physical appearances of the historical Jesus. The Incarnation was in this respect a concealment as well as a revelation. The ἐπίνοιαι corresponded to human capacity, merit, need, or moral progress. Some were a necessary answer to sin (e.g. 'Shepherd', 'Doctor', 'Redemption', 'Firstborn from the dead'); others for man's perfecting (e.g. 'Wisdom', 'Righteousness', 'Truth', 'Life').

Cels. II.64: 'Although Jesus was one, He had several aspects, and His appearance was not the same for everyone who saw Him. (Origen quotes the "I am" sayings of John 14[6], 6[35], 10[9].) That His appearance was not identical to those who saw Him, but varied according to their capacity, will be clear if we ask ourselves why, at the time He was about to be transfigured on the high mountain, He did not take with Him all the apostles, but only Peter, James and John, who alone had the capacity to look on Him thus glorified. I think too that

[42] See p. *50*, note 47.

before His ascent of the mountain, when His disciples came to Him alone and He taught them the beatitudes—I mean when rather lower down the mountain He healed those brought to Him at eventide, curing them of all illness and disease, He did not appear the same to the sick who needed His healing as He did to the fit who were able to ascend the mountain with Him. Furthermore, His 'private explanation' suggests that the disciples had a greater capacity to hear than the crowds, and so probably also a greater capacity to see—certainly with the eyes of the soul, and I should say too with the eyes of the body. Again, Judas, on the point of betrayal, bears witness that He did not always appear the same; for he said to the crowd that accompanied him, "Whomsoever I kiss, it is He", implying that they did not know Him. The Saviour Himself, I should say, makes this clear with His words, "I was daily in the temple with you teaching, and you laid no hand upon me."

'Since we hold Jesus to have been such a wonderful being, not only in respect of the divinity within Him which was hidden from the crowd, but also in respect of His body which was transfigured when He wished and before whom He wished, we conclude that before Jesus had "put off the principalities and powers" and "died to sin" (Col 2^{15}, Rom 6^2), everyone had the capacity to see Him; but after that time the crowds who formerly looked on Him could see Him no longer—He ceased to come within their capacity of vision. It was to spare them that He did not appear to all and sundry after His resurrection.'

Ibid. 65: 'I may go farther: not even to the apostles and disciples themselves was He always present or visible, for even they could not cope with the vision indefinitely.

'After He had accomplished the work of the Incarnation (οἰκονομία) His divinity became more brilliant . . . (and that is why the apostolic writings represent Him as) having been seen after the resurrection not by everyone but only by those whom He saw to have the eyes which could cope with the sight. . . .'

Ibid. 66: 'It is indeed not surprising that all the multitudes who had believed in Jesus did not see His resurrection, for Paul, writing the Corinthians whose capacity of understanding could go no further, said: "And I determined to know nothing among you save Jesus Christ and Him crucified" . . . "For you were not able to bear it; and you are not able even now, for you are still carnal" (1 Cor 2², 3²ᶠ). Accordingly the word [of Scripture], which disposed everything by divine appointment, recounted that before His passion Jesus appeared without reserve to the crowds—but not all the time; afterwards He no longer appeared without reserve, but only in such a way as His deliberate judgement suggested was fitting for each.'

Ibid. 67: '(Jesus) was sent into the world not only to be made known but to conceal Himself.[43] Even those who knew Him did not know Him completely, but some part of Him eluded them; and to others He was totally unknown. He did indeed open the gates of light to them that were in darkness and sons of night, but who devoted themselves to becoming sons of the day and of the light (1 Thess 5⁵); and our Lord came as Saviour rather to men filled with sin, like a good doctor, than to the righteous.'

Ibid. 72: 'His intention was neither that all and sundry should know everything about Him, nor that nothing should be known at all. The voice from heaven proclaiming Him to be Son of God, in the words "This is my beloved Son in whom is my delight", is not recorded to have been heard by the crowds' (Mt 3¹⁷, 17⁵).

Ibid. IV.16: 'There are, as it were, different forms of the Word, as He appears to each of those led to know Him, corresponding to their condition—the beginners, those slightly or considerably advanced, and those approaching or already in possession of virtue.'

Ibid. 77: 'His body changed in accordance with the capacity of those who saw it, and because of this its appearances could be beneficial and fitting to the needs of each viewer (so that at one time it might be said "He had no form nor beauty", and at another He might appear to the chosen three transfigured in glory). . . . This doctrine has a deeper meaning, since it proclaims that the different forms of Jesus are to be referred to the nature of the divine Word, which did not appear in the same way to the crowds as to those able to follow Him to the "high mountain". . . . To those who are still at the foot and not yet prepared to ascend, the Word "has no form nor

---

[43] Cf. *Hom. Josh.* III.5 (below, pp. *129f*).

beauty". His "form" to such people is dishonoured and defi-
cient in comparison with the words achieved by men . . . ;
. . . the teachings of philosophers . . . appear far more beautiful
than the Word of God as He is preached to the crowds. [Origen
compares 1 Cor 1²¹ "the foolishness of preaching".] . . . But
to those who by following Him have received power to go
with Him even as He climbs the high mountain, He has a
more divine form.'

Comm. Ser. Mt. 100 on 26⁴⁸ᶠᶠ: (Why did they have to be
shown which was He? Cf. 26⁵⁵! Origen refers to a tradition[44]
that) 'not only did He possess two forms, one in which He was
seen by all, another into which He was transformed before His
disciples on the mountain—but that He used to appear to every
individual in a form corresponding to his worth. . . . Nor do
I think this tradition incredible, either as regards the bodily
appearances of Jesus Himself, that He should make His appearance in different forms to men, or as regards the actual nature
of the Word, which does not make its appearances to everyone in the same way. [The suggestion is in this case that the
crowd which came with Judas was not familiar with the]
transformations . . . which marked His appearances to His
disciples.'

Princ. IV.4.2: 'Christ becomes present in each individual to
the degree that his merits have allowed.'

Hom. Num. IX.9 on c. 17 (the budding of Aaron's rod):
'Although Jesus is one in essence, He nevertheless takes different forms in the lives of the individuals in whom He works,
according to their needs. To him who is . . . apt to be slug-
gish . . . Christ becomes, in the interests of discipline, a "rod".
. . . Within the righteous man . . . Christ is said to "rise"
[from Num 17⁸, lit. "rose into blossoms"] . . . and He "rises"
until the man bears the "fruits of the Spirit" (etc., Gal 5²²).'

Hom. Jer. VIII.2 (continuation of extract above, p. *109*—
Jesus Christ is God's wisdom, power, righteousness, everything
that may be predicated of God): 'The underlying essence of
[Christ] is one, but in respect of His "aspects" the several
names apply to differences. Your conception of Christ is not

---

[44] See Chadwick (*Celsus*, p. 390, note 1), who gives other references and suggests
(from *Acts of John 93*—James, *Apocryphal New Testament*, p. 252) a Gnostic origin
for the idea.

the same when you think of Him as wisdom as when you think of Him as righteousness. In the former case you seize on His knowledge of divine things: in the latter, His power of dispensing to every man according to his desert. To think of Him as sanctification seizes on His ability to make holy those who have faith and devote themselves to God. Thus too you will think of Him as "understanding", since He is knowledge of good and evil and what is neither.'

Frag. Hom. Lk. XV (Transfiguration): 'The Word appears in different forms in accordance with each man's capacity. For some He has no form nor beauty; for others He is blooming with beauty. By those who are [still] "ascending" through lofty works and thus making for the "high mountain" of wisdom, He is conceived in His simpler form and known in carnal terms. But by the perfect He is conceived in His divinity, and their knowledge enables them to see Him in the form of God.'

Comm. Jn. I.20 (22): 'God is wholly one and self-consistent, but our Saviour (since God "set Him forth" as a "propitiation" and a "firstfruit of every creature"—Rom 3²⁵, Jas 1¹⁸) to meet many needs becomes many things—indeed I might say becomes everything that every creature capable of being liberated needs of Him. Because of this He becomes the light of men when they, darkened by evil, seek that light which shines in darkness and is not comprehended by it; He would never have become the light of men if men had not come to be in darkness. The same idea is suggested by His being the "firstborn from the dead" (Col 1¹⁸); for if we may suppose that the woman had not been led astray and Adam had not sinned, but man born for indestructibility had really secured it, He would not have descended to the "dust of death" (Ps 22¹⁵) and there being no sin He would not have died that death which sin compelled,[45] because of His love for man (φιλανθρωπία). . . . We must ask too whether He would have become a "shepherd", if man had not become "ranked with the unthinking cattle and likened to them" (Ps 48¹³, LXX). For if God saves men and cattle, He saves the latter by graciously granting (χαρισάμενος) a shepherd to those who cannot cope with the King. We must examine, putting together the titles of the Son, just which of them He took in addition—

[45] Reading ῇ with Preuschen.

which would not have grown to so great a number had the saints remained in that blessedness in which they began. He might, for example, have still been "Wisdom" alone—or perhaps "Word" and "Life"—and "Truth" in any case: but assuredly not the other forms He took in addition because of us. Happy indeed are they who needing the Son of God have yet become such as no longer to need Him as a doctor who heals the sick or as a shepherd or as redemption, but as Wisdom, Word, Righteousness, or one of the other titles that He takes for those whose spiritual maturity fits them for His noblest gifts.'

(c) THE CROSS

Christ was the true Servant of the Isaianic prophecy, who died to heal the sins of all—Gentile or Jew—by conquering the evil powers at work among us.

Cels. I.54f: 'His passion was prophesied with the reason for it, which was that it was of benefit to men that He should die for them and suffer the stripes to which He was condemned. It was also foretold that the Gentiles would "take notice of Him", although the prophets have not lived among them. It was also said that He should be seen in a "form dishonourable" in men's eyes. [Origen then quotes Isaiah 52^{13}-53^8 and insists on the direct identification of the Servant with Jesus Christ, as against any reference to Israel. For example, "with His stripes we are healed"—] are clearly words spoken by those who had been in sin and were healed by the sufferings of the Saviour, whether Jews or Gentiles; the prophet foresaw this and put these words in their mouths by the inspiration of the Holy Spirit. . . . Who is this if not Jesus Christ, by whose stripes we who believe in Him were healed, when He "put off the principalities and powers" among us, and made a show of them "openly" upon the Cross?' (Col 2^{15}.)

The death of Christ was in accord with God's purpose and of Christ's own choice—'for the sake of religion'.

Cels. II.10: 'Celsus says "He was caught": I would reply that if to be caught means that it was against His will, Jesus was not caught; for when the moment was come He did not prevent Himself from falling into the hands of men, as the "lamb of God" that He might "take away the sin of the world".'

Ibid. 11: 'He willingly gave Himself up for us all. It follows that His "arrest" was with His own consent, thus teaching us to endure such things for the sake of religion without protest.'

Ibid. 34: 'He who willingly died for the sake of religion'; 'He who willingly suffered these things for men.'

Comm. Ser. Mt. 100 on $26^{48\mathrm{ff}}$: 'If He had not wished to be captured, He never would have been; it was of His own will that He offered Himself to the hands of sinners.'

Ibid. 102 on 26⁵³: (Jesus says this) 'with a view to teaching us that it was of His own will that He offered Himself for us all.'

Sel. Gen. 22⁶: 'The Lord carried His own cross on His shoulders and suffered without the gate, compelled to suffer by no human power but of His own will and by the wish of God the Father.'

Hom. Gen. VIII.6 on 22⁸: 'For the Lord Himself provided Himself with a lamb in Christ—since "wisdom herself has built herself a home" (Prov 9¹) and "He humbled Himself even unto death". Every single thing you read about Christ you will find was done not because He was forced to do it but of His own choice.'

The death of Christ witnesses to the boundless love of both Father and Son for us while we were yet sinners and unbelievers.

Comm. Rom. IV.10 on 5⁶ᶠ: 'For we were "ungodly" before we were converted to God, and Christ assuredly underwent death for us before we believed: this . . . He would not have done unless He had possessed . . . boundless love for us, and this is true both of our Lord Jesus Christ Himself in dying for the ungodly, and of God the Father in giving His only-begotten Son for the redemption of the ungodly.'

The death of Christ gives the perfect example to man of Christian dying 'for the sake of religion'.

Cels. II.16: 'It is in no way unreasonable that the one who was to be the living model for mankind of how they should live, should have undertaken to exemplify how they should die for the sake of religion.'
(Cf. ibid. VII.17 below, p. *126* (init.).)

But underlying this historical, exemplary significance are two invisible, symbolic meanings:

(1) *By His death Christ conquered, in principle, the evil powers which held mankind in sway. His death was a ransom, paid to the devil, through which forgiveness of sin becomes possible, and hence sin and death will gradually lose their grip on mankind.*

Comm. 1 Cor., § 6 (*JTS,* IX.235): 'There are many traditional stories in the pagan world of one man's self-offering on behalf of the people putting a stop to great pestilences, floods or draughts. Is it then incredible that when the whole world was diseased and led astray, . . . One should die to destroy the pestilence of ignorance, darkness and destruction? But who could undertake such a task? No prophet, apostle or other such righteous man. It called for God's own Power to descend from heaven and undertake this death "on behalf of all" (2 Cor 5¹⁵)—and that, as it were, a public example should be made, that this death should stand as a trophy of victory over the devil. For when pagans lead their enemies in triumphal processions they put up trophies of victory over them in the form of a cross; and in this way the Cross of Christ is a trophy of victory over Satan. Hence Paul can say, "May I never boast save in the Cross" (Gal 6¹⁴), for he knew what that Cross has power to achieve—my liberation from evil, won by His dying to save me from death.'

Comm. Eph., § 4 on 1⁷ (*JTS*, III.238): ' "Redemption" or "being set free" applies to those who are imprisoned by and under the power of their enemies. We have fallen under the under the power of our enemies—namely, the "ruler of this age" and his subordinate evil powers; hence we required redemption, through the One who buys us back from our state of alienation from Him. Hence our Saviour gave His own blood as a "ransom" for us. . . . "Forgiveness of sins" follows redemption, and is indeed impossible before a man has been redeemed. First we must be redeemed from the power of the one who has taken us prisoner and holds us in his sway: freed from him—beyond the reach of his hands, so to speak—we may thus be able profitably to receive the forgiveness of sins, and healed from the wounds of sin to do the works of piety and the other virtues.'

Hom. Josh. VIII.3 on 8²⁹, where LXX reads 'he hanged the king of Gai on a *double* tree (ἐπὶ ξύλου διδύμου)': 'The cross of our Lord Jesus Christ was "double" . . . that is, it stands on two footings . . . ; on the visible plane the Son of God was crucified in the flesh, but invisibly there was nailed on that cross the "devil" and his "principalities and powers" [Col 2¹⁴ᶠ, quoted in full]. . . . Hence the cross of the Lord has two meanings: the first is given by the apostle Peter—Christ crucified "left us an example" (1 Pet 2²¹); and this second shows the cross as a trophy of victory over the devil "on which he was crucified and vanquished". [Origen quotes Galatians 6[14], adding] here too the apostle gives a double meaning to the cross; for he says two opposites have been crucified—himself (made holy), and the world of sins—on the analogy, doubtless, that we gave above, of Christ and the devil. For we are then "crucified to the world" when "the prince of this world cometh and finds nothing in us" (Jn 14[30]); and "the world is crucified to us" when we reject the evil promptings of sin.'

Ibid. 4: '(My more attentive listeners may object that, according to this allegorical reading of the Joshua story, the devil is destroyed;) how is it then that we still see the devil and the adverse powers to be such a threat to the servants of God that even the apostle Peter warns us impressively. . . . "Your adversary the devil prowls around like a roaring lion, seeking someone to devour" (5[8])?' [Origen's answer]: 'There are two advents of Christ: the first—in humility—is fulfilled; the second—in glory—is yet hoped for (Tit 2[13]). The first, in the flesh, is called in the holy Scriptures by the mystical name of His "shadow", as Jeremiah says . . . "the breath of our countenance, Christ the Lord: He of whom we said, Under His shadow shall we live among the nations" (Lam 4[20]); and also Gabriel . . . "the power of the Most High shall over-shadow thee" (Lk 1[35]). From this we understand how very many things are foreshadowed by this first advent of His, which will be fulfilled and perfected in His second. So the apostle Paul . . . "He has raised us up with Him, and made us sit with Him in the heavenly places" (Eph 2[6]): but we no-where see believers as yet, either "raised up" or "sitting in the heavenly places". These things are at the present foreshadowed through faith, that is, our minds are lifted in hope from earthly and dead works to the eternal things of the heavens, a state of things that will be fulfilled in reality at His second advent. . . . So then we must understand this matter of the devil; he is conquered, he is crucified—but only for those who are crucified with Christ. He will be crucified for all believers and equally for all mankind when that saying is fulfilled—"for as in Adam all die, even so in Christ shall all be made alive" (1 Cor 15[22]).'

Ibid. 6: '. . . what profit is it to me to know that the king of Gai was hanged on a double tree? (None at all.) But if I know that there is a double significance in the cross, on which both Christ is suspended in the flesh and the devil with his army is triumphed over, my soul will be built up through understanding the sacramental meaning (of the story of the king of Gai)'.

Comm. Mt. XVI.8 on 20[25-8]: 'But to whom did He give His soul as a ransom for many? Surely not to God. Could it be then to the evil one? For he had us in his power, until the ransom for us should be given to him—even the soul of Jesus, since the evil one had been deceived and led to suppose that he could master that soul, and he did not see that to hold Him was a trial of strength greater than he was equal to. Therefore also death, which thought to have prevailed against Him, no longer prevails against the One who has become free among the dead and stronger than the power of death, and so much the stronger that all who so wish, of those who are mastered by death, may also follow Him, death no longer prevailing aught against them. For everyone who is with Jesus is beyond the power of death. [Origen quotes 1 Pet 1[18f], 1 Cor 7[23], and proceeds]: We were redeemed, then, by the precious blood of Jesus, and there was given for us as a ransom the soul of the Son of God.'

Hom. Ex. VI.9:[46] 'We belong to . . . God, in that we were created by Him; but we have become slaves of the devil, in that we have been "sold" for our iniquities (Isa 50[1]). But Christ came and "bought us back" (Gal 3[13]), when we were the slaves of that lord to whom we sold ourselves by our sins. And thus Christ can be said to have "taken back", as it were, "His own", in the sense that He had created them; but to have "acquired",[47] as it were, "another's", in the sense that they had, by their sin, sought another lord over them.

'But [it will be said] it may quite well be true to say that Christ "bought us back", in that He paid His blood as the price for us. But in that case what price had the devil paid to buy us? . . . Well, murder is the devil's currency. . . . You have committed murder: you have, then, received the devil's

---

[46] This passage is directed against the Marcionite view that we were not originally Christ's: He 'bought' what was not His own, therefore our creation cannot have been by Him.
[47] Exodus 15[16], Latin version, '*acquisisse*' (A.V. 'purchased').

money. Adultery is the devil's currency. . . . You have committed adultery: you have received coinage from the devil. Robbery, false witness, rapacity, violence—all these are the devil's riches and his . . . treasure; for such is the money that comes from his mint. It is, then, with this kind of money that he buys his victims, and makes his slaves all those who have taken the smallest coin from such a treasury.'

Cels. VII.17: 'His death not only stands as an example of the way to die for religion, but marks a beginning and an advance in the overthrow of the evil one, the devil, who held the world under his sway. (Cf. Heb 2^{14f}, 1 Jn 5^{19}, Rev 12^9.) Signs of his defeat are that people in many places who through the advent of Jesus have escaped the demons that possessed them, and who, because of their liberation from enslavement to them, devote themselves to God, and to piety toward Him which grows daily in purity as fast as their capacities allow.'

Comm. Rom. (Gk), § 30 on Phil 2^8 (*JTS*, XIII.265); 'It is as if, for example, a free man gave himself up as a slave to the enemy general, with the purpose of getting close enough to him to liberate, by his own contrived servitude (οἰκονομικῇ δουλείᾳ) his fellow-countrymen from the danger of falling into the general's power—that is, by the strategic killing of the general and the enemy force he commanded. . . . It was in this way that Christ gave Himself up to servitude (sc. to death), with the purpose that none of those who give themselves to discipleship of His word should become a slave of death.'

(2) *Man, by continually dying with Christ, is converted from sin and set on the way to ethical perfection.*

Cels. II.69: 'The recorded events in the life of Jesus do not reveal the full truth of their meaning to a mere reader of the text as a historical narrative; for each incident has clearly in addition a symbolic significance to the more intelligent readers. Thus does His crucifixion contain the truths indicated in the words "I am crucified with Christ" (Gal 2^{20}) and "God forbid that I should boast save in the cross of my Lord Jesus Christ, by whom the world is crucified unto me and I to the world" (ibid. 6^{14}). His death was necessary because "in that He died He died unto sin once" and because the righteous man says that he is "being conformed to His death", and that "if we die with Him, we shall also live with Him" (Rom 6[10], Phil 3[10], 2 Tim 2[11]). So also His burial applies to those who are conformed to His death, crucified and dying with Him, as Paul also says, "For we have been buried with Him through baptism", and we have risen with Him (Rom 6[4]).'

Comm. Jn. VI.55: '. . . the lamb of God, sacrificed that He may take away the sin not of a few but of the whole world on behalf of which He suffered.' [Quotes 1 Jn 2[18-2] ('if any man sin, we have an advocate . . . for the whole world'); 1 Tim 4[10] ('the Saviour of all men, especially of them that believe'); Col 2[14f] ('having blotted out the bond . . .'), adding after the words, 'He hath taken it out of the way', the comment] 'that not even the traces (footprints) of expunged sins should be found.[48] And we are taught to take courage in the tribulations of this world, finding the cause for encouragement to be this—that the world has been overcome and visibly subjected to its conqueror.'

Ibid. 58: 'The sin of all, however, is not taken away by the Lamb without suffering or affliction for the sinners before its removal. For thorns have been not only scattered but deeply rooted[49] "in the hands" of every man who has become "drunk" with evil and lost the power to become sober [and Origen quotes Proverbs 26[9] from which the metaphor is taken]. I need not describe the havoc they will work in a man who has admitted such growth into the substance of His soul. A man who has given evil such a hold on the depths of his soul that he has become "thistle-bearing soil" (cf. Gen 3[18]) must be cut in pieces by the living and active Word of God, sharper than any two-edged sword and more consuming than any fire (Heb 4[12], Ecclus 48[1]). Such a soul will require to be visited by the fire which searches out the thorns (cf. Ex 22[6]) and which, by its own divinity, fastens on them but does not go on to consume the threshing-floors or the crops in the fields.'

Comm. Rom. VI.1 on 6[12]: 'Unless . . . it was in our own power that sin should not reign in us, he would assuredly not have given this precept. How then is it possible that sin

---

[48] Cf. Charles Wesley: 'He breaks the power of cancelled sin', meaning (as Origen) not merely 'He breaks the power of sin, i.e. cancels it', but 'He destroys even the lingering after-effects of the sin which He has already in principle overcome'.

[49] Reading ἐνσπαρεῖσαι and ῥιζωθεῖσαι with Preuschen.

should not reign in our flesh? If we obey the words "mortify your members . . ." (Col 3⁵), and if we "continually" bear around "the death of Christ in our own body" (2 Cor 10⁴). . . . For such is the power of the cross of Christ, that if it is placed before our eyes and faithfully held in our mind, so that the eye of the mind gazes fixedly at the very death of Christ, no concupiscence . . . , evil passion, frenzy, or envy can gain the mastery. . . .'

Ibid. IV.12: 'Christ slew the enmity in His own flesh, when by undergoing death He gave an example to mankind of fighting against sin even unto death, and thus at length by resolving the enmity in His own flesh reconciled by His blood mankind to God.'

Cels. II.44: 'The recorded sufferings of Jesus have not the slightest thing in common with those of men who have come to a bad end, e.g. through sorcery (as Celsus suggests). . . . For none could pretend that it is the work of sorcerers to convert souls from the many sins among mankind and from the flood of evil.'

Christ, as both priest and victim—the sinless offering for sinners—reconciled man to God by His blood.

Cels. I.69: 'God delivered Him up, who knew no sin (2 Cor 5²¹) as a pure offering for all sinners.'

Hom. Lev. IX.10: 'Christ . . . the true High Priest, who propitiated God to you by His blood and reconciled you to the Father.'

Comm. Ser. Mt. 88 on 26³³⁻⁵: '(Just as Peter spoke on the mount of transfiguration "not knowing what he said") so too here, . . . when he said "even if I should die with you, I will not deny you". For no man could die with Jesus the death for us all, that we may live, because all had been in sin and all had need of another to die for them, not they for others.'

Comm. Rom. III.8 on 3²⁵: 'Because He is a sacrificial victim, He becomes, by the pouring out of His blood, a propitiation in that He gives remission of past sins. Such propitiation, however, comes to each believer by the path of faith. . . . It is certain that propitiation was fulfilled by the pouring-out of the sacred blood' [and quotes Heb 9²²].

Hom. Gen. VIII.1: 'Abraham knew that he prefigured the image of the truth that was to come: he knew that from his seed would be born Christ, who would be offered as the truer sacrificial victim [sc. than Isaac] for the whole world and would rise from the dead.'

Ibid. 6: 'The fact that Isaac "carried wood for the burnt offering" prefigured the bearing by Christ of His own cross (Jn 19¹⁷). Now carrying the wood for the burnt-offering is the duty of the priest. Christ is therefore both victim and priest.'

Hom. Lev. III.1: '(Christ is both priest and victim). Christ indeed "did no sin", but He was "made sin on our behalf", when He who was "in the form of God" deigns to be "in the form of a servant", when He who is immortal dies, and He who is impassible suffers, and He who is invisible is seen; and since death and every other weakness of the flesh is imposed on us all because of our sinful state, He Himself also, who "was made in the likeness of man and found in fashion as a man", "offered as a sacrifice to God" a "calf without blemish" —that is, His immaculate flesh—unquestionably in return for the sin which He took over from us in "bearing our sins" (1 Pet 2²²ᶠᶠ, 2 Cor 5²¹, Phil 2⁷, Lev 4³, Eph 5²).'

The death of Christ brings life and salvation to believers, but punishment and death to unbelievers.

Hom. Lev. III.1: 'The passion of Christ brings life to believers . . . and death . . . to unbelievers. For although salvation and justification come to the Gentiles through His cross, to the Jews come death and condemnation' [Origen compares Lk 2³⁴].

Hom. Josh. III.5: '(The harlot [Josh 2¹⁸]) placed a scarlet cord in position in her house: this would ensure her safety when the town was destroyed. . . . scarlet, that is the colour of blood; for she knew that none can be saved but by the blood of Christ. . . . Even if someone of that people wishes to be saved, he must come to this house to find safety . . . the house, that is, . . . in which the blood of Christ is set for a sign of redemption. For among those who said "His blood be upon us and our children" (Mt 27²⁵), the blood of Christ stands for a condemnation. For Jesus was "set for the falling and rising

K

of many" (Lk 2³⁴), and hence for those who deny His "sign" His blood works punishment, for those who believe, salvation. . . . Outside this house (i.e. the Church) none is saved: to leave it makes a man responsible for his own death. Here is the sign of blood, because here too is the purification that the blood supplies. As for the sign's hanging "in the window", this, I think, draws our attention to the fact that a window affords light to a house, but that we only receive the amount of light that suffices for the sight of our eyes—not light in its pure state. Now the incarnation of the Saviour did not bring to us an unmixed sight of the deity in its fullness, but enabled us to see, through His incarnation, the light of the deity as it were through a window:[50] and that is, I believe, why the sign of safety (in Josh 2) was given through the window. By that sign let all those find salvation who are found in the house of her who was once a "harlot", after their cleansing in water and the Holy Spirit and in the blood of our Lord and Saviour Jesus Christ.'

The death of Christ was for the whole world; salvation, however, can only be for believers—that is, the Church; and the final universal reconciliation to God awaits the long, slow victory of Christ over man's enemies, the last of which is death. The cross thus initiates the birth and growth of an ultimately world-wide Christian community.

Cels. II.16: 'His death for men was of benefit to the whole world.'

Ibid. 44: 'Jesus, who was dying for the common good of mankind.'

Hom. Ex. XI.4 on Isaiah 65² [which Origen puts in the mouth of Jesus (cf. Rom 10²¹)]: 'when, lifted up upon the cross He was about the embrace with His arms the whole world.'

Hom. Josh. VI.4: '. . . through the blood of Christ this whole Church is saved.'

Comm. Rom. VII.9 on 8³²: 'The Father gave up His own Son not only for the saints . . . for the great ones, but for the least also, and for every single member of the Church. . . . God then, who gave us worth through pouring out the precious blood of His Son for us. . . .'

Comm. Mt. XVI.8 on 20²⁵ᶠᶠ (the 'ransom for many'): 'He

---

[50] Cf. above, p. *117*.

came to dwell with the human race that He might minister to us and go so far in His ministering unto our salvation as to "give His soul a ransom for many", i.e. for those who came to believe on Him. If we may suppose that all had believed on Him, He would have given His soul a ransom for all.'

Sel. Ps. 30⁹ ('What profit is there in my blood, when I go down to destruction?' LXX): 'These are the words of the Saviour, when He sees us acting utterly unworthily of the precious blood by which we were redeemed. For when some of those for whom He died remain in their sin and blasphemy, the "descent" of the Saviour "to destruction" and the out-pouring of His blood seem indeed to have been in vain.'

Comm. Jn. VI.57 (above, pp. *53*f) (it was the whole world—sinners as well as saints—that Christ reconciled to God through His death: the "enemies" were overcome not "in one sweep" but one by one—up to the last enemy, death)' (Cf. ibid. 58 [above, p. *127*].)

Cels. VIII.43 (above, pp. *82*f) (especially 'His punishment did not destroy God's messages [viz. His covenants, promises, Eph 2¹²] but . . . enabled them to be known'; the reference to John 12²⁴—the death of Jesus 'bore much fruit' [viz. the birth and growth of the world-wide Christian community]; and the citation of Romans 8³² [and John 1²⁹]).

Hom. Ex. I.4 on 1⁶f [which Origen interprets allegorically—Joseph = Jesus; and the "multiplying" of Israel, which is only subsequent to the death of Joseph, is paralleled by the growth of the Christian community being only subsequent to the death of Jesus (cf. Jn 12²⁴)].

Ibid. XI.2 on 17³ff [the 'rock', unless it is struck, gives no water. Allegorically the rock is Christ, who being 'smitten' and crucified 'let forth the fountains of the New Covenant'. Cf. 'I will smite the shepherd and the sheep will be scattered'. But for this 'smiting' we should all still be suffering 'thirst for hearing the word of the Lord' (Amos 8¹¹)].

(D) THE RESURRECTION

The Resurrection of Christ successfully exemplified to the disciples, and through them to the world, the eternal life which awaits patience in the sufferings of this life.

> *Cels.* II.77: 'He once rose from the dead and so utterly convinced His disciples of the truth of His resurrection that they show to all men through their sufferings that their gaze is fixed on the life eternal and the resurrection which has been exemplified to them in word and deed, and so can mock at all the hardships of this life.'

The Risen Christ is the beginning, the firstborn, the head of the new, regenerate creation, which not only reaches forward to us but back to Adam.

> *Hom. Num.* III.4 on 3[12ff] (allegorized as foreshadowing Col 1[18]). 'With a view to giving us the blessings of the firstborn, He Himself becomes "firstborn from the dead", that He Himself might have the primacy in everything, and may take up us, who believe in His resurrection, for His firstfruits. . . . If, indeed, we keep firm hold on the grace of these blessings to the end, aided by the mercy of our Lord Jesus Christ Himself [etc.]. . . .'
>
> *Comm. Jn. Frag.* 140 on Colossians 1[18]: 'Just as through having Adam as the first example (ἀρχή), the head, of our natural mode of birth, we are all said to have in this respect one body, even so do we register Christ as our head through the divine regeneration, which has become a pattern for us, of His death and resurrection.' [Preuschen's text.]
>
> *Comm. Ser. Mt.* 126 (above, p. *37*) (Christ's resurrection brought resurrection not only to us—the sons of Adam—but to Adam himself).

The Risen Christ leads His followers into ever deeper understanding of divine truth.

> *Cels.* V.58: 'He is not with the dead but "lives", and "goes before" (Mt 28[7]) those who are willing to follow Him, that He may show the truths that follow those He showed before,

to those who could not cope at the time of their initiation with the deeper truths.'

The Risen Christ cares for and draws to God those everywhere who have faith in the Resurrection, and whose faith issues in the ethical fruits of a new life in Him.

Cels. V.57: 'This too may be said of the Resurrection of Jesus from the dead, that it is no surprise if one or two angels were seen at the time announcing that He had risen and was providentially caring for such as to their own blessing believed in the Resurrection. It does not appear unreasonable to me that such as believe He is risen and who show considerable fruits of their belief in a strengthened life, changed from immersion in the flood of evil, should not be without ministering angels who help their turning toward God.'

Ibid. VII.35 (Celsus supposes the 'risen' Jesus to have been a phantom): 'How could a phantom which in his words— "crept stealthily" on those who saw it to deceive them, even after the moment of vision have had such a great effect on them as to convert so many souls and bring home to them the conviction that they ought to do everything with a view to satisfying God, because they will be judged by Him? And how could a so-called "phantom" drive out demons and bring about all the other tremendous results? Nor has He been limited to one place like the anthropomorphic gods of Celsus, but ranges the world, gathering and attracting by His divinity any whom He finds giving themselves to the search for the good life.'

Comm. Rom. IV.7 on 4²³⁻⁵: '(Why does Paul give us the object of our faith Him who raised Christ from the dead rather than e.g. Him who created heaven and earth? Because the former redounds far more to the praise of God than the latter). For the latter meant the making of what did not exist, the former the redeeming of what had perished. . . . the latter . . . was achieved by a mere fiat, the former by suffering. Now the pattern and image of this . . . mystery had come aforetime in the faith of Abraham. For he had believed, when he was ordered to sacrifice his only son, that God was able to raise him even from the dead; he had also believed that the transaction then set afoot did not only apply to Isaac, but that it was sacramental, and that its full meaning was reserved for that descendant of his who is Christ. It was then . . . with joy that he offered his only son, because he saw therein not the death of his issue, but the restoration of the world, the renewal of the whole creation, re-established through the resurrection of the Lord; and it was for this reason that the Lord said of him, "Your father Abraham rejoiced to see my day . . ." (Jn 8[56]).

'(Why does Paul when speaking of our faith make special mention of Christ's Resurrection, when there are so many other titles to His name—Wisdom, Virtue, the Word, Truth, Life? [Origen quotes Eph 2[6] and proceeds]): 'If you believe that Christ has risen from the dead, you must believe also that you yourselves have likewise risen with Him; and if you believe that He is seated at the right hand of the Father in heaven, you must believe also that you yourselves are situated no longer in the earthly but the heavenly scene; and if you believe yourselves dead with Christ, you must believe that you will also live with Him; and if you believe that Christ is dead to sin and lives to God, you too must be dead to sin and alive to God (Rom 6[5ff]). [Origen quotes Col 3[1-2].] This is because the man who (sets his mind on things above) shows his belief in Him who raised up Jesus . . . from the dead, and for this man faith is truly counted for righteousness. . . . In the same way . . . believers in Christ who do not "put off the old man with his unrighteous practices" (Col 3[9]) cannot have their faith counted for righteousness . . . (Hence Rom 4[25]) showing that (our sins) for which Christ was betrayed ought to be abhorred and cast off by us also. . . . For if we retain any further kinship with sin . . . , we show that we think the death of Christ Jesus of no account, because we embrace . . . the things that He subdued and conquered.

'The apostle, putting all this together, called it the "clothing of the old man"—the very body, as it were, of sin (Col 3[9f]), which he urges those to cast off who believe in Him who raised . . . Jesus from the dead; that casting off the clothing of unrighteousness they may put on our Lord Jesus, who is the true clothing of righteousness—that their lives may be worthy of their belief, and thus their faith may count for righteousness. [Again quotes Rom 4[25].] And if we have risen with Christ, who is righteousness, and we walk in newness of life, and live according to righteousness, Christ has risen for us, that we might be justified. . . . Christ, then, justifies only those who have undertaken a new life, on the model of His Resurrection, and cast off the old clothing of . . . unrighteousness as that which leads to death.'

(E) THE CONTINUING WORK OF CHRIST

The gifts of Christ to us are both intellectual and moral.

(1) *On the one hand He leads us to God, granting us wisdom, know-ledge, enlightenment, and imparting belief in that God whom He and He alone reveals.*

> *Princ.* II.9.4 [Origen is about to discuss the difficult question: how is the variety and diversity of the world consistent with the principle of 'righteousness' in accordance with which it must have been created, if it was created through Christ who *is* Righteousness (1 Cor 1³⁰)]: '(This question) is, I am sure, impossible to answer for human thought and speech, unless in humble supplication we beseech the Word Himself, who is "Wisdom and Righteousness" . . . that He may through His grace pour Himself into our minds, and deign to throw light on what is dark, to open what is shut, to reveal what is secret —which however He will only do if we are found seeking, ask-ing, knocking so worthily as to deserve to receive when we seek, to find when we ask, or for Him to order the door to be opened when we knock (1 Cor 4⁵, Mt 7⁷ᶠ).'
>
> *Cels.* II.71: 'Jesus taught us who it was that sent Him. [Origen quotes Mt 11²⁷, Jn 1¹⁸.] He revealed to His genuine disciples the true doctrine of God. . . .'
>
> *Cels.* III.1 (and passim): 'We, who through Christ believe in God.'
>
> Ibid. 34: 'Jesus, who directed our minds away from all ob-jects of sense—and led us to honour the God of the universe with an upright life and with prayers.'
>
> Ibid. 61: 'Within the divinity of the Word is power not only to help and cure those who are sick, . . . but to show to the pure in body and mind "the revelation of the mystery . . ." [Rom 16²⁵ᶠ, to which Origen adds 'both by the prophetic scrip-tures and by the appearing of our Lord Jesus Christ' (from 2 Tim 1¹⁰)]. This "appearing" shines on each one of the perfect and enlightens their mind to an unerring knowledge of the truth.'
>
> Ibid. 62: 'The divine Word was sent as a doctor to sinners, but as a teacher of divine mysteries to the already pure and sinless.'

Cels. V.I: [Origen, beginning another book of his reply to Celsus, prays that] 'God may grant that we enter on our task not with our own mind and speech, bare and empty as they are of divine inspiration, . . . but that we may receive the mind of Christ from His Father who alone gives it, and be helped to share in the Word of God'.

Ibid. 51: 'We alone demonstrate that the truth, pure and unmixed with error, lies in the teaching of Jesus Christ.'

Ibid. VI.65: 'When (Celsus) says that God is not attainable by reason, I draw a distinction. If he means the reason within us . . . (we would agree). But if, remembering that "in the beginning was the Word, and the Word was with God, and the Word was God", we demonstrate that God is attainable by *this* Word (or Reason), and comprehended not only by Him but by "any man to whom He reveals the Father" (Mt 11²⁷), we shall show that Celsus is wrong.'

Ibid. 66: (Celsus: If anyone leads people out of darkness into a bright light, they cannot endure the radiance, hence God cannot be known.)[51] 'We shall reply that those who really sit ensconced in darkness are all those who gaze on the evil works of painters and sculptors and image-makers, be-cause they have no wish to look up and ascend in their mind from the world of visible and sensible objects to the Creator of the universe, who is Light. But everyone who has followed the rays of the Word is in light, because the Word has shown him how ignorant and impious and ill-informed in divine things it was to worship these things instead of God, and has led the mind of the man who wishes to be saved to the uncreated God of the universe.' [Quotes Mt 4¹⁶, Isa 9², adding that the 'light' which has arisen is 'the God Jesus'.]

Ibid. 67: 'With the light of the Word we banish the dark-ness of impious doctrines. . . . Because the Word has opened the eyes of our soul, we see the difference between light and darkness, and choose in every way to stand in the light.'

Ibid. 68: 'Hence if Celsus asks us how we think we can come to know God and be saved by Him, we reply that the Word of God is sufficient, coming to those who seek Him or accept Him when He appears, to make known and reveal the Father,

---

[51] This is of course the old myth of Plato's 'prisoners in the cave'—the soul that passes from ignorance to knowledge is blinded and stupefied by the radiance.

who before His coming was invisible. And who but the divine Word can save and lead the soul of man to the God of the universe? He was "in the beginning with God", but because of those who cleave to the flesh and become as flesh He became flesh, that He might be received by those who are not able to look on Him as the Word who was with God and who was God; and being spoken of in physical terms, and being proclaimed as "flesh", He calls to Himself those who are flesh that first He may make them to be formed like the Word who became flesh, and then lead them upward to see Him as He was before He became flesh. Thus helped they may ascend from this physical initiation to confessing, "Even if we have known Christ after the flesh, yet now we know Him so no more" (2 Cor 5[16]).'

Ibid. VIII.4: 'That man has ascended to the God of the universe who, with no distinction, qualification or reserve (ἀσχίστως, ἀδιαιρέτως, ἀμερίστως) worships Him through His Son, the Divine Word and Wisdom seen in Jesus, who alone leads to Him those who try by every means to make themselves at home with God, the creator of all things, through excellence of word, deed and thought.'

Ibid. 59: '(We believe in the) self-revealing, living and manifest God of the universe through the One who with great power scattered the pure word of worship throughout the world.'

Prayer I.1: 'The things that cannot be comprehended by the reason of mortals because they are vast and beyond human range and far above our perishable nature, become by the will of God possible of comprehension by the abundant and immeasurable grace of God poured out on men through Jesus Christ, the minister of boundless grace toward us, and through the co-operation of the Spirit.'

Hom. Gen. XIII.3: 'Christ taught us not to seek God in one place but to know that "in every land sacrifice is offered to my name" (Mal 1[11]). For now is that time when the true worshippers worship the Father neither in Jerusalem nor the mount Garizim, but "in spirit and in truth" (Jn 4[20ff]). God dwells not in a place or in a land but in the heart . . . ; the pure heart is His abode [quotes 2 Cor 6[16]].'

Sel. Ps. 68[24]: 'In the advent of Christ all the "paths" (LXX) of God were seen by those adorned with the word of knowledge.'

Ibid. 119[169] ('Let my prayer come near before Thee, O Lord', LXX): 'We can approach (God) through Jesus Christ, and especially if we know Christ in His capacity of Righteousness, Truth, Wisdom, Resurrection, True Light. For without these we cannot approach God—nor indeed without Peace which is Christ.'

Comm. Song Songs III, pp. 214f: 'Who sees God as Christ sees Him? For He alone "sees" . . . "the Father" (Jn 6[46]), and even if it is said that the "pure in heart shall see God" (Mt 5[8]), it will be beyond question by Christ's revelation. . . . The vision that sees God is not physical but mental and spiritual; and . . . this is why the Saviour was careful to use the right word and say "no man *knoweth* the Father save the Son", not . . . "seeth". Again, to those whom He grants to see God, He gives the "spirit of knowledge" and the "spirit of wisdom", that through the Spirit Himself they may see God (Isa 11[2]). This is why He said . . . "He who hath seen me hath seen the Father" (Jn 14[9]). We . . . shall not be so stupid as to assume that those who saw the physical body of Jesus saw the Father also; otherwise the Scribes, Pharisees . . . Pilate . . . and all the crowd that cried "crucify . . . Him" . . . will have done so. . . . Many there were who looked on Him, but none is said "to have seen" Him unless He has recognized that He is the Word and the Son of God, and that in Him the Father also is at the same time recognized and seen.'

Comm. Mt. XIII.19 on Luke 9[48]: 'Since the Father is inseparable from the Son, the Father too comes to the one who has received the Son.'

Ibid. XVI.11 on 20[29-34] (allegorized—the way = the Scriptures; the blind men are Israel and Judah; their 'blindness' can only be dispersed by Christ): 'Would that we too might perceive our blindness . . . , sit at the "roadside" of Scripture, and hearing that Jesus is passing by, prevail on Him by our prayers to stop, and tell Him of our wish that our eyes should be opened. If our words are inspired by a sincere longing to see what Jesus graciously gives ($\chi\alpha\rho i\zeta\epsilon\tau\alpha\iota$) to see by touching the eyes of the soul, the Saviour will take pity on us, and in His capacity as Power, Word, Wisdom . . . will touch our previously unseeing eyes . . . straightway we shall not only receive our sight but follow Him, and our very recovery of sight will help Him to ensure that we give ourselves exclusively to following the One who made us to see, that by always following Him we may be led by Him to God, and with those eyes to which He has given sight, may see God. . . .'

Hom. Lk. IV. on 1[16]: 'John (the Baptist) "turned many of the sons of Israel to the Lord their God", . . . but our Lord Jesus Christ enlightened everyone to the knowledge of the truth, for that is His work.'

Comm. Jn. I.27 (29): 'Since one cannot be in the Father or with the Father without first ascending to the divinity of the Son, by which one can be led up to the blessedness of the Father, the Saviour is described in Scripture as the "Door".'

Ibid. 34 (39): '. . . as David says (Ps 104[24]), God has made all things in wisdom; but many things are confined to their own share of wisdom, and do not lay hold on the very wisdom itself by which they were created; and only a very few comprehend not only their own share of that wisdom but the wisdom shown in many other things. Now Christ is Wisdom-as-a-whole, and the capacity for wisdom achieved by each of the wise is actually a partaking in Christ. . . .'

Ibid. XIX.6 on 8[19], 'If ye knew me, ye would know my Father also' [Origen notes that the clauses are not reversible, any more than 14[9], 'He that hath seen me hath seen the Father'.] 'It is impossible to see God otherwise than by the Word: and he who sees the Wisdom which God created before the ages for His works (Prov 8[22]) ascends from knowledge of Wisdom to knowledge of its Father, it being impossible without the leading hand of Wisdom to come to know the God of Wisdom (and so with Truth: you understand Truth first, then God— not vice-versa).'

Comm. Rom. II,14 on 3[4] ('Let God be true though every man be a liar', which Origen notes is (in part) from Psalm 116[11], where the Psalmist's point is): 'There are many . . . systems of doctrine among men, and many philosophical inquiries for the truth; but since the Son of God must be the presupposition of all such investigations, those who have sought without first believing have not found. I however (says the Psalmist), because I believed before I sought, have found for this very reason what I was seeking. . . . And when the truth has been discovered I am not exalted in wisdom nor inflated by my own knowledge; rather is my humility the greater because I have recognized . . . that it is the Lord who teaches all knowledge.'

(2) *On the other hand, He grants us righteousness: He leads us from conversion through the progress of ethical growth to sanctification and perfection. Sin He judges and punishes, while at the same time doing battles with the demonic powers which inspire it; and in the end His triumph over evil will be complete.*

Cels. I.43: 'The goodness of Jesus toward men (ἀνδραγάθημα) was not confined to the days of His incarnation; even to this day the power of Jesus is working for the conversion and moral growth of those who believe in God through Him.'

Ibid. 47: 'The divinity [of Jesus Christ] is attested by the great number of Churches consisting of those converted from the flood of evils and dependent on their Creator and referring everything to His pleasure.'

Ibid. 68 (Celsus compares the miracles of Jesus with the works of sorcerers and Egyptian magicians): 'But the truth is that no sorcerer employs his arts to summon the spectators to moral reformation, nor to educate by the fear of God those whom his displays fascinate, nor to try and persuade his audience to live as men who will be judged (δικαιωθησομένους) by God.'

Ibid. II.8: '(Celsus' Jew) says that many others like Jesus have appeared to people willing to be deceived. Let him show us not "many", not even a few, but just one other like Jesus, who by the power within Him brought to mankind a Word and teachings which benefited life and converted from the flood of sins.'

Ibid. 29 (Celsus' Jew called Jesus a 'pest'): 'Neither the Jews nor Celsus nor anyone else could prove by demonstration that it was a "pest" who converted so many men from the flood of evils to live the natural life of self-control and the other virtues.'

Ibid. IV.15 (on Jesus the divine 'doctor of souls').

Ibid. V.12: 'If "a branch cannot bear fruit unless it abides in the vine", it is clear that the disciples of the Word, the spiritual (νοητά) branches of the true vine (the Word), cannot bear the fruits of virtue unless they abide in the true vine, the Christ of God. . . .'

Ibid. VI.45: 'From (Jesus) there flowed to mankind such a flood of conversion, healing, bettering, . . .'.

Ibid. VII.17: '. . . The prophets predicted that a certain "effulgence and image" (Wis 7²⁶) of the divine nature would come to dwell in [our] life along with the holy incarnate soul of Jesus, so that it might spread abroad a doctrine which would place on terms with the God of the universe everyone who received it into his own soul and cultivated it, and which would lead him on to the *summum bonum* if he held in himself the power of the divine Word who was to be in a human body and soul.'

Comm. Song Songs II, pp. 171f on 1¹⁴ ('a cluster of cyprus'): 'When (the Word of God) is made "Wisdom" and "Knowledge" for men, He makes them wise, learned, sturdy in their virtues— not in a moment, but by progress through stages, in accordance with their application, their keenness, their faith. . . . In the same way those for whom He is made the "true vine" (Jn 15¹) are not led to produce ripe, sweet "clusters" in a moment, . . . but first He produces in them just a sweetness of scent in the flower, that their souls, initially attracted by the grace of that fragrance, may later have strength to suffer the bitterness of the tribulations and trials that for the sake of God's Word are wrought on believers . . . (etc.). For only the perfect soul can possess such a pure and chastened sense of smell that it can detect the fragrance of the "nard", the "myrrh", the "cyprus" (Song Songs 1¹²ff) that issues from the Word of God, and so breathe in the grace of the divine scent.'

Ibid. III.175f on 1¹⁶ ('our couch'): 'This "couch", which she refers to as shared by herself and her bridegroom, seems to me to mean the human body in which while the human soul is still a tenant it is deemed worthy of consorting with the Word of God. . . . It is fitting that such a soul should have this common "couch" of the body with the Word, for the power from on High bestows grace on the body also—the gifts of chastity, continence, and other good works.'

Hom. Jer. XIV.10 on 15¹⁰ ('My strength has failed because of those who curse me', LXX), (Origen quotes Jn1⁹): 'Whoever is rational partakes of the "true Light"—and "rational" means man in general. Now . . . in some cases the strength

of the Word (or "reason") grows, in others it declines. If you
see a soul become sinful and at the mercy of its emotions
(ἐμπαθῆ) you will there witness the decline of the strength of
the Word. If you see a soul holy and righteous, you will there
witness the strength of the Word daily bearing fruit, and what
has been said about Jesus (Lk 2^{52}) will be true of these righteous
men. For the "advance" of Jesus "in wisdom, stature, and
favour with God and men" is not confined to His own person;
Jesus "advances . . ." in every man who can himself receive
such an advancement in wisdom, stature and grace.'

Comm. Mt. XII.14 on 16^{13ff} (the Kingdom of Heaven): 'The
truth may be that each virtue is a kingdom of heaven, and that
all together are the kingdom of the heavens. This would mean
that the man who lives by the virtues is already in the kingdom of the heavens, and (for example) that the saying "repent,
for the kingdom of the heavens *is at hand*" (Mt 3^2) has no
temporal reference, but a reference to actions and purpose.
For Christ, who is each and every virtue, has come to dwell
with us and speaks—and therefore the "Kingdom of God" is
"within His disciples" and not "here or there" (Lk 17^{21}).'

Ibid. 24 on 16$^{24-7}$: 'The will to go after Jesus and follow
Him is not a mere matter of ordinary good conduct: a man
has to deny himself. . . . Denying oneself means a decisive
change, a wiping out of one's previous life of sin. . . . (This
does *not* mean denying one's bad self and confirming, confessing one's good self.) If Christ is Righteousness, he who takes
righteousness on himself confesses not himself but Christ. . . .
For this reason let our every thought and idea and our every
word and deed be redolent of denial of self and witness and
confession of and in Christ. It is my conviction that every
action of the perfect man is a witness of Christ Jesus, and every
abstention from sin is that denial of the self that bears one in
the steps of Jesus. Such a man is crucified with Christ, takes
up his cross and follows the One who bore His cross on our
behalf. . . .'

Comm. Jn. Frag. 45 on 3^{29}: 'Rational being, of which the
human soul forms a part, can beget no good things of itself—
even if it can receive them. It is like a woman: it needs another to beget the virtues of action and thought that it proves
able to bring to birth. Hence I call it the bride—of no mean

bridegroom, but of Him alone who can sow the seed of good, none other than Jesus. . . .'

Comm. Rom. VIII.11 on 11^{16} ('If the root is holy, so are the branches') : '(Who is this root?) . . . Some say Abraham, others Seth, others yet another of the fathers. . . . But I know no other "root" that is holy and no other "firstfruits" that are holy except our Lord Jesus Christ. For He is . . . the first-fruits of all . . . (cf. Col 1^{15}). For on Him, as a root, all who are saved are grafted, and from Him as the holy firstfruits all the "lump" of humanity draws its holiness.'

Cels. I.60 (the demons): 'If a more divine power appears, the powers of the demons are destroyed, for they cannot look the light of divinity in the face. (Hence when Jesus was born) . . . the demons lost their power and became weak; their sorcery was exposed and their strength made impotent. This was not only at the hands of the angels who visited the earthly sphere because of the birth of Jesus, but also by the soul of Jesus Himself and the divinity within Him.'

Ibid. 67: 'The whole world of humanity is touched by the work of Jesus, for in it there sojourn the Churches of God with their members converted through Jesus from countless evils; and the name of Jesus still removes mental disorders from men—demons and diseases—and implants a wonderful mild-ness and serenity of character and a love for men and a kind-ness and a gentleness in those who . . . have genuinely accepted the doctrine of God, of Christ, and of the judgement to come.'

Ibid. III.29: 'God, who sent Jesus, brought to nothing the whole plot of the demons and made the Gospel of Jesus to triumph everywhere in the world, that men might be con-verted and set on the right path. . . .'

Ibid. VIII.31ff (above, p. *95*) (for the scope of demonic activity and God's purpose in allowing it).

Hom. Ex. VI.8: 'What do the demons fear? At what do they tremble? Beyond question—the cross of Christ, in which they are "triumphed over . . ." (Col 2^{15}). Fear and trembling, therefore, will fall upon them when they see the sign of the cross fixed in faith upon us. . . .'

Hom. Num. VII.5 on 13^{33} ('And there we saw the giants, and we were in their sight like locusts', LXX): '. . . If you compare the human and demonic species, we are "locusts" and they are "giants"—and this will be true enough if our faith is suspect. . . . But if we follow Jesus and believe His words and are filled with His faith, the demons will be as nothing in our sight.'

Ibid. 6: '. . . For He Himself says to those who follow Him in faith: "Behold, I have given you power . . ." (Lk 10¹⁹). . . . And perhaps this was in His mind when He said . . . "He who believes on Him shall do not only what He has done but even greater works" (Jn 14¹²). For I think it is in truth a "greater" work when a man while still in the flesh, frail and easily falling, overcomes in battle the giants and the legions of the demons, his only weapons being the Gospel of Christ and his own faith in it. Although it is Christ within us who conquers, the victory He gains through us He ranks as greater than the one He gains Himself.'

Hom. Josh. I.6 on 1³ (above, p. *50*) (of the diabolic powers whom we conquer through Christ).

Ibid. 7: 'Scripture does not say that "the land had rest from wars" under Moses, but under Joshua (=Jesus) (Josh 11²³). It is likewise certain that the "territory" of our own lives, the field of our struggles and tribulations, will only have rest from war by the power of the Lord Jesus. For within us are all those tribes of vices which . . . besiege the soul. . . .'

Ibid. XII.2 (above, p. *19*, note 4), 3 (above, pp. *50*f); XIV.1 (above, p. *38*) (on this 'battle of life', amplified in the following four extracts, from the same general context).

Ibid. XIII.1: 'To this day my Lord Jesus Christ wages war against the hostile powers and drives them out of the cities they had occupied—i.e. our souls—and He kills the kings who reigned in our souls, "that sin should no more reign in us" (Rom 6¹²), and that . . . our soul should become a city of God and He should reign in us—and the word should be spoken to us: "Behold, the kingdom of God is within you" (Lk 17²¹).'

Ibid. 4: 'First and foremost . . . the work of God's Word is to lay low the edifices of the devil which he has built in the human soul. For he has raised the towers of pride and the walls of self-glorying within each of us; these has the Word of God overturned and undermined, that we may fitly

L

become, as the apostle says, "God's husbandry, God's building . . ." (1 Cor 3⁹).'

Ibid. XV.4: 'Jesus . . . who destroys the vices within us and
overturns the most vile kingdoms of sin. . . .'

Ibid. 7: 'Our Lord Jesus . . . "captured the whole land"
(Josh 11²³) in the sense that from every land and all nations
the multitude of believers converges on Him. . . . "And the
land had rest from wars" (ibid.). . . . If you look at yourself,
how you came to Jesus and received from Him remission of
sins through the grace of baptism, and how within you "the
flesh wars not against the spirit nor the spirit against the flesh"
(Gal 5¹⁷), then it is true of you that your "land has rest from
wars", if only you "bear about in your body the death of Jesus
Christ" (2 Cor 4¹⁰) in such a way that all struggles within you
cease and you gain the name of "peacemaker" and "son of
God" (Mt 5⁹). But this cannot be until you have fought your
battles and conquered your enemies. Then will be given you
rest. . . .'

Comm. Mt. X.2 on 13³⁷⁻⁹ᴬ: 'The good plants that grow in
the human soul have been sown by the Word of God, who
was in the beginning with God, and are the offspring of the
Kingdom of God. . . . the devil . . . sows the so-called tares,
the evil-working doctrines. . . . In this context the "field" is
the "whole world" (verse 38), not just the Church of God.
For the Son of man sowed His good seed in the whole world,
as did the evil one his tares. . . .'

Cels. V.53: '(The Saviour) announced to men the great de-
sign of the God and Father of the Universe for them—that
those who yield to a life of pure religion ascend to God through
their great actions, and that those who turn away separate
themselves from God and take the road to destruction through
their unbelief in Him.'

Hom. Jer. XI.1-2: 'Who says the words "the whole land has
been made utterly desolate because of me?" (Jer 12¹¹, LXX).
Christ . . . ; for look at the "territory" of your life, how with
the coming of Jesus it was "made desolate"—desolate through
the "mortification of its members upon the earth" (Col 3⁵),
since the land no longer brings forth its own products, and the
works of the flesh, in which the flesh previously abounded, no
longer exist in the life of the righteous man. There is no longer

uncleanness, lasciviousness, idolatry, sorcery, etc. (Gal 5^{19f}).
[Quotes Mt 10^{34}—'I came not to send peace but a sword'.]
In very truth before He came there was no such sword on the
earth, nor did "the flesh lust against the spirit and the spirit
against the flesh" (Gal 5^{17}). But when He came and we were
taught to distinguish between the things of the flesh and
the things of the spirit, this teaching acted like a sword on the
earth and divided the flesh (the "land") from the spirit. The
land has been "made desolate", when we "bear about in
the body the dying of Jesus" (2 Cor 4^{10}), and no longer live
after the flesh but the spirit lives in us, and the purpose of
our sowing is no longer fleshly but spiritual, that our harvest
may not be of the flesh—corruption, but of the spirit—life
eternal (Rom 8^{13}, Gal 6^{8}).'

Among the specific gifts of Jesus Christ are
(1) *adoption into sonship of God.*

Prayer XXII.4 (The true sons of God are the joint-heirs with
Christ who 'believe unto righteousness') : 'Every action, word,
and thought (of such true sons), being conformed unto Himself by the only-begotten Word, imitates the "image of the
invisible God" and comes to be "in the image of the Creator"
(Col 1^{15}, 3^{10}). . . . The saints, then, being an image of an
image (i.e. of the Son), take the impression of sonship. . . .
They become conformed to Him who is "in the body of His
glory" (Phil 3^{21}), being "transformed by the renewing of the
mind" (Rom 12^{2}). If it is such as these who say in all things,
"Our Father . . .", it is clear that "he who commits sin", as
John says in his Catholic epistle, "is of the devil; for the
devil sins from the beginning" (1 Jn 3^{8}). . . . But since "for
this purpose the Son of God was manifested, that He might
destroy the works of the devil" (ibid.), it becomes possible
through the sojourn of the Word of God in our soul for the
works of the devil to be destroyed and the evil seed implanted
in us to be exterminated, and for us to become sons of God.'

Hom. Gen. IX.2: '(Abraham) was to be the father of those
who are "of faith" and who come to their inheritance through
the passion of Christ. . . .'

Hom. Jer. IX.4: 'The devil was formerly our father, before
God became our Father—perhaps indeed the devil still is; . . .

if "everyone that commits sin is born of the devil", we are born of the devil, so to speak, as often as we sin. Such perpetual birth from the devil is as wretched as perpetual birth from God is blessed; and note that I do not say that the righteous man has been born once and for all of God, but that he is so born on every occasion that God gives him birth for some good action. (This perpetual rebirth is true even of Christ—) for Christ is the "effulgence" of "glory", and such effulgence is not generated once only but as often as the light creates it. . . . Our Saviour is the "Wisdom of God", and wisdom is the "effulgence of eternal light" (Wis 7²⁶). If then the Saviour is always being born . . . from the Father, so too are you, if you have the spirit of adoption (Rom 8¹⁵), and God is always begetting you in every deed and thought you have; and this begetting makes you a perpetually re-born son of God in Christ Jesus.'

Comm. Mt. XVII.36 (above, p. 24).

Hom. Lk. Frag. 42 on 11²: 'I think that none can address God as "Father" unless he has been filled with the "spirit of adoption" (Rom 8¹⁵), and that such a son may address his Father as "Father" to do him honour—with due regard to the commandment (Mt 5⁴⁴ᶠ, "Love your enemies . . . that ye may be sons of your Father . . ."). Again, everyone that "doeth righteousness" (1 Jn 2²⁹) is born of God. So born, with the "seed of God in him" (ibid. 3⁹), because he "can sin no more", he may say "Father . . .'. Again, one is born of God not from corruptible seed but through the living and abiding Word of God, as it is written: "As many as received Him, to them gave He the right to become children of God . . . which were born not of blood . . . but of God" (Jn 1¹²ᶠ). The point of this saying is not to raise us to the level of God's nature, but that He (the Word) gives us to share in His grace, and graciously grants us His own dignity; for He tells us to call God "Father".'

Comm. Jn. XIX.5 (above, p. 25).

Ibid. XXXII.10 (7): (Doctors and teachers try to bring patients and pupils to their own level) 'but the Saviour is Lord, and the only Lord who seeks to make His servant as He is. Such is the Son of His Father's goodness and of His love. For being Lord, He worked to make His servants as their Lord, no longer to have the spirit of bondage unto fear, but to receive the spirit of adoption, whereby they cry "Abba, Father" (Rom 8¹⁵).'

Comm. Eph., § 3 on 1⁵ (*JTS*, III.237): 'The word "adoption" shows that those who are (thus) predestined by Him are not sons of God by nature. "Adoption" could not be assigned to the Saviour, but only to those who "having received the spirit of bondage to fear" (Rom 8¹⁵) have "paid the debt of fear" Rom 13⁷) and are thus become worthy of freedom—of hearing the words "I call you no longer servants" (Jn 15¹⁵)—and because of this receive the "spirit of adoption". For when a man for the first time receives the Son, at that moment he attains to the "spirit of adoption". In this way our adoption comes to us "through Christ".'

(2) *Access to God in prayer*

Cels. V.4: 'We should bring every petition, prayer, intercession and thanksgiving to the supreme God through the High-priest of all angels, the living, divine Word. We shall offer our petitions also and our intercessions and thanksgiving and prayer to that Word Himself, if we are able to appreciate the difference between the absolute and relative senses of prayer.'

Cels. VIII.13: 'We worship the one God and His only Son, His Word and image, with such supplications and petitions as we can offer, bringing to the God of the universe our prayers through His only-begotten Son. We bring them first to the Son, beseeching Him who is the "propitiation for our sins" 1 Jn 4¹⁰) to bear as High-priest our prayers and sacrifices and intercessions to the supreme God. Our faith concerning God is thus through His Son, who confirms it in us. . . .'

Ibid. 26: 'We should pray only to the supreme God, and to His only-begotten Word, the firstborn of all creation; and we should beseech His Word to bear as High-Priest our prayer which has reached Him to His God and our God, and His Father and the Father of those who live according to His Word' (cf. Jn 20¹⁷).

Prayer X.2: '(He who prays as he ought) will be (suitably) purified and thus share in the prayer of the Word of God . . . , who neglects the prayer of no one, and who prays to the Father together with him whose mediator He is. For the High Priest of our offerings and our "advocate" with the Father (1 Jn 2¹) is the Son of God, who prays for those who pray and pleads with those who plead. . . .'

Ibid. XV.1: 'If we understand what prayer really is, we shall on no account pray to any generate being, not even to Christ Himself, but only to the God and Father of the universe, to whom our Saviour Himself prayed. . . . (But this prayer to God the Father only, is) not apart from the High Priest, who was appointed by the Father. . . .'

Ibid. 2: 'The saints, when they give thanks to God in their prayers, acknowledge their thanks to Him through Christ Jesus; and just as it is not right for one who is careful to pray correctly to pray to one who himself prays, but only to the Father whom our Lord Jesus taught us to call upon in our prayers, it is equally wrong to offer a prayer to the Father without Him . . . [Origen quotes John 16²³ᶠ and adds] until Jesus taught this, no one had asked the Father in the name of the Son. . . .'

Ibid. 4: 'And it is surely fitting that the one who said "Why callest thou me good? There is none good but one, that is, God" (the Father) (Mk 10¹⁸) should also have said "Why do you pray to me? You should pray only to the Father, to whom I also pray. For you ought not to pray *to* a High Priest appointed on your behalf by the Father, and who received the office of Advocate from Him, but rather *through* this High Priest and Advocate, who can suffer with you for your infirmities, tempted at all points like you—only (because of the gracious gift of the Father) without sin. Learn then what a great gift you have received from my Father—the spirit of adoption through your regeneration in me, that ye may be called 'sons of God' and my brethren. . . . It is not fitting that those who are deemed worthy of a common Father should pray to a brother, for to the Father alone you must send up your prayers—*with* me and *through* me".'

(3) *The offer of the Gospel to all mankind*

Cels. I.32: '. . . (Jesus) who ventured so much for mankind that, as far as He was able, all Greeks and barbarians should turn from sin in expectation of divine judgement and do everything with a view to satisfying the Creator of the universe. . . .'

Hom. Lev. XII.5 on 21¹³⁻¹⁵ ('he shall take to wife a virgin from his own people' [applied by Origen to Christ—'virginity' =

the 'simplicity of the faith in Christ'—cf. 2 Cor 11³]): 'Since after the failure of the subtleties of the philosophers and the superstitions of the Jews He took to Himself the Church in its simple faith, Christ "took a wife from His own people". . . . (As for "from His own people"—) this may mean . . . that the soul of Christ was of the same stock and substance as all human souls; it may mean also that, because He calls those who believe in Him "brothers", the soul that is joined to Him in faith (as it were in marriage) is said to be "of His own people". [Origen notes that "of His own people" (at verse 13) is only in the LXX, not the Hebrew][52] and rightly so: for the Hebrews have been deprived of their kinship with God and their adoption as sons, which have been transferred to the Church of Christ.'

Sel. Ps. 24¹: 'Before the advent of Christ God was known only in Judaea; since then the whole earth is the Lord's. Before that advent "fulness" was not to be found anywhere on earth, and most of the earth was . . . emptiness; since then many would say from among the Gentile believers "from his fulness have we all received . . ." (Jn 1¹⁶), and thus themselves they have become His "fulness"—for those who are "empty" of the ordering of the Gospel cannot be the "fulness" of Christ.'

Ibid. 47²: 'Previously the name (of God) was "great" only in Israel; but since the coming of Christ He is great throughout all the world.'

Comm. Ser. Mt. 92 on 26³⁹ (One suggested interpretation would be that): 'He loved the Jews and saw what sufferings they would bring on themselves by seeking to kill Him and save Barabbas; it was thus in grief for them that He said "Father, if it be possible . . .". His further prayer "Nevertheless, not what I will . . ." would indicate the withdrawal of this petition when He saw what great blessing for the whole world would come from His passion . . . , and the words "but as Thou wilt" were said as it were from this further thought of the salvation of all mankind, which was to be won for God by His death.'

Hom. Lk. XV on 2³⁰f: ' "Mine eyes have seen Thy salvation" —which is Christ, . . . the salvation not only of the Jews but of all the world. . . . "A light to lighten the Gentiles"—Christ is the light of the Gentiles, for He was to bring the light of His teaching to them in their darkness. For now has the Father

---

[52] Although in verses 14 and 15 it is in the Hebrew also.

accepted the people of the Gentiles, giving them a covenant
of peace in the salvation that comes to them through faith in
Christ. ". . . the glory of thy people Israel", i.e. glory to Israel,
enlightenment to the Gentiles; the latter receive their first
teaching, the former the resultant knowledge. The true Israelite,
then, is everyone who knows Christ; if a man does not know
Christ he is no Israelite, for "Israel" means "the mind that
sees God". The "glory" of the Jews, then, is to believe in
Christ whom their prophets predicted—the glory, that is, of
encountering the one they had awaited.'

'We may hesitate', said Donald Baillie,[53] 'to accept all the implications of Melanchthon's famous saying that to know Christ is simply to know His benefits. . . .' In the case of Origen we may surely say that we learn more of Christ from the range of his thought on the 'benefits' than from his Christology. It was on the latter, with its real or alleged subordinationism, that the Church fastened its anathematizing eye; but one may ask whether a theology so rich and penetrating in its valuation of the gracious *work* of Christ can be summarily dismissed with any sort of justice as 'subordinationist'. The truth is rather that Origen, perhaps inevitably in his day and generation, failed adequately to crystallize in his Christology the embarrassing abundance of his thought on Christ's work—as also the implications on his own practice of prayer[54] and worship.

In these discussions of the work of Christ Origen's *Scriptural fidelity and insight* are at their height. His lists of Christ's Titles are no mere random discharges of learning; they control his whole exposition. His own suggestion that Christ is also αὐτο-βασίλεια, the 'Kingdom in Person', springs from real appreciation of the New Testament theology of the Kingdom, and would exclude from the start the later (and disastrous) Roman identification of the Kingdom with the Church. His determination to find Christ everywhere in the Old Testament leads to some curious exegesis: the 'priest' who is 'chief among his brethren', for example, who is to 'take a virgin wife from his own people' (Lev 21 [above, pp. *150*f]) would not readily suggest Christ to most expositors. But the defect is in the application, not the principle; and a theologian who can lay the Old Testament—and the 'Wisdom of Solomon'—under contribution will give us a far

---

[53] *God was in Christ*, p. 159.
[54] Cf. the section above on 'Access to God in Prayer' (pp. *149*f). *Prayer* XV forbids Prayer to Christ; yet, as Jay says (op. cit., p. 126, note 3), '(Origen's) devotion to Christ led him both himself to pray boldly to Christ and to encourage others to do so'. *Cels.* V.4 distinguishes the 'absolute and relative' senses (κυριολεξία, κατάχρησις) of prayer, the latter only being appropriately offered to Christ. But it is surely very difficult to attach any meaning to this distinction. If 'relative prayer' to Christ merely signifies 'prayer to the Father through the mediation of Christ', nothing is gained (or proved) by the distinction. If O'Meara is thinking of this passage when he suggests (op. cit., p. 10) that the prayer which Origen forbids to Christ is solemn or liturgical prayer only, one may comment that it is a pity Origen did not express himself more clearly. The real motive behind Origen's restriction seems to be Christological; in *Prayer* XV he goes on to explain that the Son is 'distinct from the Father both in nature and person (κατ' οὐσιάν καὶ ὑποκείμενον), hence prayer to Him is inappropriate.

truer and richer picture of Christ than a Marcionite. His summary of the work of Christ at *Cels.* V.33 (above, pp. *111*f) is given in the very words of Isaiah 2²ᶠᶠ; he sees the crucified Christ as the true Servant of the Isaianic prophecy (above, p. *121*); his expositions of Christ as the Wisdom of God and the 'effluence' of His glory take him to the Wisdom Literature; Christ as the priest-victim and Christ as the conqueror of the demons takes him to the Old Testament sacrifices and the battle-stories of Joshua. Some of his most characteristic writing is inspired by the book one would have thought most alien to his ascetism, the Song of Songs⁵⁵ (cf. e.g. p. *142* above).

It is indeed Origen's consistent claim that through Christ has come for the first time a real understanding of the Old Testament Scriptures.

> *Comm. Jn.* XIII.48: 'That which was hidden from the generations of old and even from Moses and the prophets has been revealed to the holy apostles in the days of Christ's sojourning, since He has poured on them the light of the knowledge of the whole of Scripture.'
>
> *Hom. Ex.* XII.4: 'It is He who "opens the Scriptures" (Lk 24³²) and so kindles the hearts of the disciples.'
>
> *Hom. Jer.* X.2 (with reference to Ex 15²⁵): ' "The Lord . . . threw a tree in the water and the water became sweet"; but when the "tree" (Cross) of Jesus comes and the teaching of my Saviour makes its dwelling with me, the Law of Moses is "sweetened"—its taste to one who thus reads and understands it is sweet indeed.'
>
> *Hom. Gen.* XV.7 on 46⁴ ('The hand of Joseph shall close your eyes'): 'The true "Joseph", our Lord and Saviour, just as He placed His physical hand on the eyes of the blind man and restored him the sight he had lost (Mt 20³⁴), even so has placed his spiritual hands on the eyes of the Law—eyes which had been darkened by the literal interpretations of the Scribes and Pharisees—and restored them vision: thus may those to whom the Lord opens the Scriptures be granted spiritual sight and understanding of the Law.'
>
> *Comm. Jn.* I.6 (8): 'Before Christ came, the Law and the

---

⁵⁵ Jerome, introducing his translation of Origen's two homilies, writes: 'Origen, who in his other books had surpassed all others, in the "Song of Songs" surpasses himself.'

THE GRACE OF GOD THE SON

prophets, because the One who makes clear their mysteries had not yet come, could not proclaim the gospel as we have defined it. But when the Saviour came and willed that the Gospel should become incarnate, through the Gospel He made the whole (Scripture) into Gospel; . . . before the Gospel which began with the coming of Christ, none of the things of old was Gospel. But the Gospel—i.e. the New Covenant—rescued us from the dead hand of the letter and granted us by the illumination of knowledge the new light of the spirit, that light which is even now untouched with age, that light which while proper to the New Covenant yet now shines in the whole of Scripture. It is pre-eminently necessary that the name "Gospel" should be given to that which made even what had been supposedly peculiar to the old Covenant into Gospel.'

It is unfortunate that this new and spiritual understanding, which turns the Law into Gospel and renders its bitterness sweet, turns out to be the method of allegory.

Cf. *Hom. Ex.* V.1 (Paul laid down for the Gentile Church the correct method of interpreting the Old Testament): 'His intention was that the disciples of Christ should differ from those of the synagogue, in that while they by false interpretation of the Law did not receive Christ, we by its spiritual understanding should show that it was really given for the instruction of the Church. [The Jews understood the journey of Israel in the wilderness only in its literal sense: Origen quotes 1 Cor 10$^{1-4}$:] . . . what the Jews take as merely the crossing of the sea Paul calls baptism; what is to them the cloud is to Paul the Holy Spirit; . . . and the manna which the Jews understand as merely food for the stomach . . . Paul calls "spiritual food" [Origen supports this by the words of Jesus at Jn 3^5, 6$^{49-51}$]. . . . Then indeed, Paul comes into the open and pronounces of the following rock . . . "the rock was Christ". . . . Surely it is the right course to keep the rule thus given us in the other cases (otherwise we should desert the example of Paul and revert to the "Jewish fables" of Titus 1^{14}).'

But whatever we may think of allegory, Origen's *purpose* is to find Christ throughout the Old Testament, and he is eminently justified in claiming Dominical sanction for this.

The ease with which Origen moves among the whole body of Scripture and draws from its fullness at will is nowhere more evident than in his discussions of the work of Christ,[56] where the many-sidedness of his theme gives full reign to his eager erudition. He falls no doubt into serious error from his besetting sins of undue literalism and irresponsible allegory; but his knowledge of *Scripture-as-a-whole* saves him from some of the more serious errors of his successors—even down to our own day. There is, for example, no dichotomy of the Father's justice and the Son's love in his discussions of the Atonement. Nor is his presentation of the work of Christ unbalanced by an unduly 'incarnational' or 'soteriological' emphasis: the Incarnation and the Cross are seen in the light of each other.

Nowhere is this more evident than in his eschatology. He is widely regarded as an unbalanced 'universalist'—the notorious advocate of the ultimate salvation of the devil. Now if the real gravamen of the charge against universalism is that it 'cuts the nerve of ethical endeavour', Origen may confidently plead his innocence: no theologian is more responsive to the ethical implications of the Gospel than he. If his universalism is a symptom of his 'optimism of grace', this may be pleaded as a merit. But my real point is that to confine his eschatology to the question of universal salvation is to do him serious injustice, and to ignore, among other things, his profound and Scriptural doctrine of the 'Two Advents'. We have quoted some examples of this above.[57] Compare with these—

Hom. Lk. Frag. 22 on 9²⁸ᶠᶠ (Transfiguration): 'That the glory which appertains to the very being of God is not to be seen or approached by any creature, was shown by the disciples' inability to bear even the physical reflection of it which was shown them on the mountain—they fell to the ground. One only sees the Word transformed into His glory when one ascends with Him and is exalted with Him and sees Him as the Word-in-Person and as the High-Priest who has converse with and prays to the Father. But since the time had not yet come

---

[56] Cf. e.g. *Hom. Lev.* III.1 (above p. *129*). At *Comm. Jn.* XIII.48 he justifies his words (quoted above p. *134*) by a string of quotations—all excellent—from Matthew 13¹⁷, 12⁴², Ephesians 3⁵ᶠ, Daniel 8¹⁷, Isaiah 29¹¹ᶠ. These are mere random examples.
[57] *Comm. Mt.* XII.29 (above p. *113*); *Cels.* I.56 (pp. *113*f); II.38 (p. *114*); *Comm. Jn.* XIII.62 (60) (p. *114*); *Hom. Josh.* VIII.4 (p. *124*), cf. ibid. 3 (pp. *123*f).

for Him to have perfected His body with immortality incorruptible, He was seen in corruptible garments—but with them He was dazzling bright; for when the righteous are raised in glory at the second coming of Christ they will have no visible garments, but a dazzling bright covering will clothe them. And just as the appearance of the garments (of Jesus) was not made different in kind by the Transfiguration, even so the appearance of the saints at the resurrection will be much more glorified than the one they had in life—but not different in kind.

'Those who stood with Jesus (at the Transfiguration) appeared glorified to the disciples, Moses representing the Law and Elijah the prophets (for Christ was Lord of both Law and prophets). He then that has apprehended the spiritual law and the "wisdom hidden in a mystery" (1 Cor 2⁷) of the prophets sees Moses and Elijah in glory.'

Here, surely, is anticipated some of the best modern thought on what is perhaps best termed 'inaugurated eschatology',[58] and this passage gives the key to Origen's whole approach. Compare, for example:

Hom. Josh. VIII.4 (above, p. *124*); *Hom. Num.* XXIII.11 (on the feast of booths, or tents): 'God rejoices . . . over you, when He sees you dwelling in this world "in tents" . . . i.e. with a mind and purpose which is *not* fixed and grounded on this earth, or yearning for earthly things, or looking on the shadow which is this life as a guaranteed and eternal possession, but (as it were) passing through this world and hastening to that true home-country of paradise whence you are come, and saying "I am a passing guest, a sojourner, like all my fathers" (Ps 39¹²).'

Sel. Ps. 119¹¹⁷: 'As long as we are in this world, the words "I shall be safe" cannot be completely fulfilled—only when we live with the angels of God, when "God's statutes" will be practised face to face with Him, in true reality, not a shadow thereof.'

Hom. Ezek. II.5: 'We have a "pledge of the Holy Spirit" (2 Cor 1²²), whom we shall receive in His fullness "when that is perfect is come" (1 Cor 13¹⁰): and likewise we have a "pledge of the resurrection", the fact being that none of us has yet risen in the perfection of resurrection.'

[58] C. F. Dodd, *The Interpretation of the Fourth Gospel*, p. 447, note 1.

Comm. Mt. XV.22f on 19²⁷ᶠ (the Regeneration): 'This is the Regeneration of that new coming-into-being when a new heaven and earth is created for those who have renewed themselves, and a new covenant and its "cup" is given. Of that Regeneration what Paul calls the "washing of Regeneration" (Tit 3⁵) is the prelude (προοίμιον), and that which is brought to this "washing of regeneration" in the "renewing of the Spirit" is a symbol (μυστήριον) of that newness. It might also be said that whereas at our natural birth "none is pure from defilement, even if he only lives one day" (Job 14⁴, LXX), . . . in the "washing of regeneration" everyone who is "born again" "of water and the spirit" (Jn 3³, ⁵) is pure from defilement— but (if I may venture to put it so) only "in a glass darkly" (1 Cor 13¹²). But at that other Regeneration, when the Son of man shall sit upon the throne of His glory, everyone who achieves that Regeneration in Christ is totally pure from defilement, sees Him face to face, having passed through the washing of regeneration to that other one. The latter can be understood by reflection on the words of John, who baptized "with water unto repentance", concerning the Saviour: "He shall baptize you with the Holy Spirit and with fire."

'Further, in the washing of regeneration we were buried with Christ [quotes Rom 6⁴]; but in the Regeneration of the washing through fire and the Spirit we become conformed to the "body of the glory" (Phil 3²¹) of the Christ who sits on the throne of His glory. . . .'

These are but samples of a profoundly biblical eschatology that runs through the whole of Origen's writings. We note with appreciation his understanding of the Transfiguration and of Christian baptism as prime examples of 'inaugurated eschatology', and the First Advent of Christ as intelligible only in the light of the Second; nor do we miss his biblical setting of the Christian life— conceived as always with a strong ethical colouring—in the eschatological framework of the Work of Christ: incarnation, death, resurrection, glorification, Second Coming in triumph— the whole integrated for Christ and for the Christian into a pattern which allows development in degree but not in kind. It is surely in the light of this eschatological pattern that Origen's defence of universal salvation should be construed.

I have dealt at some length with the biblical background of this part of Origen's theology, because fidelity to the Bible means fidelity to Grace. We must now look briefly at the several sections into which I have divided his thoughts on the work of Christ.

Incarnation

The most noteworthy feature here is the elaborate doctrine of the ἐπίνοιαι, the 'aspects' in which Christ was revealed or imparted to men at the Incarnation. There is an immediate suggestion here of the doctrine of the 'accommodation' of God in providence (above, pp. *103*ff), but the resemblance is superficial. Perhaps because of the more biblical setting of the doctrine, the Stoic *apatheia* keeps its distance; it is not suggested that the 'appearances' of Christ were false to His real nature. It is true that at one point Origen dabbles with speculations that have a decidedly Gnostic ring (cf. *Comm. Ser. Mt.* 100 [above, p. *118*, and the reference to Dr Chadwick in note 44]). But this does not effect the essence of the idea, which is surely designed to 'earth' the divinity of Christ in the varying degrees of sin and ignorance that characterize humanity.[59] Physically this *was* true of the Incarnate Word in Jesus; spiritually it *is* true of the eternal nature of the Divine Word. His Incarnation was in this respect a concealment as well as a revelation (*Cels.* II.67 [above, p. *117*], *Hom. Josh.* III.5 [above, pp. *129*f]), in so far as man's finitude and his sin render him unable to bear the unveiled glory of Eternal Light.[60] It is to be admitted that Origen's exegetical literalism (a necessary complement in that unique mind to his fantastic allegorism) leads him to suspicious suggestions about the varying physical 'forms' of Jesus. This should not obscure his real purpose and achievement.

---

[59] Cf. *Hom. Jer.* VIII.2 (above, pp. *118*f;) *Hom. Jer.* VIII.5 ('These treasures are in Christ' from whom 'one man becomes wise, another faithful, another has knowledge' and so with all the other χαρίσματα).

[60] *O how shall I, whose native sphere*
Is dark, whose mind is dim,
Before the Ineffable appear,
And on my naked spirit bear
The uncreated beam?
There is a way for man to rise
To that sublime abode ;
An offering and a sacrifice. . . .

This famous hymn of Thomas Binney is pure Origenism.

'The ἐπίνοιαι corresponded to human capacity, merit, need, or moral progress' (above, p. *115*). Here, once again, is the old query of the relative standing of grace and merit. The dominant note in the above extracts is that of 'capacity' (χωρεῖν), and we may presume (as we did in the section on Providence) that Origen would not have denied that this 'capacity' is itself God-given. But what of *Comm. Ser. Mt.* 100 (above, p. *118*)—'He used to appear to every individual in a form corresponding to his worth' (*unicuique apparebat secundum quod fuerat dignus*); *Princ.* IV.4.2 (above, p. *118*)—'Christ becomes present in each individual to the degree that his merits have allowed' (*quantum ratio indulserit merit-orum*); and *Hom. Jer.* VIII.2 (above, p. *119*)—'His power of dis-pensing to every man according to his desert' (τὴν τοῦ κατ' ἀξίαν ἀπονεμητικὴν δύναμιν)? These passages would indeed suggest a limitation of grace by merit, and the 'curse of the law' from which the Gospel has set us free would again be casting its shadow. We learnt early not to expect perfect consistency in Origen on this question—possibly because it had not yet become a theological issue; and we may plead here that, if questioned, Origen would have interpreted the 'merit' passages with refer-ence to the more regulative categories of 'capacity' and 'need'. We should, however, welcome more frequent assurances that this very capacity and need are 'of grace'.[61] This whole notion of Christ's self-revelation in 'aspects' to meet our needs or capacity or anything else needs constant correction by the equally Scrip-tural presentation of Christ as the sovereign Word of God, the new wine that bursts the old bottles, the eschatological Son of Man, in whom the Grace of God is brought to bear with over-riding majesty on His creatures. We welcome Origen's recogni-tion that some of the ἐπίνοιαι are a necessary answer to sin, others for man's perfecting—in other words, that there is grace justifying and grace sanctifying. We should welcome an equally

[61] *All the fitness He requireth*
Is to feel your need of Him:
This He gives you . . .
        (Joseph Hart, *MHB* 324)

Jesus, if we aright confess
Our heartfelt poverty,
We own the conscious want of grace
Itself a gift from Thee.
        (Charles Wesley, *MHB* 785)

It is a measure of the greatness of Charles Wesley as a theologian that in this matter of grace-merit, as in most others, he *never slips*.

consistent emphasis that man remains to the end infinitely indebted to the divine forbearance—that 'justification by faith' not
only strikes the opening chord of the symphony but constitutes
the determinative 'ground-bass'[62] of the harmony from first to
last.

The Cross

The section-headings given above (pp. *121*ff) show a many-
sidedness of Origen's theology of the Atonement which is without parallel in the early centuries, and which springs from his
comprehensive fidelity to the *Bible-as-a-whole*. Perhaps the heart
of his doctrine lies in the dual symbolism—the twin 'invisible
meanings'—of the conquest by Christ of the demons and of our
'dying with Christ'. Many readers will remember the discussion
by Rashdall of the 'ransom' passages, and his endeavour to ex-
culpate Origen from more than a small share in the guilt of the
later theologians of the 'fish-hook' and the 'mouse-trap' devil-
deception school.[63] It would be truer to admit that Origen is
allowing his literalism to run him into absurdity, as he so often
does. The Marcan word 'ransom' is notoriously a metaphor that
should not be pressed; but no metaphor is safe when either the
literalism or the allegorism of Origen is brought to bear on it.
Of more importance than this is the general view that Origen
shared with the New Testament writers of human life as an
ethical conflict in which the powers of heaven and hell—the
angels and demons—are invisibly but actively present and engaged. We are perhaps less disposed to dismiss this mythology
as 'Jewish old clothes' than were our fathers. We have learnt
much from Aulén and Tillich—from the 'Christus Victor' of the
former and the doctrine of demonism as 'structural evil' of
the latter.[64] We can appreciate Origen's firm grasp of the
agonizing dualism of the moral universe—of the reality and the

---

[62] An illustration used in his lectures by Prof. E. Gordon Rupp.

[63] Rashdall, *The Idea of Atonement*, pp. 259ff, to which H. E. W. Turner, *The Patristic Doctrine of Redemption*, pp. 55-6, is a needful corrective.

[64] Cf. Tillich, *Protestant Era*, xxxv-v —'demonic' is a symbol of the 'structure' (*Gestalt*) of evil beyond the moral power of goodwill; every individual good action is inescapably involved in such evil just because it is part of the 'pattern' of life. There is also a 'divine structure'—grace; and history is a continuous conflict between the two. Evil and grace are inescapable just because they are 'structural'.—This puts into language, which (as always in Tillich) might be clearer, our instinctive sense of the supernatural 'overtones' of the drama of the ethical conflict.

M

eternal reach of evil; his refusal to simplify the issues by any concession to the shallower dualism of Marcion (*Hom. Ex.* VI.9
[above, pp. *125*f]); and his conviction of the victory of the good—
of the grace of God in Christ—won in principle by the Cross
and in actuality at the Consummation.

Origen was the first Christian theologian in any real degree
to understand and apply the Pauline doctrine of the crucifixion
of the believer with Christ[65] through baptism, with its 'inaugurated
eschatology' of the new life in the Risen Christ which sets the
believer on the path to perfection. Formally, the integration of
this doctrine with the nailing on the Cross of the devil and his
powers is attempted at *Hom. Josh.* VIII.3 (pp. *123*f): the visible
crucifixion of Christ is to the invisible crucifixion of the evil powers
as is the crucifixion of the believer (made holy) to the sin of this
world which he is thus renouncing;[66] the relation is one of divine-
human analogy, and Christ crucified is an 'example' to the faithful
believer of that victory over the powers of hell which He achieved
by conquering the arch-demon in the decisive, 'eschatological',
conflict, and which as each believer is crucified with Christ he
appropriates in *his* personal struggle against the sins with which
the devil seeks *his* destruction. 'The devil is conquered, he is crucified—but only for those who are crucified with Christ. He will
be crucified for all believers and equally for all mankind when
that saying is fulfilled—"for as in Adam all die, even so in Christ
shall all be made alive" '—and this will mark the Second Coming
of Christ in glory.

I believe that this dual symbolism marks the real centre of
Origen's understanding of the Cross, and that everything else he
says—his use of the Servant-analogy, his emphasis that the death
of Christ was of Christ's own choice and God's own purpose ('for
the sake of religion'), his references to divine love and Christian
martyrdom, his description of the priest-victim and the benefits
of His sacrifice, his warning that the Cross brings punishment
and death to unbelievers, and his vision of final universal

---

[65] Cf. *Comm. Eph.*, § 15 on 3[18] (*JTS*, III.411f) ('length, breadth, height and depth'):
'All these are embraced by the Cross of Christ, through which "He ascended on *high*
. . . and descended to the *depths* of the earth" . . . and made His course "to the ends of
the earth", reaching its *breadth* and *length*. And he who has been "crucified with Christ"
. . . comprehends the "breadth and length and depth and height".'

[66] Cf. *Comm. 1 Cor.*, § 6 (*JTS*, IX.235): 'If I have "died to the world", I am "crucified to the world" with Christ. But if I "live to sin", I have not yet attained to the
blessing of the Cross'.

reconciliation to God's through the long, slow victory of Christ in the lives of generations of believers which is the real inner history of the long, slow growth of the Church into a world-wide Christian community—should be understood in the context of the crucifixion by Christ of the devil and by the believer in Christ of his sin. I am not suggesting that such an integration of doctrine was consciously present in Origen's mind whenever he turned to interpret some aspect of the Atoning work. He takes each passage of Scripture as it comes, and as a result there is hardly any historical insight into the Cross which is not represented somewhere in his writings. But the systematizing is there, even if unconscious—partly in his uniform modes of scriptural understanding, and partly in the experience, the learning, the cast of mind and temperament which went to make him the man he was.[67]

Three comments may be added to this attempted estimate of Origen's thought on the Cross:

(1) Origen's thought is here, as always, ethical through and through. Note the passage about the devil's currency (*Hom. Ex.* VI.9 [pp. *125*f]): the mythological language of the double financial transaction—our selling ourselves to the devil and Christ's ransom for our re-purchasing—is treated as a kind of ethical shorthand. The profound diagnosis of sin is above all evident in such a passage as *Comm. Jn.* VI.55 (p. *127*), with its likening of the sinful soul to 'thistle-bearing soil' which must be cut to pieces by the penetrating sharpness of God's Word and visited by His fire, not without suffering or affliction for those whose sin is thus purged and broken. Origen's curious exegesis of Joshua 8[29] (*Hom. Josh.* VIII.3ff [pp. *123*ff]) ends with the significant comment that the mere historical knowledge of how the king of Gai died is of 'no profit to me': its real value is as a sacramental pointer to the ethical victory of Christ on the Cross—this is how 'my soul will be built up'. A theologian whose entire bent of mind is as ethical

---

[67] Cf. Brunner on Barth: 'You understand Barth best when you take him not so much as a systematic theologian but as one who has first one insight and then another which he puts into words as they come, without worrying whether they fit closely together in a system. . . . this is a sign of spiritual vitality and ample freedom' (*SJT*, IV.2.124-5). It may be; but there is an underlying unity of system in the great *'Dogmatik'* to which Brunner does less than justice. Origen, of course, takes none of the Barthian delight in consciously shocking his disciples with some outrageous affirmation which (like the harmonic 'shocks' in Beethoven) *prima facie* upsets everything but is finally seen to be totally in keeping with the unfolding pattern of thought. This is the difference between the Reformed prophet and the Eastern ascetic.

as this needs an overriding doctrine of divine Grace to save him from moralism and legalism, and this on the whole Origen achieves, in these passages at least.

(2) There is (perhaps inevitably) a relative under-emphasis on divine Love in these passages. When his biblical text of the moment speaks of Love, Origen will dutifully expound it (cf. *Comm. Rom.* IV.10 [p. *122*]). But his central conviction of the 'double symbolism' and the victory over the devil and sin leaves little room for such conceptions of divine Love as St Paul develops in 1 Cor 13;[68] and we noted above (p. *48*) that the balance of Origen's thought on Grace in general leans toward *power* rather than Love. Here again the ascetic is speaking, and the intense inner conflict of supernatural powers, with the human soul as the battle-ground and human salvation or death as the prize, does not blend easily with the Fatherly love which goes on forgiving to the last agony of the dying Saviour.[69]

(3) Something must be said of Origen's notorious doctrine of the efficacy of the blood of martyrs. This is set out in passages such as the following:

> *Martyrdom* 30: 'Let us also remember our sins, and that without baptism it is impossible to obtain remission of sins (cf. Acts 2[38]), and that according to the precepts of the Gospel one cannot be baptized a second time in water and the Spirit for the remission of sins, but that we are given the baptism of martyrdom. . . . And you must consider if, just as the Saviour's baptism of martyrdom cleanses the world from guilt, ours too may work for the healing of many by such cleansing. For as those who served at the altar set up by the law of Moses were thought to procure through the blood of goats and bulls remission of sins for the people, so the souls of those "who have been beheaded for their testimony to Jesus" (Rev 20[4]) do not serve in vain at the altar in heaven but procure for them that pray remission of sins. We learn too that just as Jesus Christ the High Priest offered Himself as a sacrifice, so the priests whose High Priest He is offer themselves as a sacrifice (Heb

---

[68] Which I have always understood as a picture not of ἀγάπη in the abstract but of Christ dying on the Cross.

[69] Cf., however, *Comm. Rom.* (Gk), § 28 on 5[5-9] (*JTS*, XIII.362), where Origen interprets συνίστησι ('commends') as 'establishes': 'By the death of Jesus everything that stood in the way of the "establishment" of God's love towards us was removed from us.'

5, 7, 8, 10), for which reason they are seen at their rightful place
—the altar. But while some of the priests were without blemish
and offered in their divine service sacrifices that were without
blemish, others were sullied with such blemishes as Moses listed
in "Leviticus" (21[17ff]) and were kept away from the altar. Who
then is the priest without blemish, if not he who upholds the
confession to the last and who fulfils in every detail what we
mean by martyrdom?'

Ibid. 50: 'Perhaps too, just as we were ransomed by the
"precious blood of Jesus" (1 Pet 1[19]) who has received "a name
above every name" (Phil 2[9]), so some will be ransomed by the
precious blood of the martyrs; for the martyrs are more highly
exalted than they would have been if to their righteousness
had not been added martyrdom.'

Comm. Jn. VI.53 (35) on 1[29]: '(in the interpretation of which)
we start from the dispensation (οἰκονομίαν) of the bodily Advent of the Son of God into the life of men and so understand
the "lamb" as none other than the Man. For He was "led
as a lamb to the slaughter . . ." (Isa 53[7]) [and Origen quotes
Jer 11[19], Rev 5[6]]. He then was the lamb whose slaughter
cleansed the whole world from guilt in a way that is too mysterious for telling. . . .' Ibid. 54 (36): 'The other sacrifices,
which the [Old Testament] Law symbolizes, are akin to this
Sacrifice, as are also (in my view) those in which the blood of
the noble martyrs is poured out, for they are not seen by John
the disciple to stand at the heavenly altar in vain (Rev 6[9]). . . .
We must regard the blood of the holy martyrs as freeing us
from harmful powers; their endurance, for example, and their
confession even unto death, and their zeal for religion serve
to blunt the edge of the plots the powers lay against a man in
his sufferings. . . . Such is the kind of service that the death
of the most pious martyrs must be understood to do, many
people receiving benefits from their death by an efficacy that
we cannot explain.'

Cels. I.31: '. . . He who was crucified accepted death willingly for the race of mankind, in the same way as those who
have died for their own countries to check the spread of epi-
demics or famines, or the destruction caused by tempests at
sea. For it is likely that the nature of things allows, in a mysterious manner that most people cannot understand, the

possibility that the voluntary death of one righteous man for the community will avert by expiation evil demons who cause plagues or famines or tempests at sea etc.'

Ibid. VIII.44: 'Since the souls of those who die for Christianity, and which depart from the body in glory for the cause of religion, have destroyed the power of the demons and rendered their plot against men ineffective, I infer that experience has taught the demons that they are worsted and conquered by the martyrs of the truth, and that they have feared to return and seek vengeance.'

(Cf. *Comm. Rom.* II.1 (p. *51*): Of those 'whose sins have been remitted through the grace of baptism, or covered through their penitence, or to whom sin is not to be imputed because they have won the glory of martyrdom'.)

Martyrdom 28 (p. *52* and note 50) (where martyrdom is a kind of counterbalance, repayment, for the gifts of God to us).

Three ideas seem to run through these passages:

(*a*) Martyrdom is 'akin' to the sacrifice of Christ, and it has two parallels: the Mosaic priests, and those who in any community die to avert or lessen peril from the people. The first parallel suggests that the martyrs by serving at the altar of heaven procure cleansing from guilt, remission of sins for 'those who pray'; the second that they neutralize the power of the demons.

(*b*) Martyrdom is a qualification that is higher than righteousness, and it alone makes possible the purity of sacrifice that will qualify it to avail.

(*c*) Whereas the sacrifice of Christ was 'for all'—'for the whole world'—the sacrifice of martyrdom is of limited avail—'for some', 'for many'.

It hardly needs to be proved that none of these ideas is scriptural, nor in any way a legitimate application or development of New Testament doctrine. They offend against two of the cardinal principles of Grace—that there is but One Mediator, over against whom stands the world (saints, martyrs, sinners) awaiting redemption, and that merit has no place in the scheme of salvation, since *coram Deo* we are all one (saints, martyrs, sinners) in our unrighteousness. To put penitence and martyrdom on a level with the 'grace of baptism' as means for the remission of sins (*Comm. Rom.* II.1 [above] is to destroy grace by equating it with good works. To suggest that the only difference between the Cross and human sacrifice is in the range of their saving power is to destroy the infinite qualitative distinction between God and man that the Scriptures presuppose. We are not saved by some sacrificial principle that Christ exemplified to perfection and others, like martyrs, validly but in a lesser degree; we are saved by Christ. In this disastrous doctrine of martyrdom we can perceive the seeds of later heresies that Origen would have disowned with horror—and of course Origen does not stand alone in the guilt of setting these heresies afoot.

It seems to me that here is a prime example of that *inconsistency* of doctrine which we have continually noted in Origen and which *in him* earns the leniency due to the pioneer. Origen in reality knows full well that there is but One Mediator, that none is so pure as to offer a blameless sacrifice. Cf. for example *Comm. Rom.* VI.1 (pp. *127*f), *Comm. Ser. Mt.* 88 (p. *128*), and in the *Exhortation to Martyrdom* itself the emphatic assertion that concludes c. 12: 'One only has proved able to give an "exchange" for a soul previously lost—He who purchases us with His precious blood.' ('Exchange' here is from Matthew 16[26]—'what exchange shall a man give for his own soul?') But these 'inconsistencies' of Origen were apt to be absorbed by later theologians and developed to a degree that proved far more disastrous than the overt 'heresies' for which Origen was condemned. The doctrine of martyrdom is a cardinal instance of this.

The Resurrection

Little comment is called for on these passages. As with the Cross, there is a visible and an invisible significance—the historical example of the eternal life which crowns the patient endurance of the sufferings of this life, and the spiritual founding of a new, regenerate creation, which (being eternal) reaches back to Adam as well as forward from the empty tomb—for we, as the sons of Adam, share in that corporate humanity which the Risen Christ will redeem *as a whole*. The fruits of His rising from the dead are at once intellectual and moral—the deeper understanding of divine truth, and the faith that issues in the ethical fruits of the new life in Him. The pattern of His death and resurrection is thus 'earthed' in the lives of His believers, and the Risen Christ ranges the world, winning everywhere for God those who are seeking the good life. The long passage quoted above from *Comm. Rom.* IV.7 (pp. *133*ff) is as fine an example of Origen's biblical theology as may be found, with its vindication of the Resurrection as a greater miracle than the Creation, its tracing back of the vision of the Resurrection and its cosmic significance to Abraham, its 'inaugurated eschatology' of the new life in glory for the believer, its firm ethical grounding of the whole doctrine, and its elevation of the Resurrection to a position of primacy among the objects of our faith.

The Continuing Work of Christ

In this section my task of *selection* has been at its most difficult. In all these passages Origen is taking the Incarnate work of Christ and applying it to all nations and all ages—that which was 'once-for-all' becomes the available and regulative pattern of salvation for that new family of the redeemed which was inaugurated by the Cross and the Resurrection and will be co-extensive with humanity when He comes again in glory.

The balance of the intellectual and the ethical, which we noted above, is maintained with surprising consistency. There is no concession to the natural theology or the philosophical agnosticism of Celsus; there is equally no concession to ethical relativism. All is of Christ, and because of this the knowledge is truth and the ethical goal is perfection. Origen might rest his claim to be a 'theologian of grace' on his treatment of these themes with more than usual confidence; the occasional inconsistency and the careless expression are there, but grace is truly abounding.

One of his prime convictions is that our sonship of God is by adoption—that sonship is of grace. So many other theologians have worked on the easy assumption that Christianity 'means' that God is Father of all and all men are His sons that it seemed right to let Origen declare his own biblical orthodoxy here. Our *dual* sonship—of the devil and of God—and the life-long tension between the two lie at the heart of the ethical struggle.

The question most obviously suggested in connection with Prayer has been mentioned above (p. *153*, note 54). It seemed fitting to conclude the whole section with renewed stress on the *universalism* of at least the *offer* of salvation. Here Origen is the true son of St Paul. With all his stumblings and inconsistencies, he knew in whom he had believed, and in the strength of that conviction preached his Saviour to all mankind.

§ 3. THE GRACE OF GOD THE HOLY SPIRIT

This theme may best be introduced by reproducing the relevant passages from *Princ.* I.3, which is devoted to the Person and Work of the Holy Spirit.

> *Princ.* I.3.1: '. . . we believe that the only possible way of explaining and bringing to human knowledge the higher and more divine doctrines concerning the Son of God is by means of the Scriptures which were inspired by the Holy Spirit (both Old Testament and New Testament).'
>
> Ibid. 4 (Quotes Isa 42[5]: 'He who gives Spirit to the people on earth, and Spirit to them that walk upon it.'). 'For unquestionably everyone who "walks upon earth", i.e. every earthly and corporeal being, partakes of the Holy Spirit, which he receives from God'. . . . 'All knowledge of the Father, whom the Son reveals, is gained in the Holy Spirit. [Quotes Mt 11[27] for the revelation by the Son, and 1 Cor 2[10] for the revelation through the Holy Spirit.] Further: when in the gospel the Saviour mentions the divine and deeper doctrines which His disciples could not yet receive, He says . . . (Jn 16[12f], 14[26]). We must then, understand that as the Son, who alone knows the Father, reveals Him to whom He wills, so also the Holy Spirit, who alone "searches the deep things of God" reveals God to whom He wills.'
>
> Ibid. 5: 'It seems right to inquire why he who is "born again through God" (1 Pet 1[3]) unto salvation has need of Father, Son and Holy Spirit, and will not attain salvation without the Trinity as a whole; and also why it is impossible to become partaker of the Father or the Son without the Holy Spirit. In this part of our discussion it will of course be necessary to describe the special working of the Holy Spirit, as also the special working of Father and Son.'
>
> [Koetschau inserts here a Greek fragment quoted by Justinian.] 'The God and Father, who holds the universe together, works on every existing being, for He imparts to each one from His own being the existence that he has. The scope of the Son's working is less (for He comes second as compared with the Father), and effects rational beings only: the working

of the Holy Spirit is still more restricted, and applies only to the saints.'

Ibid. 6: 'That the working of the Father and Son applies to both saints and sinners is evident from the fact that all rational beings are participants in the Word of God—i.e. in reason—and because of this bear about implanted within them certain seeds, as it were, of Wisdom and Righteousness, which is Christ. (All things that exist—rational or irrational, and, among the rational, righteous and sinners—derive their being from the Father; and Christ is "in the heart" of all men [cf. Rom 10⁶⁻⁸] because He is the Word (reason), in sharing which men are rational.)

Ibid. 7: (But Gen 6³, LXX, 'My Spirit shall not remain in these people for ever, because they are flesh' shows that) 'God's Spirit is taken away from all the unworthy. (Cf. Ps 104²⁹ᶠ, "Thou shalt take away their spirit and they shall die and revert to their earth; Thou shalt send forth Thy Spirit and they shall be created, and Thou shalt renew the face of the earth" —i.e.) after sinners and unworthy people have been removed and wiped out, the Holy Spirit creates for Himself a new people and "renews the face of the earth", when through the grace of the Spirit men "put off the old man with his doings" and "begin to walk in newness of life" (Col 3⁹, Rom 6⁴). This is why it is fittingly said of the Holy Spirit that He will not dwell in all men, nor in those who are "flesh", but in those whose "earth has been renewed". In consequence the Holy Spirit was bestowed through the laying-on of the apostles' hands after the grace and renewal of baptism (Acts 8¹⁸, Tit 3⁵). Also our Saviour after the resurrection, when "old things had now passed away and all things had become new" (2 Cor 5¹⁷), Himself being the "new man" (Eph 2¹⁵) and "firstborn from the dead" (Col 1¹⁸), says to the apostles, themselves also renewed by faith in His resurrection, "Receive the Holy Spirit" (Jn 20²²). This is of course what our Saviour Lord Himself was referring to in the gospel, when He said that "new wine" could not be "put into old wineskins" (Mt 9¹⁷), and ordered that new wineskins be made, i.e. that men should walk "in newness of life" (Rom 6⁴), in order that they might receive the new wine, the newness of the grace of the Holy Spirit.

'Thus the working of the power of God the Father and Son

extends discriminately over every creature, but we find that participation in the Holy Spirit is had by saints only. . . . It is a consequence of this, I think, that "he who has sinned against the Son of Man is worthy of forgiveness" (Mt 12^{32}), because he who shares in the Word (or reason) would appear, if he ceases to live according to reason, to have fallen into ignorance or folly and thus to deserve pardon; but he who has once been held worthy to share in the Holy Spirit and then turns backward is by this very fact and deed said to have "blasphemed against the Holy Spirit" (ibid.).'

Ibid. 8: '. . . When therefore (rational beings) obtain first their existence from God the Father, then their rational nature from the Word, and thirdly their holiness from the Holy Spirit, they are made capable of receiving Christ in His capacity of Righteousness, because they have now been sanctified through the Holy Spirit; and those who have merited the attainment of this degree of progress through the sanctification of the Holy Spirit obtain just as surely the gift of wisdom through the power of the working of the Spirit of God.'

(The passage concludes in words quoted already—above, pp. 73f—and concludes:)

'That this may come to pass, and that those who were made by God may be present unceasingly and inseparably with Him who is, it is the work of wisdom to instruct and educate them and lead them to perfection, by the strengthening and the unceasing sanctification of the Holy Spirit, through which sanctification alone they can attain to God.'

The ideas expressed in this section of *De Princ.* may be traced through the whole range of Origen's writings. I set them out here, in what seems to be their order of importance, with representative illustrations and expansions.

The grace of the Father applies to all creation; the grace of the Son to all rational beings; but the grace of the Holy Spirit is restricted to the saints—the regenerate. It must thus be deserved; the recipients must be (for example)—

(1) *Those who merit it through faith in Christ or through thirsting after and longing for God.*

(2) *Those cleansed by the Law, who have known and fulfilled the commandments of God.*

(3) *Those who are faithful, gentle, humble, pure in heart—whose lives are praiseworthy for their good deeds, their virtues, their love.*

(4) *Those who have laid aside bad habits and innate vices.*

Hence the reception of the Holy Spirit does not follow baptism automatically. Baptism itself must be preceded by the attainment of purity 'coram hominibus' through self-discipline, and is only a stage on the long, hard way to the sanctification and salvation bestowed by the Holy Spirit.

Princ. I.1.3: '(The Holy Spirit) is a sanctifying power, a share of which all are said to have who have deserved to be sanctified through His grace.'

Ibid. II.11.5: 'The grace of the Holy Spirit . . . is given to the faithful.'

Hom. Lev. VI.2: 'You, who wish to receive holy baptism and to earn the grace of the Spirit, must first submit to the cleansing of the Law—must hear the Word of God, cut out your innate vices and lay aside . . . your barbarous habits, that in gentleness and humility you may be able to receive in addition the grace of the Holy Spirit.'

Hom. Num. III.1: ' "Not all who are descended from Israel belong to Israel" (Rom 9[6]), nor are all who have been washed with water straightway washed with the Holy Spirit, just as (on the other hand) not all who are enrolled as catechumens are outside the sphere of the Spirit. Cornelius was a catechumen, and before he came to the waters he deserved to be granted the Holy Spirit. Simon had received baptism, but because he was insincere in seeking this grace he was denied the gift of the Holy Spirit (Acts 8).'

Ibid. VI.3 on 11[25] ('The Spirit rested on them and they all prophesied'): 'We read that the Spirit rests not on all men whatsoever but on the holy and blessed; For the Spirit of God rests on the "pure in heart"[70] and on those who purify their souls from sin, just as He does not dwell in a body given over to sins—even if He has dwelt in it in the past; for the Holy Spirit cannot tolerate the partnership and company of an evil spirit. For there is no doubt that when we sin an evil

---

[70] Matthew 5[8], where however the Holy Spirit is not mentioned. Cf. *Comm. Jn.* XXXII.8: 'The hour had now come when the Holy Spirit dwelt on those disciples how had become pure.'

spirit comes and makes play in our heart, whosoever we be. . . .
Hence our sin "grieves the Holy Spirit" (Eph 4³⁰), but our
righteous and holy deeds prepare Him a "resting-place" in us.
Hence (in Numbers 11) . . . to say that the Spirit rested on
the seventy elders is to declare the praiseworthiness and goodness of their lives.'

Ibid. XI.8 on 18⁹ (literally 'sanctified holy-things'): 'My
interpretation is that the Holy Spirit is so holy as to be above
"sanctification"; for *His* holiness comes not from some outside source, thus making Him holy—He was always holy. . . .
But every creature will be "sanctified unto holiness", either
through the Holy Spirit who deems it fitting to make him so,
or through his own merits.'

Hom. 1 Sam. 18 on 2⁵ ('the barren has borne seven'): 'My
soul within me was "barren"—it bore not the "fruits of
righteousness" (Jas 3¹⁸). But now, when through faith in
Christ it has merited the grace of the Holy Spirit, and the
"spirit of wisdom . . . and fear of the Lord" (Isa 11²ᶠ)
has filled it, "the barren" has beyond question "borne
seven". . . .' [N.B. The spirit at Isa 11² has *seven* predicates.]

Sel. Ps. 119¹³¹ ('I opened my mouth and panted (drew
breath), because I longed for Thy commandments'): 'He who
through his actions has opened his heart, draws in the Holy
Spirit who reveals to him the mysteries of God. The "mouth"
of my soul is my understanding. Closing this to evil thoughts,
I opened it to good ones, and drew in the Spirit of understanding, grace and wisdom. The cost of the grant [χορηγία] of
the Spirit is the recital and execution of the commandments
of God: no sooner is our mouth opened than the Spirit is
drawn in from heaven.'

Comm. Song Songs, III, p. 213: '. . . The Holy Spirit, from
whom those who thirst after and long for God obtain "spiritual
graces" (Rom 1¹¹) and heavenly gifts.'

Hom. Ezek. VI.5 on 16⁴ ('You are not washed with water
unto salvation'): 'Not all are "washed unto salvation". Those
of us who have received the grace of baptism in the name of
Christ are "washed", but I cannot tell which are washed
"unto salvation". Simon was "washed" . . . but because he
was not washed unto salvation he was condemned by the one
who said to him in the Holy Spirit "your money perish with

you" (Acts 8²⁰). It is tremendously hard for him who is washed to be washed unto salvation. Hearken, ye catechumens . . . and prepare yourselves while you are still catechumens and unbaptized . . . : he who is washed but not unto salvation receives the water but not the Holy Spirit. He who is washed unto salvation receives both.'

Hom. Lk. XVII on 2³⁶: 'Anna appears to have been fittingly a prophetess, since the Holy Spirit had been able to find a place within her because of her holiness and purity. . . . His dwelling within her was no random proceeding.'

Comm. Jn. XXXII 7(6) on 13¹⁰: (Why wash the already clean?) 'He washed their feet because, although they were clean by human standards they were not so *coram Deo*. For without the help of Jesus none is pure before God, even if previously by some discipline or other he had been deemed to have made himself pure. But in those who have already gained purity on human standards, and gone on to be washed in His baptism and have their feet washed by Him, the Holy Spirit can make His dwelling and the power from on high as a garment. . . .'

Ibid. *Frag.* 37: 'The Holy Spirit comes only to the virtuous and stays far from bad men. . . . Apart from and alien to the bad, it fills those who have faith and love.'

The Scriptures (Old Testament and New Testament) were inspired by the Holy Spirit, and the grace of wisdom and knowledge granted by that Spirit is necessary for their understanding, especially as regards—

(a) *The reasons which underly the facts of the* κήρυγμά.
(b) *The sacramental, spiritual (i.e. allegorical) interpretation of Scripture;*
(c) *The deeper doctrines—the divine mysteries—of God. Granted such grace, a Christian teacher can teach the same things, and in the same way, that Jesus taught.*

Princ. Pref. 3: 'The holy apostles, in their preaching of the faith of Christ, took the doctrines they believed to be essential and handed them down without any kind of reserve to all believers —even to those with little aptitude for the investigation into divine knowledge. The reasons, however, for their assertions they left to the inquiry of those who should merit the excelling gifts of the Spirit, and especially those who should have acquired through the Holy Spirit Himself the grace of speech, wisdom, knowledge. . . .'

Ibid. 8: 'The Scriptures were written through the Spirit of God, and they possess not only the meaning which lies on the surface but another which is too deep for most of its readers; for the contents of Scripture are the outward forms of certain sacramental truths—the images of divine things. The whole Church is agreed that while there is but one law, and it is spiritual, the spiritual significance is only appreciated by those who are granted the grace of the Holy Spirit in the word of wisdom and knowledge.'

Ibid. II.7.2: 'Through the grace of the Holy Spirit this most wonderful of all His numerous gifts is made manifest—that whereas in previous times only a few, hardly any indeed beyond the prophets themselves, could understand the writings of the prophets or the Mosaic Law in any sense beyond the mere literal meaning of the words, or rise to any appreciation of their higher, spiritual significance: in these days believers beyond number, who may indeed not all be able to explain with order and clarity the logic of the spiritual interpretation, yet with few exceptions need no convincing that circumcision should not be understood literally, nor the sabbath rest, nor the pouring out of an animal's blood, nor the fact that God gave answers to the inquiries of Moses about these things. This insight is beyond question prompted by the working of the Holy Spirit in them all.'

Hom. Gen. IX.1 on 22$^{15-17}$: (—we now approach 'deep waters') 'we who with our small accomplishments and limited intelligence presume to embark on such a vast sea of mysteries. But if the Lord deigns . . . to give us a favouring breath of His Holy Spirit, we shall make the harbour of safety.'

Hom. Lev. VI.6: 'The proper tasks of a priest are twofold: to learn of God by reading and frequently meditating on Holy Scripture, and to teach the people. But let him teach what he has learned from God—not "from his own heart" (Ezek. 13^2) or from human understanding, but the things the Spirit teaches. . . .[71] And so we, meditating on [the Old Testament

---

[71] Cf. *Hom. Ezek.* II.2: 'If a man teaches the same things in the same way that Jesus . . . taught, he speaks not "from his own heart" but by the Holy Spirit.'

narratives], recalling them to mind day and night, and continuing instant in prayer, should pray God that He may deign to reveal to us true knowledge of what we read, and to show us how we may keep the spiritual law, both in our understanding and in our actions. So may we deserve to obtain spiritual grace, enlightened by the law of the Holy Spirit.'

Ibid. XIII.4: 'We [as contrasted with the heretics] say that there is one and the same Holy Spirit in the Law and the Gospels.'

Ibid. XIII.6: 'Let us take pains to avoid being found unworthy of so great and sublime an understanding [viz. the mystical interpretation of Leviticus 24[1ff]], but rather that our soul should first become a "holy place" in which we may receive the holy mysteries by the grace of the Holy Spirit, from whom everything that is holy has received its sanctity.'

Hom. Num. XXVI.3: 'It is the Holy Spirit who tells the deeds of which we read. . . . For whence could Moses tell of what has been done since the beginning of the world or what was in store at its end, unless through the inspiration of the Holy Spirit? Whence could he prophesy of Christ, unless the Holy Spirit told him? . . . The meaning of the narrative [in Numbers] and the real truth hidden under this veil, can only be known in full clarity, as I hold, by the Holy Spirit, who inspired the words, and by our Lord Jesus Christ, who said of Moses "he wrote of me" (Jn 5[46]), and by Almighty God, whose venerable counsel is revealed to mankind not by open disclosure but under the veil of letters.'

Comm. Song Songs, Prol., p. 77: '(The true student of Scripture will achieve his aim) if . . . in his search he knocks on the "door of wisdom" (Col 4[3]), asking God that it may be opened to him and that he may deserve to receive through the Holy Spirit the word of Wisdom . . . and become a participator in that wisdom.'

Comm. 1 Cor., § 11 on 2[12-15] (*JTS*, IX.240): 'The apostolic writings show us how one is taught by the Holy Spirit. For it is "by comparing spiritual truths with spiritual"—collating this passage (of Scripture) with that and bringing together parallel sayings—that as it were the "mind" of Scripture is revealed. . . . This means not merely understanding the "truths of the Spirit' which inspired Isaiah, but gaining possession of

N

that same Spirit which "locked" (Isa 22²²) and "sealed" (Isa 29¹¹) the writings of Isaiah. For if the Spirit has not "opened" the words of the prophets, the imprisoned truths cannot be opened.'

The Holy Spirit, by granting us wisdom and knowledge, reveals to our minds the secrets of the natural universe, the how and why of natural events—and even leads us in thought to the supercelestial region. He leads our minds to God by adding clarity and certainty to our ideas about God and revealing to us the mysteries of God's love.

Princ. II.7.3: '. . . the Holy Spirit, in whom is every kind of gift. For to some is offered by the Spirit the word of wisdom, to others the word of knowledge, to others faith (cf. 1 Cor 12⁸ᶠ); and thus in the life of individuals who can receive him, the Spirit Himself becomes, and is apprehended as, just that which is needed by the man who has earned the right to participate in Him.'

Ibid. I.7.3: 'The inquiry into these matters [i.e. whether sun, moon and stars are living beings with souls, and what will happen to them "after the consummation of this age"] may appear somewhat overbold; but because we are motivated by eagerness to make the truth our prize, it does not seem out of place to seek out and put to the test what is open to us by the grace of the Holy Spirit.'

Ibid. II.7.4: 'By the guidance of the Spirit (he who has earned the right to participate in Him) has come to know the *raisons d'être* of all things—why and how they happen.'

Cels. VII.44: '(Even an uneducated Christian) . . . in his prayers out-climbs the whole world . . . and comes in thought to the supercelestial region, being guided by the divine Spirit.'

Ibid. VI.17 (Quotes Psalm 18¹¹: 'God made darkness His hiding-place'): 'By this it is made clear that the ideas about God which are open to human understanding on its own merits are without clarity or certainty, since God hides Himself as if in darkness from those who cannot bear the radiance of knowledge of Him and who cannot see Him—partly because of the defilement of the mind that is bound to a human "body of humiliation" (Phil 3²¹), partly because of its limited power to comprehend God. . . . That the prophet may show the profundity of the doctrines about God, which is beyond the reach of those who do not possess the Spirit that searches all things, and searches even the deep things of God (1 Cor 2¹⁰), he says "The great deep like a garment is His covering" (Ps 104⁶).'

Comm. 1 Cor., § 10 (*JTS*, IX.239): ' "The Spirit searches everything, even the deep things of God" (1 Cor 2¹⁰). . . . The soul of man cannot search "everything", and a greater Spirit was necessary within us . . . that we, by the mingling of this Spirit with us, might search along with Him "everything, even . . .".'

Cels. IV.95: 'We pray that there may shine "in our hearts" the "light of the knowledge of the glory of God" (2 Cor 4⁶), through the Spirit of God dwelling in our imagination and picturing to us the things of God. "For as many as are led by the Spirit of God, they are the sons of God" (Rom 8¹⁴).'

Sel. Ps. 43³ ('Send me thy light'): 'That is, the light sent out from (the Father) into the mind of those who are called to redemption—the understanding through the Spirit, which leads those who are thus enlightened to God.' (Cf. *Sel. Ps.* 119¹³¹, p. *174*.)

Comm. Song Songs, Prol., p. 74 ('God is love'; hence—): 'Just as "none knoweth the Father but the Son and he to whom the Son is willing to reveal Him", even so none knows love save the Son. . . . Further, . . . only the Holy Spirit "proceedeth from the Father", and hence knows the things that are in God (just as the "spirit of a man knoweth the things that are in man"). Here then the "paraclete, the Spirit of truth, who proceedeth from the Father", ranges, searching for any souls worthy and fitted for His revelation of the greatness of this love which is from God.' (Mt 11²⁷, Jn 15²⁶, 1 Cor 2¹¹.)

The ethical gifts of the Holy Spirit are set out by St Paul (Gal 5²²)— love, joy, peace, patience, etc.—in a word, all the virtues. The evil spirits working within a man strengthen the dishonourable passions of 'the flesh': the Holy Spirit upholds the righteous, and helps human nature in its weakness to grow strong in 'the spirit'. All human good—public laws and institutions as well as moral standards—is given by God through the Holy Spirit.

Hom. 1 Sam. 10 (Quotes Rom 5²⁰ and adds): 'When the grace of God has driven out the evil spirits, it leads in the Holy

Spirit, and the soul which had been filled with an unclean spirit is thereafter filled with the Holy Spirit.'

Sel. Ps. 37[17] ('The Lord upholds the righteous'): 'Nothing upholds the righteous as does a spiritual grace-gift.' (Cf. Rom 1[11].)

Comm. Mt. XVI.27 on 21[17-22]: 'Jesus "was hungry", i.e. constantly seeking to share in the fruits of the Holy Spirit in the life of the righteous; His food, if one may put it so, the "figs" that He eats in His hunger, is the love growing in the life of him who bears it—that love which is the first "fruit of the Spirit"—and joy, peace, longsuffering, etc. (Gal 5[22]).'

Ibid. 29: '(If the "figs" were the fruits of the Holy Spirit, what about Mark 11[13], "it was not the season for figs"?) It is better to display the fruits of the Holy Spirit when circumstances make it difficult than when everything is easy.' (Origen compares Matthew 5[44f], 'Love your enemies', etc.)

Hom. Lk. XI on 1[80] ('grew and became strong in spirit'): 'To grow and to become strong are different things. Human nature is weak, and if it is to become strong, needs the help of a stronger. Whose help? The Spirit's. This means that he who would be truly strong must "become strong *in spirit*". The majority become strong in and according to the flesh, but the athletes of God (2 Tim 2[3ff]) become strong in spirit, and because of this become valiant against the "mind that is set on the flesh" (Rom 8[7]). For the Spirit wrestles with the flesh, and the man's spirit which that Spirit strengthens wins the victory.'

Ibid. XXII on 3[5ff]: 'Everyone without faith is a deep and hollow "valley": belief in Christ fills him with the fruits of the Spirit—that is, with the virtues.'

Ibid. *Frag.* IX on 6[43]: 'The "good tree" is the Holy Spirit, the "bad tree" is the devil and his servants. He who has the Holy Spirit shows forth His fruits, which the apostle enumerates (at Gal 5[22]). He who has the opposite power bears the fruits of "dishonourable passions" (Rom 1[26]), "thorns and thistles" (Heb 6[8]).'

Comm. Rom. IX.24 (p. *42*): (all human good, including moral standards and public laws and institutions, comes from God and is given through the Holy Spirit).

It is the Holy Spirit that empowers the Christian ministry of the Word (and Christian miracles, although these are disappearing): but the Spirit is above all active in prophecy—Jewish and Christian (for the same Christ-given Spirit is at work in both Old Testament and New Testament). The prophets were chosen by Providence on ethical grounds, and granted mental illumination, brighter radiance of soul, and even purity of the body. The presence of the Holy Spirit in the prophets has been proved by the accuracy of their forecasts.

Hom. Josh. II.1 ('Moses my servant is dead'): 'We must understand in what sense Moses is dead before we can perceive the sense in which Jesus reigns. Look then at Jerusalem overthrown, the altar deserted, no signs of sacrifices . . . offerings . . . libations . . . priests . . . ; you must then say "Moses the servant of God is dead". . . . But look at the Gentiles coming to the Faith, Churches a-building, altars not sprinkled with the blood of cattle but consecrated by the precious blood of Christ—priests and Levites ministering not the blood of bulls and goats but the word of God through the grace of the Holy Spirit: you must then say that Jesus has succeeded Moses. . . .'

Hom. Lk. IV on 1[17] ('in the spirit and power of Elijah'): '(The relationship between Elijah and John the Baptist was *not* "metempsychosis")[72] for to Elijah there came Spirit and power, or (one may say) a spiritual grace-gift, as to each of the prophets; and the Spirit which was in Elijah came to be in John.' (Later, Origen defines 'in the spirit' as 'in the prophetic grace'.)

Ibid. XVII (p. *175*) (Anna the prophetess).

Cels. IV.21: 'Since the prophets who foretold much in the future are shown to have told the truth about much which has now come to pass, and to have given proof that there was a divine Spirit in them, clearly we ought to believe them—or rather the divine Spirit in them—concerning things still in the future.'

Ibid. VII.4: 'The Jewish prophets, illuminated by the divine Spirit as far as was servicable to their prophesying, were the first to enjoy the visitation of the superior Spirit to them. Because of what I may term the touch of what we call the "Holy" Spirit upon their soul they gained clearer mental perception

---

[72] Inaccurately 'reincarnation'.

and brighter radiance of the soul and even of the body, which no longer warred against the life-according-to-virtue, because it was mortified in respect of the "mind of the flesh" (Rom 8⁶ff). For we are persuaded that the "deeds of the body" and the enmities arising from the "mind of the flesh" which is opposed to God, are done to death by the divine Spirit.'

Ibid. 7: 'Of the Jewish prophets some were wise before they received the gift of prophecy and divine inspiration, others became wise through the mental illumination that the actual gift of prophecy bestowed. These were chosen by Providence to be entrusted with the Divine Spirit . . . on the ground of the unexampled and finely-toned freedom of their lives—such a quality as would face danger and death without fear.'[73]

Ibid. 8: 'It is general knowledge that the Holy Spirit has forsaken (the Jews) because they were guilty of impiety against God and against Him who was foretold by their prophets. But signs of the Holy Spirit were manifested at the commencement of the teaching of Jesus, and more still after His ascension, though later they became less. There are indeed to this day traces of (the Spirit) in a few men whose souls have been purified by the Word and the actions which He inspires.'[74]

Sel. Lam. 4²⁰: 'The Spirit that worked in the prophets was Christ . . . it is Christ who has given us the Spirit of prophecy.'

The grace of the Holy Spirit has an especial place in Prayer. *Of his own resources man can neither understand prayer nor pray as he ought. Before prayer can be understood the Father must shed light on it, the Son must teach it, and the Spirit work within us. Before we can pray as Jesus did, we must be taught by Jesus and hear the prayer of the Holy Spirit, who because of His love for us makes up the deficiencies of our own prayers by His intercessions with the Father—intercessions which vary in intensity with our ethical deserts. Our own constant prayers result, for example, in the conception by our previously barren minds through the Holy Spirit of true and saving thoughts.*

Prayer II.3: 'We "do not know how to pray as we ought" (Rom 8²⁶); and Paul goes on to tell us whence the deficiency

---

[73] Chadwick ad loc. compares *Hom. Jer.* XV.1: '. . . the exceptional qualities of the prophets—their freedom, courage, watchfulness.'

[74] The reference here is to Christian miracles. On their occasional survival in the Church of Origen's day, cf. Chadwick ad loc. (p. 402, note 1) and *SJT*, VII.2.133ff.

may be made good for the man who, although he lacks this knowledge, yet tries to make himself worthy of having what is lacking supplied—"The Spirit itself makes intercession for us to God with groanings . . .". And the Spirit that cries in the hearts of the blessed "Abba, Father" (Gal 4⁶) . . . makes intercession for us to God . . . because of His great love and fellow-suffering [συμπάθειαν] for man, taking up our lamentations. . . . And this Spirit, not content with making intercession to God, intensifies His intercession and "more than makes intercession"[75] in the case, I believe, of those who are "more than conquerors" (Rom 8³⁷). . . . Probably He makes intercession-and-no-more not for those who are more-than-conquerors, nor for the conquered, but for those who conquer-and-no-more.'

Ibid. 4: '(Akin to the Romans 8 passage is 1 Corinthians 14¹⁵—"I will pray [and sing] with the Spirit, and I will pray [and sing] with the understanding also".) For neither can our understanding pray unless the Spirit prays first, as it were in its hearing [and so with singing]. I believe that it was through seeing that human weakness is incapable of praying as one ought to pray, and realizing this above all when he heard the wise and mighty words spoken by the Saviour in His prayer to the Father, that one of the disciples of Jesus said to the Lord when He had finished praying "Lord, teach us to pray . . ." (Lk 11¹) (and *not* because the prayers of saints before Christ were not inspired by the Holy Spirit—they were!).'

Ibid. 6 (Origen's own prayer for divine help in expounding Prayer): 'Since then to expound prayer is such a difficult task that one needs the Father to shed light upon it and the Word Himself, the firstborn, to teach it, and the Spirit to work within us that we may understand and speak worthily of so great a theme, I beseech the Spirit, praying as a man (for I do not lay to my own credit the capacity for prayer), before I begin to speak of prayer, that it may be granted me to speak fully and spiritually (etc.).'

Ibid. XIII.3: 'How many things are there which each of us

---

[75] ὑπερεντυγχάνει (Rom 8²⁶) = 'intercedes for,' the prefix ὑπέρ signifying 'on behalf of'. ὑπέρ can, of course, mean 'excessively'; but to take ὑπερεντυγχάνει here as 'intercedes excessively', 'more than intercedes', as Origen does, in order to gain a link with Rom 8³⁷ ('more than conquerors'), is quite unjustifiable.

can recount, if he remembers with gratitude benefits done him and wishes to praise God for them? For souls long barren[76] knowing of the sterility of their own minds and the barrenness of their own understanding, have conceived by the Holy Spirit through constant prayer and brought forth words of salvation, filled with true ideas.' (Cf. *Hom. Lev.* VI.6 (pp. *176*f), *Comm. Song Songs*, Prol., p. 77 (p. *177*), *Cels.* VII.44 (p. *178*), ibid. IV.95 (p. *179*).)

If the gift of the Holy Spirit is abused or disparaged by evil speech, thought or action it is withdrawn.[77] Indeed, only on one—Jesus—has the Spirit descended in its fulness and never thence departed, because only He was personally sinless. From all others—prophets, saints, the faithful in general —the Spirit is at times removed; nor is any lawful human institution (e.g. marriage) such that the Spirit can grace its whole course with His presence. Correspondingly, when the Spirit comes to a man, His practice is to help, not to compel.

Princ. II.10.7: (on Luke 12[42-6]: the punishment of the unjust stewards—'cut asunder'—must mean the separation of spirit and soul; and if spirit = the Holy Spirit, the passage means that) 'when, either through baptism or through the grace of the Spirit, the word of wisdom or of knowledge or of anything else is given freely, and later abused . . . the gift of the Spirit will straightway be taken from the soul, and the part that is left (i.e. the substance of the soul) will be . . . separated from the Spirit, with whom, by joining itself to the Lord, it should have been "one spirit" (1 Cor 6[17]).'

Hom. Gen. XV.3: 'Because the divine fire can be from time to time extinguished even in the saints and the faithful, hear the apostle Paul prescribing for those who have deserved to receive the gifts and graces of the Spirit—"Quench not the Spirit" (1 Thess 5[19]).'

Hom. Num. VII.2 on 12[1-10], q.v.: ' "The cloud withdrew", and immediately (Miriam) was covered with leprosy—a demonstration that if a person has the grace of the Holy Spirit and then disparages or "speaks against" it, it withdraws from him . . . and immediately his soul is covered with leprosy.

[76] The metaphor is taken from the literal barrenness of Hannah.

[77] Cf. *Comm. 1 Cor.*, § 45 on 10[5] (*JTS.* X.29): 'The apostle's point is that it is not the mere reception of God's gift which saves the recipient, but the persevering in worthy possession of it. . . .'

For that whole people, too, had possessed the grace of God, but when later they blasphemed the true Moses—our Lord Jesus Christ—the "cloud withdrew" from them and passed over to us on that "high mountain" when our Saviour was "transfigured" and the "glittering cloud overshadowed" His disciples. . . . But we too should beware lest perchance we put to flight this cloud by evil speech, action or thought; for then will the leprosy of sin be seen in us, when the grace of God has deserted us.'

Hom. Lk. XXXIX on 19[11ff]: ' "Take the mina from him"—that is, the grace of the Holy Spirit, since while he is in possession of it he cannot be punished.'

Hom. Num. VI.3 on 11[25] (pp. *173*f. The passage continues): ' "The Spirit rested on all who prophesied"—on none of them, however, as He did on the Saviour [and quotes Isa 11[1-3], q.v.]. . . . Note that on no other is the Spirit said to have rested in this sevenfold way.[78] [Origen also quotes John 1[33] —the Spirit descending "and remaining": no one else, says Origen, is said to have the Spirit not only descending on him but remaining.] For because (Jesus) is the only one who never sinned (1 Pet 2[22]), in Him alone the Holy Spirit "remained". For if He is the object of that unique and tremendous affirmation—"He did no sin"—it is implied that everyone else had been under sin—including the prophets. . . . Now it may appear incredible that the prophets, after receiving the Holy Spirit, could ever sin; but look at Moses himself . . . , assuredly the greatest . . . of the prophets. He himself gives proof of his sin: . . . "Hear me, ye unbelievers; shall we bring you forth water out of this rock?" (Num 20[10]) . . . i.e. he *did* trust in the power of God and say that God *is* able to bring forth water from this rock; but with a certain weakness, springing from lack of trust, he said "Shall . . . ?" These were the words of one who spoke not by the Holy Spirit, but by the spirit of sin. [Origen also quotes the words of David at Psalm 51[11], "Take not thy Holy Spirit from me", and gives an example about Solomon.] (And as regards ordinary people: for example) marriage according to the law is not in itself sinful; but at the moment of consummation the presence of the Holy Spirit is withheld—even if the male partner is deemed

---

[78] Spirit of wisdom, understanding, etc. (see Isa 11[2]).

a prophet.[79] There are many other actions in which human ability suffices on its own, and the presence of the Holy Spirit is neither necessary nor desirable.'

(Cf. *Hom.* II in 1 Sam, pp. *32*f.)

Sel. Judg. 11²⁹ᵗ, q.v.: 'If the "Spirit of the Lord was upon (Jephthah)", how did he come to make such an inappropriate vow? . . . Did the Holy Spirit commit an error? Certainly not. The Holy Spirit came to him to help him, not to suggest the objectionable vow. It was Jephthah who went wrong. . . .'

---

[79] Cf. *Hom. Gen.* V.4: 'Marital intimacy is irreverent.'

In estimating Origen's doctrine of the Grace of the Holy Spirit, we must first seek his view of *the respective contributions in the sphere of Grace of the Father, Son and Holy Spirit.*

Princ. I.3.5 (p. *170*) (on the *range* of the workings of the Father [all creation], the Son [rational beings], the Spirit [the saints, the regenerate]).

Comm. Jn. II.10 (6) (pp. *46f*) (the Spirit makes available the 'raw material' [ὕλη] of grace-gifts, which the Father 'makes active' and the Son 'tends').

Princ. IV.4.5 (32): 'As by participation in the Son of God a man is adopted into the ranks of God's sons, and by participation in God's wisdom he is made wise, so also by participation in the Holy Spirit he is made *holy* and spiritual.'

Prayer XXVIII.3: 'Above all (our other obligations), we are the creation and fashioning of God (the Father), and so obliged to preserve a certain disposition toward Him—to love Him with all our heart, strength and mind (Lk 10²⁷); unless we honour this obligation, we continue to be God's debtors, sinning against Him. . . .⁸⁰ But we are also debtors of Christ, who purchased us with His blood, just as every slave is a debtor of his purchaser, since so much money has been given for him. Again, we are in debt to the Holy Spirit, which debt we pay when we do not "grieve" Him by whom we are "sealed unto the day of redemption" (Eph 4³⁰), and if we grieve Him not we bear the fruits that are required of us, since He Himself is with us and quickens our soul.'

Hom. Ezek. VI.6: '(In my exposition here) I shall take an example from men: then, if the Holy Spirit grants it, I shall proceed to Jesus Christ and God the Father.'

Princ. IV.2.2: '(The Scriptures) were composed, and have come down to us, from the inspiration of the Holy Spirit, by the will of the supreme Father, through Jesus Christ.'

Prayer II.6 (p. *183*) (we cannot expound Prayer unless the Father sheds light on it, the Son teaches it, the Spirit works within us).

---

⁸⁰ Do we, then, cease to be God's debtors if we *do* love Him?

Hom. Ezek. II.2 (p. *176*, note 71) (if a man teaches the same things in the same way that Jesus taught, he speaks 'by the Holy Spirit').

Hom. Num. IX.9 (on Numbers 17, the budding of Aaron's rod): 'Everyone who believes in Christ first dies then is reborn; and here is another lesson, in the subsequent budding of the dry rod. The first shoot is the first confession a man makes in Christ. Then come the leaves, when the reborn man has received the gift of grace from the sanctification of the Spirit of God. Thereafter he bears flowers when he has begun to make headway—to be graced with refinement of character, to put forth the bloom of mercy and kindness. Finally he brings forth the fruits of righteousness, by which he not only lives himself but offers life to others too. For when he reaches perfection and puts forth the word of faith, the word of the knowledge of God, and so benefits others, this is bearing fruits by which others may be nourished.—This is the way the various types of believers are produced from the rod of Aaron, who is Christ [and Origen equates these four types with those in 1 John 2$^{12-14}$, which are to him not age-divisions but stages in the soul's progress]. [See the rest of this passage above, p. *118*, especially "in a truly righteous man . . . Christ is said to 'climb' (Num 17^8, 'climbs into flower') until he bears 'the fruits of the Spirit . . . (etc.)' (Gal 5^{22})".]'

Comm. Rom. III.8 on 3^{25f} [the 'propitiatorium', understood as 'mercy-seat'. This, says Origen, goes back to Exodus 25^{17f}, where the 'mercy-seat made of pure gold' = the pure and holy (human) soul of Jesus. The 'cherubim' = the 'fulness of knowledge', which is to be found (*a*) in the Word of God (Col 2^3), (*b*) in the Holy Spirit (1 Cor 2^{10})—i.e. 'on that mercy-seat, the (human) soul of Jesus, dwell the Word of God—the only-begotten Son—and his His Holy Spirit'].

Princ. II.7.3: 'The Gospel shows (the Holy Spirit) to be of such power and majesty that it says the apostles could not yet receive those things which the Saviour wished to teach them until the Holy Spirit should have come, who could pour Himself into their souls and enlighten them concerning the nature and faith of the Trinity.'

Putting together these passages, along with the *locus classicus* from

Princ. I.3 (pp. *170*ff), we can see a doctrine emerging somewhat as follows:

(1) The Father gives existence to all that is; the Son redeems the rational creation; the Holy Spirit sanctifies the regenerate.

(2) The grace of the Holy Spirit is the power of God working *within* us: the Father remains *without* and *above* us, and the Son *mediates* between God and man. This principle may be exemplified:

(a) *Intellectually.* The Holy Spirit leads our minds to the Son and the Father: He enlightens us concerning the nature and faith of the Trinity. The Father is revealed *by* the Son, but all knowledge of Him is gained *in* the Holy Spirit.

(b) *Ethically.* The Father creates, the Son redeems, but the Holy Spirit within us quickens our souls that we may bear ethical fruits.

(c) *The Scriptures.* Their composition was authorized by the will of the Father, made possible through Jesus Christ, but implemented from the inspiration of the Spirit.

(d) *Prayer.* The understanding and practice of prayer requires that the Father should shed light on it, the Son should teach it, the Spirit work within us.

Thus, although the Father 'makes active' the gifts of divine grace for us, and the Son 'tends' them, the Spirit 'provides the raw material'—makes them available within us.

(3) The Christian path to perfection is marked by stages—conversion, rebirth, growth in grace, perfection itself. The first two stages are made possible through the grace of Jesus Christ; then the Spirit, with His sanctifying power, brings forth the growing refinements of character that culminate in that perfection of righteousness and wisdom which is the second reception of Christ, and which bears fruits from which others may be nourished. It is in accordance with this that the human soul of Jesus was the throne both of the Divine Word—the Son—and of the Holy Spirit, as bringing to mankind the promise and potency of the whole process of justification, sanctification, and evangelism.

This doctrinal scheme (if it may be so called) is illustrated in a curious passage from *Comm. Jn.* II.11 (6), which among other things seeks to explain why it is the sin against the Holy Spirit that should be unforgivable.

'In certain passages of Scripture (e.g. Isa 48[16], Mt 12[32]) the Spirit is, as it were, ranked higher than Christ. May not the explanation in the one case be, however, that it is not because of His higher ranking that sin against the Holy Spirit cannot be forgiven, but because those who partake in Christ and receive pardon on repenting from their sins include all rational beings, whereas those who are deemed worthy of the Holy Spirit cannot reasonably expect pardon when even with His unique concomitant inspiration for good they still fall away from and turn their backs on the counsels of the indwelling Spirit? (And as for Isaiah 48[16]—the Spirit sends Christ, not vice-versa) not as if the Spirit were naturally higher than He, but because the Saviour was made less than the Spirit through the divine plan [οἰκονομία] of the incarnation of the Son of God. [Origen quotes Hebrews 2[9] for this "lessening" of the Son of God.] Or possibly one might say too that the creation, including mankind, in order to be freed from the enslavement of corruption, needed the incarnation of blessed and divine power which could put this world right. This duty fell, as it were, on the Holy Spirit, but He could not sustain it, and put forward the Saviour who alone could undertake so great a task: hence when the Father—the Supreme Power—sent forth His Son, . . . the Holy Spirit sent Him too, with the promise that at the right moment He would descend on Him and work with Him for man's salvation.'

(On the unforgivable sin against the Spirit, cf. *Princ.* I.3.7) (p. *172*).

The strength of Origen's doctrine of the Grace of the Holy Spirit.

In the first place, we have throughout Origen a serious and sustained attempt to evaluate part at least of the Biblical witness on a theme which even today awaits a treatment really commensurate with that accorded at every stage of Church History to Christology. Origen was not only, to all intents and purposes, a pioneer in this, but in him we can trace the seeds of that developed pneumatology which the Eastern Church, as against the Roman and Protestant, makes its boast.

We note, for example, the high seriousness of his doctrine of sanctification; his keen sense of that inevitable human sin which perpetually jeopardizes this especial provision of God for the saints; his conviction that the Holy Spirit is a divine Person, and not a mere influence (still less, Stoic-wise, a 'substance'), and that the grace of the Holy Spirit is hence throughout a matter of personal relations; the closeness with which the work of Christ is complemented at point after point by the work of the Spirit, and the whole Christological pattern thus reproduced in the setting of the new perspective which pneumatology affords.

Cardinal instances of this last feature are given above in the passages concerning the Scriptures and the doctrine of Prayer, and in the careful balancing of the intellectual and the ethical— of Wisdom and Righteousness—in the whole series of extracts. It would be possible in addition to parallel the more detailed Christological insights we noted by similar thought on the work of the Spirit.[81]

The consistent emphasis on the *indwelling* of the Spirit is perhaps the most successful feature of Origen's doctrine. To the passages given above many others might be added, e.g.:

Comm. Rom. IV.5 (p. *45*) [on the 'firmness' of God's promises, stronger than any legal enactment and written by the Spirit on the heart of the believer].

Cels. VI.70: 'God is always giving a share in His own Spirit to those who are able to partake of Him . . . dwelling (sc. the Spirit) within those who are worthy. . . .'

Ibid. V.1: 'It is God's work to dwell unseen, by His Spirit and by the Spirit of Christ, in those in whom He judges it right to dwell.'

The weakness of Origen's doctrine of the Grace of the Holy Spirit.

The great flaw is surely the restriction of the grace of the Holy Spirit to the saints—the regenerate. This restriction results from Origen's failure to take in the *whole* of the biblical witness to the Spirit, and the unwarranted isolation of one feature of this witness from its total context most unhappily allows the fullest and least defensible exercise of Origen's favourite aberration—the doctrine of merits.

The cosmic drama of redemption, cast on the stage of history and recorded in the biblical narrative from Genesis to Revelation, is reproduced in the personal life of every believer. The Holy Spirit brooded over the face of the waters as the curtain rose; He was active throughout the whole chequered story of

---

[81] E.g. 'inaugurated eschatology': *Comm. Rom.* I.1: 'Just as the knowledge, which is now given to the holy, is given but "in a glass darkly", and so prophecy and the other gifts of the Spirit, the same is true of the liberty which is now available for the holy. It is not yet full liberty, but as it were "in a glass darkly".'

Israel, and most active where the genius of Israel responded most nearly to the call of God—in the life and witness of the prophets. He was preparing the world for the coming of Christ—from those far-off days when the morning stars sang together and all the sons of God shouted for joy, right down to those surpassingly wonderful moments when a little group of God-fearing people listened with awe to the glad tidings brought by the angel Gabriel. The final warning and promise is sounded by John the Baptist, and the One is born on whom the Spirit descends as a dove, and whose baptism is with the Holy Spirit and with fire. During that Incarnate life the Spirit, as it were, recedes into the background,[82] only to return at Pentecost with new and over-whelming power, to guide the infant Church in every critical decision and to guard it in every danger, to inspire the apostolic prophets of the New Israel, our promised Paraclete until the day when the Spirit and the Bride say 'Come . . .'.

This is the drama that is equally played out in the inner his-tory of the Christian soul. It is to the Holy Spirit that the Father entrusts what we may call our 'pre-evangelism': it is He who nurtures our yearnings for the divine, and who inspires every upward movement of the human spirit—aesthetical, ethical, philosophical, mystical. It is He who convicts us of our own helplessness to 'climb the heavenly steeps', and brings home to us the folly of trusting in our own merits. It is He who inspires the fundamental questions to which Christ alone can give the answers. All this may be called the 'Old Testament stage' of Christian belief. Then there comes the shattering moment of conversion—the entry of Christ into a life already awaiting Him, but whose whole pattern of question and expectancy is trans-formed by the sudden revelation that all our upward strivings and questionings of the eternal need a radical rethinking and 'regeneration' in the light of Him who has come. 'Calvary is the only gateway to Pentecost.' Thereafter the Holy Spirit can abide with those whose baptism into the death of Christ has fitted them to receive the peace, righteousness, joy and all the other gifts which that Spirit, who has brought home the Sacri-fice of Christ to all believers, nurtures with deepening root until

---

[82] I still think the answer Dr Flew gave to this problem to be the most satisfying. 'The whole conception of the Spirit in the Old Testament must needs be baptised into the death of Christ. Calvary was the only gateway to Pentecost.' (*Jesus and His Church*, pp. 70-1.)

the final goal of sanctified perfection is achieved. But the Cross is never left behind; and to the last moment the Spirit does but apply the one hope, the one justification, the one saving grace even of the saints in heaven—Christ crucified.

Origen's doctrine of the restriction of the grace of the Spirit to the regenerate takes, in effect, one part only of this whole process—the post-Pentecostal—and holds it in splendid isolation, and by so doing cuts it adrift from its biblical setting of preparation, 'pre-evangelism', and necessary grounding in the Cross. The biblical *context* of sanctification is wholly of grace; Origen is free to give it another context, almost wholly of merit.

A glance through the passages collected above makes this only too clear.

Princ. I.3.8 (p. *172*): 'Those who have merited the attainment of this degree of progress through the sanctification of the Holy Spirit'; ibid. I.1.3 (p. *173*): '(All have a share in the Spirit) who have deserved to be sanctified through His grace'; *Hom. Lev.* VI.2 (p. *173*): 'You, who wish to . . . earn the grace of the Spirit'; *Hom. Num.* VI.3 (p. *174*): 'To say that the Spirit rested on the seventy elders is to declare the praiseworthiness and goodness of their lives'; ibid. XI.8 (p. *174*): 'Every creature will be "sanctified unto holiness, *either through the Holy Spirit who deems it fitting to make him so, or through his own merits*" '; *Sel. Ps.* 119[131] (p. *174*): 'The cost of the grant of the Spirit is the recital and execution of the commandments of God'; *Hom. Lk.* XVII (p. *175*): 'The Holy Spirit had been able to find a place within (Anna) because of her holiness and purity'; *Comm. Jn. Frag.* 37 (p. *175*): 'The Holy Spirit comes only to the virtuous and stays far from bad men'; *Hom. Lev.* VI.6 (p. *177*): 'So may we deserve to obtain spiritual grace'; *Comm. Song Songs*, Prol., p. 77 (p. *177*): (of Bible-students deserving to receive through the Holy Spirit the word of Wisdom); *Princ.* II.7.3 (p. *178*): 'The Holy Spirit becomes . . . just what is needed by the man who has earned the right to participate in Him'; *Comm. Song Songs*, Prol., p. 74 (p. *179*): 'The Spirit . . . searches for any souls worthy and fitted for His revelation of God's love'; *Cels.* VII.7 (p. *182* and note 73) (moral qualifications for the prophetic grace); *Hom. Gen.* XV.3 (p. *184*): 'Those

o

who have deserved to receive the gifts and graces of the Spirit';
and cf. *Prayer* XXVIII.3 (p. *187* and my note).

Two passages are especially noteworthy:

Prayer II.3 (pp. *182*f), where the intensity of the Spirit's intercession varies with the ethical attainments of those for whom
He intercedes. A sound doctrine of Grace would surely suggest
that such variation of intensity, if it has any meaning, should
be in *inverse* ratio to human merit—'those who are conquered'
in the battle of life needing that intercession (on this reading)
far more than the 'conquerors', and the latter far more than
the 'more than conquerors'. It is true that such a doctrine of
Grace would go further and deny the validity of *any* such ratio,
direct and inverse. The prayer of or for the 'more than conquerors' must begin, like any others, with a confession of sin
and helplessness before God. But Origen loses on both counts:
he brings in his scale of merits, and he misapplies it.

Hom. Num. VI.3 (p. *185*): 'Because Jesus is the only one who
never sinned, in Him alone the Holy Spirit "remained".' In
everyone else it is intermittent because they sin [and Origen offers
some not very convincing examples of the sin of Moses, etc., to
prove his point]. Such a human institution as marriage is a good
thing, and the Holy Spirit is present; but the subsequent marital
intimacy occasions His retirement.[83] 'There are many other actions
in which human ability suffices on its own, and the presence of
the Holy Spirit is neither necessary nor desirable.'

This portrayal of the Holy Spirit like a maiden on the village
green flitting from swain to swain to find one she can trust, is
surely the *reductio ad absurdum* of the whole scheme of merit-
theology. One would like to ask Origen, very seriously, what
sin Jesus had committed when the cry was forced from Him:
'My God, My God, why hast Thou forsaken Me?' In the presence of sin the Word of God through the Holy Spirit may judge,
may pardon, may heal: sinners might be considerably more at
ease if He merely withdrew. 'Depart from me, for I am a sinful
man', cried Peter. 'Fear not . . .', said Jesus. In these matters

---

[83] Cf. *Comm. Rom.* (Gk), § 3 (*JTS*, XIII.213) 1[11f]: 'There are some "grace-gifts"
which are *not* "spiritual", e.g. marriage. For a spiritual gift could never hinder
prayer, but marital intimacy prevents it. But marriage *is* a "grace-gift", as the
apostle shows (at 1 Cor 7[7]).'

'the Lord is the Spirit' (2 Cor 3^{17}), for there is but one divine answer to sin. And as for marriage, Origen is of course seeing the Spirit in his own celibate image; the doctrine of the *essential* sinfulness of marital intimacy is very far from biblical. Origen may well suggest that in these matters 'human ability suffices in its own', and leaves him to pursue the truth of pneumatology in less distasteful fields.

We have previously suggested that Origen's real fault in this matter of grace-merit is inconsistency—failure to think through the whole doctrine in terms of the total biblical witness; and sure enough in this section too he contradicts himself again and again with no sense of incongruity.

> *Princ.* I.3.4 (p. *170*): 'Unquestionably every earthly and cor-poreal being partakes of the Holy Spirit'; ibid. 5: 'It is im-possible to become partaker of the Father or the Son without the Holy Spirit'; ibid. 7: 'Through the grace of the Spirit men . . . "begin to walk in newness of life" ' [contrast, a few lines later: 'Men should "walk in newness of life" in order that they might receive . . . the grace of the Holy Spirit']; *Hom. Lev.* XIII.4 (p. *177*): 'There is one and the same Holy Spirit in the Law and the Gospels'; ibid. XIII.6 (p. *177*): 'Let us take pains . . . that our soul should first become a "holy place" in which we may receive the holy mysteries by the grace of the Holy Spirit, from whom everything that is holy has received its sanctity'; *Hom. Lk.* XI (p. *180*): 'The Spirit wrestles with the flesh, and the man's spirit which that Spirit strengthens wins the victory'; *Comm. Rom.* IX.24 (p. *42*): (All human good . . . is given through the Holy Spirit); *Prayer* II.4 (the prayers of saints before Christ were inspired by the Holy Spirit). (p. *183*)

These passages could be indefinitely multiplied; contrast, for example:

> *Comm. Rom.* I.5: 'He is called the Spirit of holiness because he offers holiness to all', with *Cels.* IV.7: 'In each generation the wisdom of God enters souls which she finds holy and makes them friends of God and prophets. Indeed one could find in the sacred books men in each generation who were holy—and receptive of the divine Spirit.'

Origen's exposition of the unforgivable sin against the Holy Spirit (*Princ.* I.3.7 (p. *172*), *Comm. Jn.* II.11 (6) (pp. *189*f) is based on the theology of merits. Sin against the Word (or 'reason'—Λόγος) argues mere ignorance or folly, which is pardonable. But sin against the Holy Spirit is the sin of the saints, who ought to have been above such things, blessed as they are with His 'unique concomitant inspiration for good'. Contrast with this facile moralism a passage in which Origen makes the startling suggestion of a '*Kenosis*' of the Holy Spirit Himself.

> *Comm. Mt.* XIII.18 on 18¹⁻⁶ (a suggested interpretation): 'Let us ask what child it was that Jesus called to Him and set in the midst of the disciples. May it not have been the Holy Spirit, humbling Himself and called by the Saviour to take His stand in the midst of the minds of the disciples? And may He not desire us to forswear all other examples and turn to those suggested by the Holy Spirit—that is, to become as the children (i.e. the apostles) who were themselves converted and likened to the Holy Spirit, the children whom God gave to the Saviour . . . (Isa 8¹⁸)? Entry into the kingdom of heaven will thus be possible only to those who have turned from earthly things and been likened to the children who have within them the Holy Spirit—that Spirit which Jesus summoned to descend from His native perfection down to mankind, and set Him as a child in the midst of His disciples. . . . Such a humbling of oneself as that child represents is an imitation of the self-humbling of the Holy Spirit for man's salvation.'

It is true that here Origen is only making a suggestion, acceptance of which would necessitate rather drastic revision of other passages, e.g. *Comm. Jn.* II.11 (6): 'The Saviour was made less than the Spirit through the divine plan of the Incarnation' (pp. *189*f). But such a doctrine of the self-humbling of the Holy Spirit would itself suggest a very different and far more biblical explanation of the unforgivable sin (although Origen does not proceed to make it). The sin against the Holy Spirit is unforgivable because He is God's instrument of pre-evangelism. To reject Christ is serious enough, but to reject God's means of enabling us to receive the challenge of Christ—to 'blaspheme' the very spiritual faculty which God gives us to perceive the

meaning and relevance of Christ's offer of salvation—is wilfully
to close and stop the eyes and ears of the soul by which alone
forgiveness can be apprehended. Origen never really faces the
implications of 1 Corinthians 12³, 'none can say that Jesus is
Lord except by the Holy Spirit'. If he did, he would be able
to set even the unforgivable sin in a context of grace instead
of merit.

We previously (p. *64*) drew attention to a disturbing feature
in Origen's thought—his *grading* of grace-gifts into higher ranking and lower. His standing exegesis of 1 Corinthians 12⁸ makes
what is in St Paul a mere enumeration into an 'order of merit'.
E.g. *Cels.* III.46: 'In his list of God's gifts of grace, Paul ranks
first the gift of wisdom, second—and inferior to the first—the
word of knowledge, and third—presumably lower still—faith.'
Throughout the *Contra Celsum* Origen is concerned to rebut the
charge that Christianity has nothing to offer to the 'intellectuals',
and his defence is in the main twofold: Christianity *does* at any
rate cater for the 'simple', for its offer of conversion through
simple faith is far better than leaving them until such a time as
they can rise to intellectual apprehension themselves—it does at
least give them, in their inability to understand the Scriptural
and rational grounds for Christian philosophy, the '*Ipse dixit*' of
Jesus in which to put their trust. Indeed, the unique miracle
of Christianity is just this successful conversion of the 'irrational'.
But this is only part of the story. Christianity *does* cater for the
'intellectuals' also. It is scriptural teaching that reason and wisdom are far better than mere faith, and the Incarnate Word of
God offers not merely healing to sinners but knowledge of the
divine mysteries to the pure and sinless. Wisdom is a higher gift
than redemption, and the Cross itself cannot *complete* our salvation, which must needs include the sanctification of the Holy
Spirit before it is perfected.

Two texts from St Paul (1 Cor 2² [cf. *Cels.* II.66, pp. *116*f] and
2 Cor 5¹⁶) are cited in this connexion, as in the following specimen
passages:

Hom. Ex. XII.4: 'Although He did in very truth take unto
Himself physical flesh from a virgin, and in it suffered the
Cross and inaugurated the Resurrection, there are other words
of the apostle that we must remember (2 Cor 5¹⁶). Here his

purpose is to challenge his hearers to a finer, spiritual under-standing in place of the mere literal reading of the law; and hence he says that the man who is willing to remove the veil from his heart is turned to the Lord (ibid. 3¹⁶)—not, that is, to the Lord in the flesh, . . . but to the Lord who is the Spirit. . . . [Origen illustrates this by quoting 1 Cor 2², spoken] to certain people whom he knew to be unaccomplished, . . . and that is why he did not say to them that the Lord is the Spirit or . . . that Christ is the Wisdom of God. For they could not have recognized Christ in His capacity of Wisdom, only as the cruci-fied. But his later words (1 Cor 2⁶ᶠ) were spoken to those who had no need of apprehending the Word of God in so far as He was made flesh, but in His capacity of "wisdom hidden in a mystery".'

Hom. Josh. III.2: 'It is possible, I think, that the advent—the incarnation—of Jesus does not give us complete and perfect knowledge; nor indeed does He reveal to us of Himself such knowledge in its fulness and entirety through His cross . . . and resurrection. We have need of another to unfold and re-veal this in its totality [quotes Jn 16¹²⁻¹⁴]. . . . For although through the Lord and Saviour repentance and conversion is preached and remission of sins is given to all believers, . . . it is still true that perfection, the highest range of all good, de-pends on the subsequent deserving to receive the grace of the Holy Spirit.'[84]

It is scarcely necessary to point out how completely Origen misin-terprets St Paul in the first of these passages, or that the correlation of the Incarnate, crucified Saviour with 'imperfect knowledge', as compared with perfect knowledge and the Holy Spirit, misreads disastrously the Paraclete passages in St John. This is indeed the final example of the corrosion of grace by merit. The shadow of 'dual standards', the heresy of 'intellectualism', broods more

---

[84] Cf. Hanson, *Origen's Doctrine of Tradition*, pp. 165f, who quotes a similar pass-age from *Comm. Jn.* II.3 (of 'those who "know nothing except Jesus Christ and Him crucified", thinking that the Word who became flesh is the whole content of the Word, and know only Christ after the flesh; of this sort is the majority of those who are accounted believers'.) Hanson's pertinent comment is that one suspects from this kind of doctrine that for Origen the Incarnation was ultimately an unfortunate necessity rather than something to be gloried in. Yet cf. *Comm. Inéd. des Psaumes*, p. 82 [L, 3]: 'The mystery of the Incarnation, than which there neither has been nor can ever be a greater.')

darkly here than anywhere else in our discussions. It is true that the 'perfect', in their enviable enjoyment of the higher graces of the Spirit, have not dispensed with Christ altogether, but it is Christ 'in His capacity of Righteousness' (*Princ.* I.3.8, p. *172*), no longer Christ the Redeemer. 'Mere faith' has been left behind—lost in Wisdom, and no longer even relevant. The sanctified have graduated, and the text-books they used as schoolboys lie forgotten in the lumber-room of the past.

How distant is all this from the evangelical fervour of those who have caught the real spirit of the New Testament Gospel of Salvation! William Cowper, for example:

> *E'er since by faith I saw the stream*
> *Thy flowing wounds supply,*
> *Redeeming love has been my theme*
> *And shall be till I die.*

Elizabeth Rundle Charles:

> *Never further than Thy Cross . . .*
> *Till amid the Hosts of Light*
> *We, in Thee redeemed, complete,*
> *Through Thy Cross made pure and white,*
> *Cast our crowns before Thy feet.*

—and (inevitably) Charles Wesley:

> *Each moment applied*
> *My weakness to hide,*
> *Thy blood be upon me and always abide:*
> *My Advocate prove*
> *With the Father above,*
> *And speak me at last to the Throne of Thy love!*

For, in truth—and this is something Origen never understood —faith which is lost in *Wisdom* is no longer faith at all: its questions are answered, its ignorance made good. But faith which is lost (as St Paul loses it) in *Sight* is still faith—only faith transformed into adoration. And likewise with the grace of the Holy Spirit, who leads us into all truth: the truth is indeed the Wisdom of God, open to the matured insight of the saint. But it is the truth of the Cross.

CONCLUSION

I HAVE SOUGHT in the above pages to allow my author to state his own convictions on what I conceive to be the heart of the Christian faith—the doctrine of Grace. On every theme the paragraph-headings have been drawn up in practically his own words, and the range of selective illustration has been as generous as space would allow. The danger of arbitrary selection has been constantly borne in mind, but I trust my quotations have at least been representative of some of the main currents of thought of a bewilderingly subtle and comprehensive theologian.

My choice of themes may be more questionable. The master theme of Grace needs no defence; but my difficulty has been that no single feature of Origen's thought is ultimately irrelevant to my quest. Some readers for example will have looked straightway for a discussion of the doctrines on which Origen was condemned (cf. p. *11*); except by implication he will not have found it. This is because I am not convinced that the anathematizers were asking the right questions; I have indeed more than a suspicion that Origen's real defects as a Christian theologian undercut the overt controversies, and were shared by his accusers themselves. Other readers will have sought an exposition of the doctrines on which Origen is generally supposed to have the most to offer—be it for imitation or warning: the allegorical interpretation of Scripture, Subordinationism, the mystical ascent of the soul to union with God and ultimate 'deification'. Some remarks on allegory have been ventured—although my real interest throughout has been the emerging doctrines, not the method by which they are 'deduced' from Scripture; and subordinationism and deification have been rigidly excluded. They would have demanded a book to themselves; but I must put it on record that deification is, in my view, the most serious aberration to be found not only in Origen but in the whole tradition to which he contributed, and nothing that modern defenders of ἀποθέωσις like Thornton and Mascall have urged has shaken in the slightest my conviction that here lies the disastrous flaw in Greek Christian thought. As for Subordinationism, I have indicated above that Origen's Christology hardly does justice to his own thought (p. *153*), and it seemed worth-while to disentangle, as it were, the Grace from the Person, if only to cast a clearer light on the latter than Origen's own Christology affords.

It only remains to summarize the main points that have arisen in the footnotes and discussions above.

(1) GRACE

The definition of Grace (p. *48*) which the numerous references of Origen seem to suggest is all the more impressive because he never consciously formulates it. It underlies not only his overt use of χάρις, but a whole range of most illuminating 'grace-words' or synonyms, and justifies us in seeking the true content of Grace in Origen in his whole presentation of the work of God the Father, Son, and Holy Spirit for us and within us. He can condense it all into a phrase—like the αὐθεντικῶς οὐ δουλικῶς of *Comm. Lam. Frag.* 116 (pp. *31*f), or a sentence—like the οὐδὲν γὰρ χρηστὸν ἐν ἀνθρώποις ἀθεεὶ γίνεται of *Cels.* I.9 (p. *80*). He can speak the language of the Reformation in a way that would gladden the heart of Luther himself (cf. p. *62*). We did indeed note a shift of emphasis from God's Love to God's Power (p. *48*), which came out most noticeably in the central conception of the Cross as Christ's victory in the cosmic ethical drama (p. *164*). Possibly this is the ascetic speaking, and although Origen dutifully expounds the 'love of God' which motivated the whole Salvation-process (pp. *56*ff), we note that it is nearly always φιλανθρωπία rather than ἀγάπη. But Origen successfully avoids the major temptations indicated by Manson and Torrance (pp. *14*ff, *63*f); grace is throughout initiated by God, its determinative enactment is in Scripture, centrally in the Person and Work of Christ. Origen's Stoic affinities have not led him to depersonalize what is essentially a matter of personal relationship; even when he speaks of grace as transmissible (pp. *46*f), it is God who retains its sovereign disposal. Nothing is more to the credit of this Christian Hellenist than his spurning of the classical connotations of χάρις and his absorption of the new wine poured into the old (if still beautiful) wineskins by the innovating genius of St Paul. (Cf. p. *48*).

P

(2) PHILOSOPHY AND RELIGION

Origen, the 'Christian Platonist of Alexandria', where philosophy and religion met in liberal and informed speculation; Origen, who like Justin Martyr before him and Karl Barth long after, would deprecate as 'no good thing' the rejection of Greek culture, and who not only acknowledges the Christian debt to Plato (pp. *28* note 16, *58*), but owes much of equipment and method to him (cf. p. *2*)—would he escape the pillory of Cullmann and his disciples for any theologian who has any truck with philosophy whatsoever? Does he stain the purity of the κήρυγμά with illegitimate and corroding speculation? Or has he a positive contribution, by way of method at least, to our own approach as Christians to the problems thrown up by the world?

We have suggested throughout that the true category of relationship between philosophy and religion is that of *question and answer* (cf. p. *19* note 4), and that justice is at best done to Origen by looking at his work in this light. It was, after all, the impact of the Greek spirit on the Church of the first five centuries that produced the Creeds—by way of pointing at the κήρυγμα the questions (transcendence, unity of the Godhead, etc.) which the new light of the Gospel enabled it to answer, even if the question itself was apt to be transformed in the process by a revelation of its fallacious presuppositions. We saw (ibid.) how Origen, on such a question as transcendence, can use almost the very words of the pagan Greeks in a sense that his Christian presuppositions wondrously transform—like the pedestrian melody of some forgotten songster which the 'plagiarizing' Handel can transmute to gold. We see Origen at his best in this respect in his discussions of Providence (pp. *75*ff). Here the Stoic influence is at its height—and so too, or nearly so, is Origen as a Christian theologian. Christianity is not necessarily impartial as between the rival philosophies of mankind, and Origen allies himself (though not uncritically—e.g. p. *101* note 33) with that philosophy whose questions can be answered in words which bring home the Gospel to a hungry and inquiring world.

His weaknesses are twofold: his criticism does not go far enough, and there are regions where even his subtle and penetrating mind has not learnt to make way for the grace of God.

The cardinal instance of the former is his acceptance of that curse of the Greek theologians—the Stoic apatheia (p. *105*f), and of the latter his speculations on the Creation (*71*ff). His very failures, however, are as instructive as anything in his writings— not least, perhaps, because of the surprising modernity of the issues with which he deals (e.g. the Gnostic criticisms of the doctrine of Creation, the Stoic speculations on the problem of evil). It would be a salutary exercise to disengage in a modern Christian philosopher like L. S. Thornton or Paul Tillich the points on which the question limits and 'corrodes' the answer from those in which the answer transforms and 'baptizes' the question into the new life of the Gospel. This is the method and manner of approach we have sought to employ with Origen.

(3) THE BIBLE

We made it clear from the start (*9*ff) that our interest in Origen's biblical interpretation was the doctrine resulting from it—or possibly imposed by it. We have certainly afforded his twin vices of unbridled allegorism and pedantic literalism ('atomistic inspirationalism', as we ventured to call it—p. *28* note 14) plenty of scope for demonstrating their absurdity (cf. pp. *25*, note 10, *28*, note 14, *44*, note 37). Indeed, we find ourselves longing for the inclusion in Origen's impressive accomplishments of even the slightest sparkle of humour, as well as the insight to recognize that God may use, in the Bible as elsewhere, fallible human beings with human passions and weaknesses. But we have not allowed ourselves to be blinded to the real achievements of Origen—his almost unrivalled knowledge of the Bible, and his ease of movement within its whole compass (p. *156*); his almost fanatical eagerness to show his loyalty by complex patterns of citation on each and every issue; and his genuine and startlingly modern canons of interpretation—that God reveals Himself through the impact of the thought-forms and type-events on the heart and mind of the reader of the *Bible-as-a-whole*, and that the key to every passage of Scripture, Old and New Testament (and Apocrypha) alike, is *Christ* (pp. *8*ff; *154*ff). These two canons, properly applied (as Origen usually does not) undercut the whole Fundamentalist-Liberal controversy, still unhappily and unnecessarily kept alive amongst us by scholars who could go back to Origen with considerable profit.

His doctrine of Grace in Scripture has a double edge: it was Grace that inspired its writing, and grace that enables its understanding (pp. *28*ff). This is worked out impressively with reference to Christ (pp. *153*ff) and the Holy Spirit (pp. *175*ff). As we read these passages we cannot but lament again and again the perverse ingenuity and the hopeless wrong-headedness that almost turn our author's gold to dust. As an exegete of a given passage, he is often exasperatingly at sea—although, as Dean Inge and Professor Dodd have warned us, we neglect his Commentary on John and the scarcely less able Commentary on Matthew at our peril.[1] But in his search for the *principles* of biblical theology and exegesis he asked the right questions and gave many of the right answers. He is not above the occasional straining of a text to fit a preconceived idea (cf. p. *26*, note 12); but although his lack of historical and critical insight allows—or necessitates—his bringing his doctrine to his text rather than extracting it from it, the doctrine itself issues from an astonishingly comprehensive understanding of the totality of the biblical witness—of the Word of God which is Christ.

A word of special commendation is due to his eschatology. One can be so obsessed by 'universalism' and the 'salvation of the devil' as to miss the profoundly biblical insight of 'inaugurated eschatology' (pp. *156*ff, *168*, *191* note 81) which runs through the body of his writings.

(4) INTELLECTUAL AND ETHICAL EMPHASES

No Christian theologian has been more keenly alive to the ethical implications of the Gospel than Origen. We noted the place of Grace in the granting and nurturing of the ethical qualities of this life (p. *39*); the vindication of free-will—of the validity of human response to God's challenge—in the scheme of Providence (pp. *98*f); the ethical *motif* of the theology of the demons (pp. *161*f); the ethical conditioning of the efficacy of the Cross (pp. *163*f). We have set out in due tabulation the *balance* of the intellectual and the ethical in Origen's exposition of the Continuing Work of Christ (pp. *136*ff) and the Grace of the Holy Spirit (pp. *178*ff).

At the same time we have noted with growing apprehension a *grading* of the gifts of God which leaves the ethical progressively

[1] A modern translation of these Commentaries with notes is much to be desired.

lower in the list of graces than the intellectual, and the first hints of a 'dual standard' for saints and sinners which, if made fundamental, would vitiate the whole notion of Grace at its source. (Cf. pp. *40, 61*f, *64, 197*ff.) We suspected at first merely the intellectual snobbery of the Professor. At the end we had come to sense a radical and vicious misunderstanding of the eternal validity of the Cross and the very nature of human faith. It is true that Origen is here, as usual when he goes wrong, transgressing the legitimate implications of his own central position, and that he is saved by his very inconsistency. But we see here the seeds of later heresies far more serious than any with which Origen was charged—the depersonalization of Grace into qualitatively differentiated virtues, the devaluation of the divine currency to the terms of human achievement, the failure (in the most vital field of pneumatology) to see the Biblical witness *as-a-whole*.

(5) GRACE AND MERIT

Here, lastly, was the rock of offence on which we have struck almost from the beginning. At times Origen speaks with Pauline assurance of 'sufficient, sovereign, saving Grace', meeting but far transcending our needs, creating and sustaining the very response we offer. At other times, with no sense of incongruity, he makes grace and merit so complementary as to cast an iron-curtain of human capacity, human desert, human achievement around the free Grace of the Almighty—if not actually reversing his triumphant αὐθεντικῶς οὐ δουλικῶς, at least opening the way for the later (and supreme) heresy of Pelagius. (Cf. pp. *22*ff with *25*ff; and see *61*f; *63*f; *72*f on Creation; *97*f on Providence; *98*f on Freewill; *160*f on the ἐπίνοιαι of Christ; *164*ff—cf. *62*—on the efficacy of the blood of martyrs; *172*ff on the 'meriting' of the Holy Spirit; *184*ff on the withdrawal of the Holy Spirit from the unworthy; *191*ff on the context of merit for the whole doctrine of the Holy Spirit.) It is clear that our search for Grace in Origen has led us to put our finger on a cardinal flaw of his theology.

Certain palliatives of Origen's guilt may be advanced. I think I could demonstrate in detail how his Latin translators heighten the element of merit beyond his intentions. Colourless uses of verbs like ἀξιῶμαι ('I attain to . . .') become fully-blown presumptions of human merit; the Latin love of antithesis in the very pointing of a phrase almost dictates the recurrent '*mereri gratiam*' ('deserve grace') when Origen merely meant 'receive grace'; '*merito*', which suggests 'by right', is often used where Origen merely meant 'correctly'.

But the real defence is itself an accusation—that Origen is not consistent with himself. (To the passages listed above add pp. *72*f, *106*, *153* note 54, *167* for Origen's cheerful inconsistency on a variety of questions.) Yet we must recall, here above all, that Origen is a pioneer. His self-imposed task is to bring the whole range of human thought and action within the sphere of the Gospel. The task is ultimately beyond him, as it is beyond everyman; and his failure is not the less instructive because his very inconsistencies so patently advertise it.

The tragedy is that the Church did not diagnose until the Reformation the radical disease of merit-theology. The traducers of Origen did not even suspect it—rather did they share it. Augustine himself was a comparatively lone figure, and the reaction against Augustinianism was from this point of view quite as significant as the rejection of Pelagius. It is to be hoped that the new insights of 'Biblical Theology' in our own day—shared by scholars of all Christian communions—will not only guard us from the perils of Origenism, but bring us closer to each other as we ever move nearer to that living, redemptive, sanctifying Grace which is Christ, and which through the Holy Spirit is destined in the Providence of God to take possession of all human life and thought and feeling as its own.

We would fain take leave of Origen on a happier note. We would think of him in his real calling of leading his followers to Christ—lecturing and preaching to those eager young people of Alexandria and Caesarea who without him would have been lost in the allurements of pagan philosophy, and not less to the Christians of simple faith whom he felt (and rightly) the Gospel could feed with the rudiments of divine truth when neither secular prophets nor the hard impact of a hostile world left them any other hope or consolation. We would recall his 'optimism of grace'—his universal offer of salvation—to a generation still largely in the grip of fear. We would compare his single-minded and sacrificial devotion to the Word of God with the cowardice of Rufinus, the self-righteousness of Jerome, the cold and calculating ambition of Cyril of Alexandria. He ranks with Athanasius as the greatest gift of early Eastern Christianity to the world. We have learned from him; and even if we find it hard to love him, he compels the admiration and even the devotion of all who seek the truth of Christ, and long His glorious matter to declare.

INDEX OF NAMES AND SUBJECTS

INDEX OF PASSAGES FROM ORIGEN